Practical Liferay

Java™-based
Portal Applications
Development

Poornachandra Sarang, Ph.D.

Practical Liferay: Java™-based Portal Applications Development

Copyright © 2009 by Poornachandra Sarang, Ph.D.

ISBN-13 (pbk): 978-1-4302-1847-0

ISBN-13 (electronic): 978-1-4302-1848-7

9 8 7 6 5 4 3 2 1

Lead Editor: Steve Anglin
Development Editor: Tom Welsh
Technical Reviewer: Alexander Wallace
Editorial Board: Clay Andres, Steve Anglin, Mark Beckner, Ewan Buckingham, Tony Campbell, Gary Cornell, Jonathan Gennick, Jonathan Hassell, Michelle Lowman, Matthew Moodie, Duncan Parkes, Jeffrey Pepper, Frank Pohlmann, Ben Renow-Clarke, Dominic Shakeshaft, Matt Wade, Tom Welsh
Project Manager: Richard Dal Porto
Copy Editor: Nina Goldschlager Perry
Associate Production Director: Kari Brooks-Copony
Production Editor: Laura Esterman
Compositor: Linda Weidemann, Wolf Creek Publishing Services
Proofreader: Dan Shaw
Indexer: Ron Strauss
Cover Designer: Kurt Krames
Manufacturing Director: Tom Debolski

Distributed to the book trade worldwide by Springer-Verlag New York, Inc., 233 Spring Street, 6th Floor, New York, NY 10013. Phone 1-800-SPRINGER, fax 201-348-4505, e-mail orders-ny@springer-sbm.com, or visit http://www.springeronline.com.

For information on translations, please contact Apress directly at 2855 Telegraph Avenue, Suite 600, Berkeley, CA 94705. Phone 510-549-5930, fax 510-549-5939, e-mail info@apress.com, or visit http://www.apress.com.

Apress and friends of ED books may be purchased in bulk for academic, corporate, or promotional use. eBook versions and licenses are also available for most titles. For more information, reference our Special Bulk Sales–eBook Licensing web page at http://www.apress.com/info/bulksales.

To my wife, Nita

Contents at a Glance

Contents

CHAPTER 10   Publishing Dynamic Content 261

About the Author

DR. POORNACHANDRA SARANG has worked in various capacities in the IT industry for more than 20 years. He provides consulting and training in enterprise architecting, solution architecting, and design and development to worldwide clients through his business, ABCOM Information Systems (http://www.abcom.com). He has served as a consultant to Sun Microsystems for several years, and his recent engagements include director of architecture for Kynetia, a software architecture and development firm based in Madrid. He earned Microsoft's Most Valuable Professional (MVP) award two years in a row.

Dr. Sarang has spoken at several international conferences on Java™, CORBA, XML, and .NET technologies organized by O'Reilly, SYS-CON, Wrox, Sun, and Microsoft in countries such as India, the United States, the United Kingdom, Switzerland, and Singapore. He has been invited to deliver keynote speeches at Microsoft Architect Summits and other prestigious events. He has written several research papers, journal articles, and books.

Dr. Sarang has been a visiting professor of computer engineering at the University of Notre Dame in the United States, and he currently serves as an adjunct faculty member of the computer science department at the University of Mumbai, where he teaches post-graduate courses, provides project guidance to post-graduate students, and guides Ph.D. students. His current research interests include distributed systems, mobile computing, and algorithm development. You can reach him at profsarang@gmail.com.

About the Technical Reviewer

ALEXANDER WALLACE was born in the city of Saltillo, Coahuila, Mexico, where he went to college and graduated with honors in 1995 as an industrial engineer. In 1997 he moved to Austin, Texas, where he worked for multiple companies developing software, architecting enterprise applications, and leading software-development teams. In 2006 he moved back to his hometown, where he now owns an enterprise and web software-development company with clients in the United States and Mexico, specializing in the Liferay Portal framework and many other leading Java™ technologies. You can reach him at aw@siiesa.com.mx.

Acknowledgments

I would like to acknowledge the efforts of Vijay Jadhav, who provided valuable help in testing the portal developed in this book, validating the setup and configuration procedures described in each chapter, and helping format the manuscript. I express my gratitude to the technical reviewer, Alexander Wallace, who did an extremely thorough review of the entire manuscript and provided invaluable comments throughout the editorial process to improve the book's content. I would like to thank Nina G. Perry for her efforts in improving the overall quality of the book by doing an excellent job of copy editing the manuscript. Finally, I would like to thank the entire Apress editorial team, without whose efforts this book would not have been possible. I would especially like to mention Steve Anglin (lead editor), Tom Welsh (development editor), Richard Dal Porto (project manager), and Laura Esterman (production editor), whose constant support made this book possible in a short period of time.

Introduction

Liferay is a popular open source framework that you can use to create attractive web portals. A web portal can consist of a wide variety of applications such as blogs, document management apps, wikis, discussion forums, and shared calendars. Liferay lets you offer these kinds of features on your portal by providing a runtime environment for hosting Java™-based portal applications, also known as *portlets*. It offers a container where you assemble the portlets, configure them, and set their look and feel. In addition to the portlets offered by Liferay, you have access to third-party portlets created by user communities. To create a successful portal based on Liferay, you need a definitive guide that can take you through the various Liferay applications and teach you how to put together a portal quickly and easily.

Who This Book Is For

You are probably reading this book because you are interested in creating your own portal based on Liferay, or because you want to maintain or enhance your existing Liferay portal. Either way, this book meets your requirements by covering Liferay and its various applications in depth. You'll get a thorough introduction to the operation and function of a number of Liferay applications, including step-by-step instructions on how to install and use them on your own portal.

How This Book Is Structured

This book is a comprehensive guide to Liferay. It deals with every aspect of obtaining, installing, configuring, and maintaining it.

- Chapter 1, "Introducing and Installing Liferay":

  This chapter defines what a portal is, describes the various types of portals, explains their advantages, and gives a brief overview of the various tools available to create them. Finally, it introduces Liferay itself. You'll get an introduction to Liferay's important features and its internal architecture, after which you'll learn to install and test Liferay on your machine.

- Chapter 2, "Creating Portal Pages":

  This chapter describes the basics for setting up a portal, using a case study that will serve as the example portal throughout the book. You will learn to create a portal, define portal pages, set page layouts and themes, and download and install third-party plugins.

- Chapter 3, "Managing Portal Users":

  A portal is used by a number of people, quite likely in a distributed organization. But simply creating users is not enough to run a portal efficiently; you need to give your portal an organizational structure, manage user accounts, establish access policies, and more. You can also create communities of users who share common interests, e-mail those communities, send them event reminders, and so on. This chapter covers user management in depth.

- Chapter 4, "Creating Discussion Forums":

  This chapter shows you how to set up discussion forums for your users. As a portal creator, you can create discussion categories according to the users' areas of interest. You can enable users to create their own discussion threads, to read posts made by others, to comment on existing posts, and to post replies. As a discussion-forum facilitator, you can publish a list of recent posts, provide portal statistics, ban and unban users, tag contents, and so on. This chapter will help you master all these techniques.

- Chapter 5, "Facilitating Collaboration":

  Using discussion forums is one way to allow user collaboration, but you can also facilitate several other kinds of collaboration in your portal. For example, this chapter explains how to let users receive and send e-mail without leaving the portal. You can also allow users to send SMS messages, chat with other online users, and locate users to create their own discussion groups.

- Chapter 6, "Incorporating Blogs":

  This chapter introduces you to Liferay's application that facilitates blogging. You will learn how to set rights and permissions to blog entries and replies, and you'll discover how to publish a list of recent bloggers and display blog aggregations.

- Chapter 7, "Establishing a Wiki":

  Wikis offer another fashionable way of publishing your knowledge for the benefit of other users. In this chapter, you will learn to set up a wiki on your portal. You'll find out how to create nodes, add pages and subpages, set up the pages' look and feel, assign permissions, manage page hierarchies, track modified pages, get rid of orphan pages, and so on.

- Chapter 8, "Implementing a Shared Calendar":

  As a portal administrator, you might organize events for your portal's user communities. Using shared calendars, you can define and announce such events on your portal. You will be able to create single events as well as recurring events. And if you move your entire portal from one server to another, you will be able to move the entire event database to a new server.

- Chapter 9, "Managing Content":

  Any large site should be able to accommodate the publication of important documents for its user communities. This chapter covers Liferay's tools for managing documents and images. You will learn to set up document libraries, create hierarchies, upload documents, set user permissions, publish a list of recently added documents, create archives, and more.

- Chapter 10, "Publishing Dynamic Content":

  This chapter focuses on publishing content that changes periodically, such as news and announcements. You'll find out how to publish and manage such items on your portal.

- Chapter 11, "Enhancing Your Portal":

  As the other chapters have described, Liferay provides a number of applications that you can use to give your portal its core functionality. But Liferay has become so popular that many Liferay users have developed useful tools that can help you enhance your portal even further. You'll learn to integrate these external tools into your portal, including applications that other developers have built using the Java Portlet Specification and Google's Gadgets API.

- Chapter 12, "Doing Portal Administration":

  Any portal requires proper administration. And as the number of users grows, administrative tasks become more demanding. Fortunately, Liferay provides tools for managing a portal and controlling its activities to ensure user satisfaction. In this chapter, you will see how to perform several administrative tasks using Liferay's admin tools.

Prerequisites

A web developer who creates and maintains web sites will easily be able to create a sophisticated web portal after reading this book.

Contacting the Author

Dr. Sarang is a founder and director of ABCOM Information Systems, a firm specializing in IT consulting and training (http://www.abcom.com). You can reach him at drsarang@abcom.com for consulting and training assignments. Dr. Sarang is also associated with the University of Mumbai as a post-graduate faculty member and advisor for Ph.D. students. For academic-related work, you can reach him at profsarang@gmail.com.

CHAPTER 1

∎∎∎

Introducing and Installing Liferay

Web portals have become commonplace in today's online world. While surfing the Internet, you often open web portals without even realizing it. So what's a portal, anyway? Why are portals so important? How do you create your own portal? Are there any frameworks and tools that are suitable for creating portals? What kind of management is required to maintain a portal? How do you administer a portal? You will find answers to these and many other questions in this book, which walks you through an example of creating and managing a typical web portal.

In this chapter, you'll first learn what a portal is. You will then be introduced to Liferay, a popular open source framework for creating portals. You'll learn to install Liferay on your machine and create a portal of your own as you read through the book. This chapter comprises the following sections:

- What Is a Portal?
- Kinds of Portals
- Portal Advantages
- Creating a Portal with Liferay
- Liferay Features
- Under the Hood
- Installing Liferay
- Testing the Liferay Installation

What Is a Portal?

You have already encountered a web portal if you've used Yahoo!—one of the world's best-known and most-used portals. Yahoo! Sports, Yahoo! Finance, Yahoo! Movies, and Yahoo! Music each aggregate the contents provided by their partners. This is exactly what a portal does: it provides a single point of entry to widely distributed information on the web, and it offers a unified way to access that diverse information.

Some portals allow users to decide what they want to display on their portal pages. In many of these cases, the portal designer will customize the user's page contents and generate them dynamically. Regardless of whether the customization is done by the portal designer or the user, portals provide an easy way to configure desired content on a personal web page. Plus, portals provide a consistent look and feel. Users can take advantage of diverse applications in the same manner, making it easy for them to access information from various sources.

Now let's look at the formal definition of a "portal." If you search for "portal definition" on Google, you'll pull up several definitions that all convey the same meaning. Wikipedia (http://en.wikipedia.org/wiki/Web_portal), the popular free encyclopedia, provides the following definition:

> *A web portal is a site that provides a single function via a web page or site. Web portals often function as a point of access to information on the World Wide Web. Portals present information from diverse sources in a unified way. Apart from the search engine standard, web portals offer other services such as e-mail, news, stock prices, infotainment, and other features. Portals provide a way for enterprises to provide a consistent look and feel with access control and procedures for multiple applications, which otherwise would have been different entities altogether.*

The Wikipedia definition is probably the most comprehensive one. As it states, a web portal gives a user access to contents generated by diverse applications in a unified way.

Here's another definition from Sun Microsystems, which defines "portal" in its Java Portlet Specifications (JSR 286) as follows:

> *A portal is a web-based application that commonly provides personalization, authentication, [and] content aggregation from different sources and hosts the presentation layer of information systems.*

This definition states that a portal is a kind of web application that aggregates content from different sources—web sites or web applications. The content generated by these web sites can be static or dynamic. For example, a sports-related portal might generate a web page that aggregates and presents information from several sports web sites. If a user decides to gather further information from one of the displayed web sites, she can simply visit that web site by navigating to it from the portal page. After doing that, she can return to the portal page with ease and continue navigating to the other web sites if desired.

Some of the displayed web sites might require the user to sign on, in which case a portal can offer the capability of single sign-on. Single sign-on means that once the portal authenticates the user, it applies the same credentials to all the applications displayed on the portal page so that the user can access them. In some cases, a portal simply communicates to an aggregated application that the user is authenticated, and the application trusts that.

As stated in the Sun Microsystems definition, a portal provides personalization, whereby the user can decide what applications should be initially displayed on the personal portal page. The user can configure this page any time by adding and removing different applications.

Different web sites offer several other definitions, all of which describe portals as user-customizable web sites that serve as gateways to diversified content arising from various sources. However, these definitions neglect to describe an important feature of today's portals:

they provide collaboration among their users. Most of the Web 2.0 features such as wikis, blogs, video sharing, and even social networking are available on today's portals.

Generally, these new types of portals give users tools and applications to create sites for social networking and collaboration. I'll describe one such portal, uPortal, later in this chapter. The Liferay portal that we'll explore also falls into this new category of portals.

Now that I've defined what a web portal is, I'll discuss two real-life examples: Yahoo! and Google.

Example Portal: Yahoo!

To understand what a portal is and how to customize its contents, look at what Yahoo! provides to a user. When you open the Yahoo! web site, you see a screen similar to the one shown in Figure 1-1, assuming that you are in the United States (http://us.yahoo.com).

Note The Yahoo! pages shown in this section vary by region. Depending on your location in the world, the menus and their locations appear in different places. So do not get alarmed if the menus discussed here do not appear in the shown location. You will need to locate the appropriate menu to proceed further.

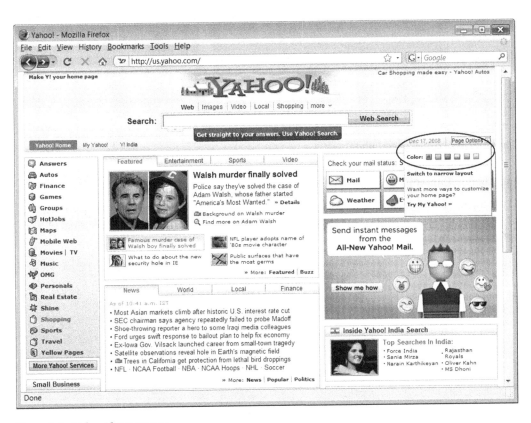

Figure 1-1. *Yahoo! home page*

On the right-hand side, you will see the *Page Options* drop-down menu. One of the options in the drop-down list is *Try My Yahoo!*, which allows you to customize your Yahoo! page (see Figure 1-2).

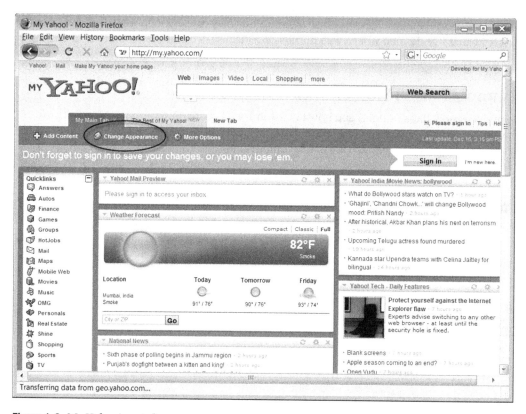

Figure 1-2. *My Yahoo! portal page*

Aggregating Contents

At the top of the page, you will find a toolbar that allows you to add content to the page and change its appearance. When you click the *Add Content* menu option, you will see a list of options as shown in Figure 1-3.

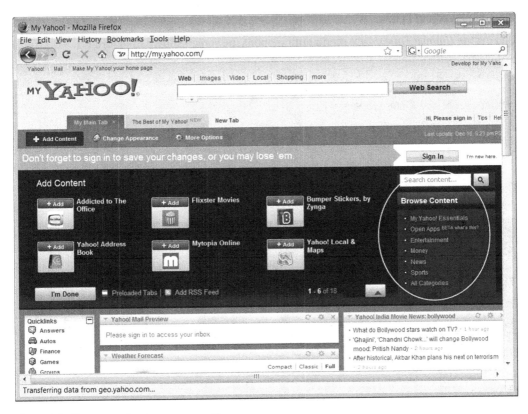

Figure 1-3. *Content-selection menu option*

Click the desired item in the displayed list to add it to your page. Before adding an item, you can preview it by hovering the mouse over it and clicking the *Show Preview* link that's displayed. You can add multiple items to the page.

Once you've added an item, you can relocate it on the page simply by selecting it and dragging it to the desired position. You can remove any of the added or existing items from the page by clicking the "x" symbol shown in the top-right corner of each. After deleting the undesired items, you can relocate the remaining items to your liking.

Once you've finished adding items to your page, click the *I'm Done* button to return to full-page view. You've just configured the entry-point page that provides easy, uniform access to several distributed applications on the web.

Now, you'll change the page's appearance—its look and feel.

Changing Look and Feel

Clicking the *Change Appearance* menu option opens the screen shown in Figure 1-4.

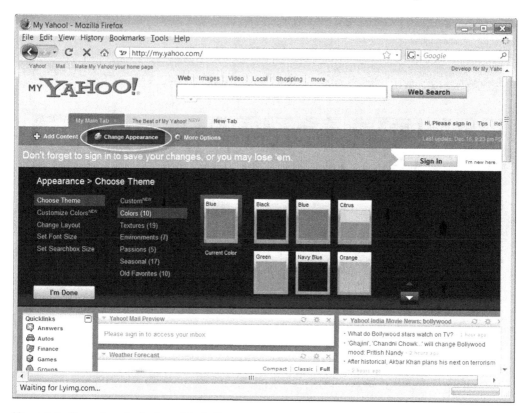

Figure 1-4. *Changing the look and feel of a page*

Here, you will find options for changing the color, layout, font size, and search-box size. Select the color of your choice from the displayed colors. You can also select textures, environments, and so on from the displayed menu choices. To change the layout, click the *Change Layout* option and select the size and number of columns from the choices offered. After selecting a different column layout, you might want to rearrange the display items to your liking. Likewise, you can configure font size and search-box size by clicking the respective menu choices.

Try out the other configuration options. If you want your changes to persist, you should sign on before making them.

You've used a portal that lets the user aggregate desired home-page content and you've set the page's look and feel. Now consider Google, another popular portal in the market.

Example Portal: Google

When you open the Google home page, you will find an *iGoogle* link on the right-hand side (see Figure 1-5).

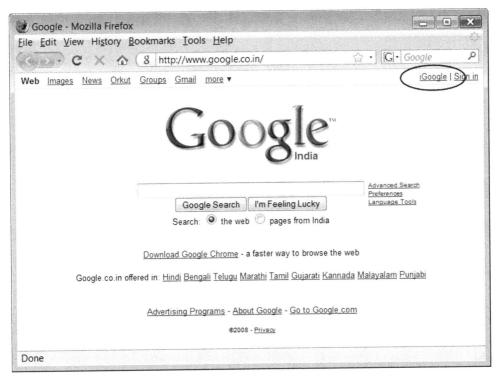

Figure 1-5. *Google home page displaying the iGoogle link*

Clicking this link opens the Google portal page that you can customize to suit your needs (see Figure 1-6).

Figure 1-6. *A typical Google portal page*

The iGoogle portal allows you to add more pages. Note the *Add a tab* link next to the *Home* tab. Clicking the *Add a tab* option opens a dialog box that asks for the tab name.

■**Note** The *Add a tab* menu appears as a link or as an option in a drop-down list, depending on your location. Google's user interface varies from country to country, and the company can change it any time without notice. So do not get alarmed if your screen looks different from the one shown here. You will need to search for the menu options discussed in this book on your own Google portal page.

Entering a character in the displayed edit control opens a drop-down list showing the available predefined tabs, as shown in Figure 1-7.

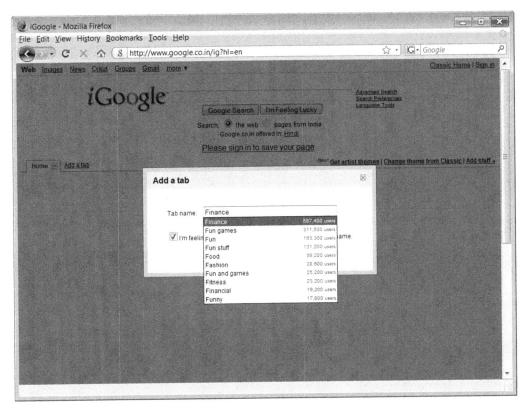

Figure 1-7. *Selecting from predefined tabs*

Google provides the user with several tabbed pages pertaining to different categories. Simply type a letter in the *Tab name* edit box to drop down a list of predefined tabs starting with that letter. The list also shows the number of users who have used each tab on their portal pages. Google tracks the tab names created by users worldwide and provides these as suggestions whenever you try to find a name for your new tab.

If, for example, you select the *Finance* tab, a preconfigured Finance portal page would open (see Figure 1-8), provided the *I'm feeling lucky* check box in the *Add a tab* window is checked.

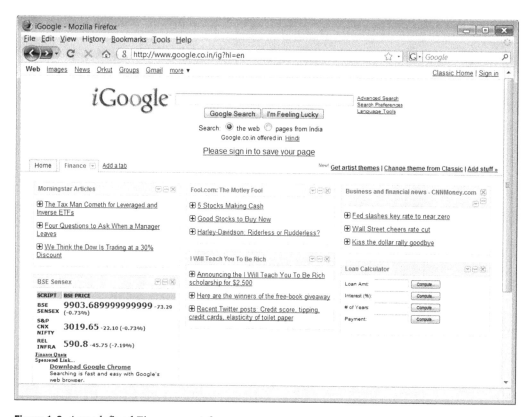

Figure 1-8. *A predefined Finance portal page*

You will find many finance-related applications displayed on this tabbed page. Likewise, you can add multiple tabbed pages by selecting a category of your choice for each page. In addition to using the preconfigured pages, you can add tabs that you create yourself. If you type in a tab name that does not exist in the predefined list, Google adds a blank tabbed page to your iGoogle portal. For example, entering the tab name **DrSarangHome** opens a page like the one shown in Figure 1-9.

Note You can use your own name for creating a blank portal page. You can also create a blank page with an existing name by unchecking the *I'm feeling lucky* check box in the *Add a tab* window.

Figure 1-9. *A blank portal page*

You can now add various applications of your choice to this page. The easiest way to do so: select an existing application from any of the other tabbed pages and drag it to the newly created tab. This moves the item from the existing page to the new page. To add new applications to the page, click the *Add stuff* link on the right-hand side of the page to pull up a list of available items. You can add a Google gadget or theme to the page, for example. To add a gadget, browse the sequential list displayed on the page or search for a specific gadget using the search box on the right. For example, searching for **world time clock** results in a page similar to the one shown in Figure 1-10.

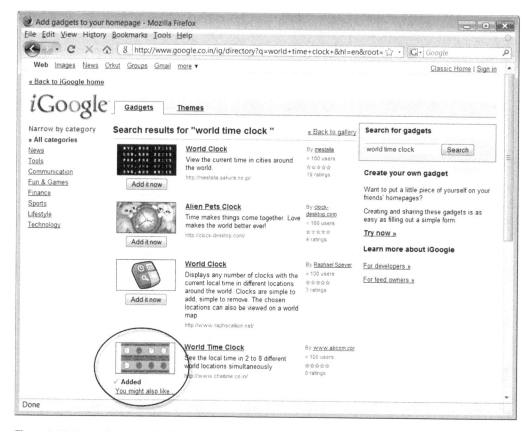

Figure 1-10. *Page showing the list of searched gadgets*

You can now select the world time clock of your choice from the displayed list and add the application to your portal page by clicking the *Add it now* button. You can add multiple gadgets to the page in this manner. When you're finished, return to the home page by clicking the *Back to iGoogle home* link displayed on the top-left corner of the page.

To change the page's theme, click the *Add stuff* link and select the *Themes* tab (see Figure 1-11).

Figure 1-11. *Page showing available themes*

After applying applications and a theme, you will find a screen similar to the one shown in Figure 1-12 when you return to your iGoogle home page. This page displays the Summer Time theme (although the theme name might differ, depending on your location).

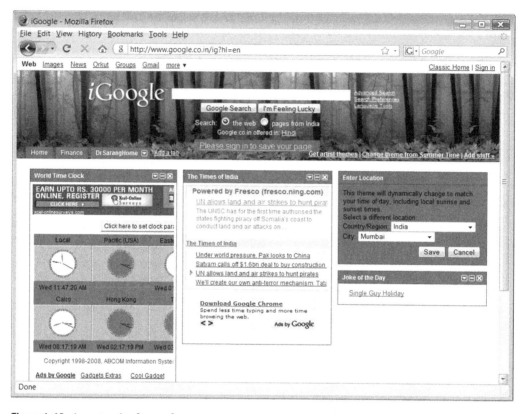

Figure 1-12. *A customized portal page*

Your home page should now display the applications you selected and the theme you applied. You can relocate the applications on the page by clicking and dragging them.

From these two example portals, Yahoo! and Google, you can easily appreciate the power of web portals. Other web portals include Excite, Lycos, Netscape, MSN, AOL, and AltaVista. You probably have visited one or more of these sites, but you might not have realized that you were using a web portal.

The aim of this book is to teach you how to create your own portals similar to the ones I've described so far and other portals on the web. Before I go into the details of creating a portal, however, I'll describe the kinds of portals you might like to create.

Kinds of Portals

Wikipedia classifies portals into several different types:

- Personal portals
- Academic portals
- Regional web portals
- Government web portals

- Corporate web portals
- Domain-specific portals
- Sports portals

These classifications are essentially based on the use of each portal type.

Note Wikipedia is a collaborative encyclopedia maintained and edited directly by several worldwide users. The preceding classifications were in effect at press time, but they're subject to change. Regardless of how these classifications change, you should know the different kinds of portals, which I'll describe next.

Personal Portals

A personal portal is a portal that an individual can customize to meet his or her requirements and suit his or her tastes. Examples of these include My Yahoo! and iGoogle, which you saw earlier in this chapter. These portals are easily customizable, and the customization information is stored in the individual's user account. A user needs to log on to the account to regenerate the personalized page. A personal portal generally aggregates the contents provided by several distributed applications hosted by various worldwide sources, but it doesn't necessarily meet business-driven requirements such as support for various kinds of input devices like PDAs, cell phones, and so on.

These kinds of portals are best if you are not satisfied with the preconfigured portals on the web and you'd like to create customized pages with the look and feel of your choice.

Academic Portals

An academic portal addresses the needs of academicians. An example of a typical academic portal is uPortal (http://www.uportal.org/), a sharable portal under development. Unlike Yahoo! and Google, uPortal is portal *software*. Whereas Yahoo! and Google provide customizable portal sites, uPortal provides a platform for collaboration. Several institutions of higher education have joined together to create uPortal, which is freely downloadable and based on standard technologies such as Java, XML, JSP, and J2EE. It supports collaboration with the help of several community tools such as chat, forums, surveys, and so on. It basically provides "an abridged and customized version" of the campus web presence.

Another example of an academic portal is the Austrian Academic Portal (http://www.portal.ac.at/index-en.html). This portal—a straightforward portal site like Yahoo! and Google—is a gateway to Austrian institutions that teach science and humanities, research, education, and culture. Anybody wishing to pursue studies in Austria in the specified fields would find this portal useful.

You'll find several such academic portals for each country. For example, if you wish to get information on education in Switzerland, you can visit the education portal SWITCH (http://www.switch.ch/).

Regional Web Portals

A regional web portal provides information pertinent to a specific geographic location. Such information might consist of weather forecasts, street maps, local news, and shopping. One such popular regional web portal in India is Rediff (http://www.rediff.com). It provides regional information related to travel, local news, stocks, matrimony, Bollywood, and so on.

A similar regional portal for China is SINA (http://www.sina.com), which is available in both Chinese and English. It offers information about business, sports, lifestyle, and entertainment. Other countries and regions within countries offer portals, such as Greece (http://www.in.gr) and the South East of England (http://www.southeastofengland.com/). The former targets only users who read Greek.

Government Web Portals

Many governments worldwide provide portals for their citizens. One such portal is The National Portal of India (http://india.gov.in), which provides useful government-related information to its residents, information for entrepreneurs who are setting up businesses in India, and tourist information for visitors and students.

A portal hosting government-related information for the United States is USA.gov (http://www.usa.gov). This portal provides information for citizens, businesses and not-for-profit organizations, government employees, and visitors. Because the United States is a large country, many of its states have set up their own regional portals, such as Clark County Now, A Regional Portal for East Central Illinois (http://www.clarkcountynow.com) and the State of Illinois Business Portal (http://www.business.illinois.gov).

Corporate Web Portals

Corporate web portals, also known as *intranet portals*, have become a widely accepted standard among corporations. These corporate intranets provide a consolidated view of the company's information to its employees and often allow employees to personalize and customize the site's content display.

Today's corporate portals also allow the creation and publication of workflows that facilitate better collaboration among the company's divisions. They permit the creation of wikis that allow the users to share knowledge, thereby increasing the company's overall productivity. Generally, these portals provide single sign-on to its employees; once a user is authenticated at the entry point, he can navigate the organization's departments using the privileges assigned to the specific login role.

Such corporate web portals might expose part of their contents to external users through the Internet. In such cases, these portals are called *extranet portals*.

Corporate web portals for big companies are likely hosted on the company's internal servers; portals for smaller organizations might be hosted on external servers supplied by service providers.

Domain-Specific Portals

Portals geared toward a particular industry are called *domain-specific portals*. For example, a portal for real-estate agents brings a region's agents to a single site and allows consumers to buy and sell their properties. A single real-estate agent could even create a portal for facilitating the buying and selling of real estate.

Examples of real-estate portals in the U.S.A. include HomesWEB (`http://www.homesweb.com/`) and RealEstateBig (`http://www.realestatebig.com/`), and the U.K. offers SeLoger (`http://www.seloger.co.uk`). Examples of such portals in India include MagicBricks (`http://www.magicbricks.com/`), Makaan (`http://www.makaan.com/`), and Propertymart (`http://www.propertymart.co.in/`).

Note The sites presented here are simply examples of domain-specific portals; their inclusion does not mean they outperform other sites in their domain.

Sports Portals

Several portals cater to the needs of sports lovers. A typical example of a sports portal is ESPN STAR Sports (`http://www.espnstar.com`), which covers tennis, hockey, international cricket, and motorsports. Other popular sports portals, to name a few, are Sky Sports (`http://www.skysports.com/`), Sportal (`http://sportal.nic.in/`), and Sify Sports (`http://sify.com/sports/`). The last two specifically cater to sports in India. All these portals cover various aspects of different sports, such as live scores, live matches, replays, game analysis, and so on.

Now that you've seen the classifications of web portals depending on their use and application, consider some of the advantages offered by portals over conventional web sites.

Portal Advantages

I've mostly discussed portals in terms of content aggregation and page-layout customization. But I also hinted at extended functionality that portals can offer: collaboration among user communities. In fact, a portal designer can create different user communities on a single portal and ask users to register for each of them. The designer can present different content, a different look and feel, and different collaboration features that depend on the community to which the user belongs. You might find these kinds of collaboration features in a portal:

- *Group discussions*: You can host group discussions on your portal, whereby the users can discuss a topic in a message board that you establish. This kind of collaboration offers several advantages over conventional group e-mail discussions. Users can join or leave the discussion at any time without affecting others who have currently logged in, and they can archive discussion threads for later viewing.

- *Blogs*: A portal can allow the user to publish opinions in a blog, just as users can do on Blogger (`http://www.blogger.com`) or Windows Live Spaces (`http://home.spaces.live.com/`). The blogs can be made public for others to view, so general users can read the views of senior-level users who offer insight into industry and market trends, for example.

- *Document sharing*: A portal can allow sharing of existing documents and other media such as photographs. This feature would require proper document management.

- *Wikis*: Your portal can host wikis, which enable users to create web pages, edit them, and link them together. Wikis function like a shared notebook whereby users can share their ideas collaboratively.

- *Shared calendars*: A portal can also host shared calendars, which can prove useful in managing both company-hosted and user-hosted events. This feature lets users schedule meetings and send invitations.

As you can see, a portal can provide several features to facilitate collaboration among its users, thus providing a richer user experience than conventional web sites can offer.

Creating a Portal with Liferay

Now that you've seen what a web portal is and what benefits it offers over conventional web sites, I'll show you how to create one. A portal, as I mentioned earlier, consists of a wide variety of applications that might or might not relate to one another: blogs, document management apps, wikis, calendars, and so on. Obviously, no single vendor can provide all the necessary tools to integrate those features into your web portals. You will thus need to incorporate tools from different vendors. These tools might use diverse technologies, which could pose an integration challenge because the portal's applications need to work together.

Many vendors provide tools for creating portals and servers to host the portals. Some of the popular tools and servers are Oracle WebLogic Portal, IBM WebSphere Portal Server, Sun Java System Portal Server (also known as GlassFish Web Space Server), and Microsoft Office SharePoint Server. Among open source technologies, Liferay is a popular portal server.

Liferay Portal essentially provides a framework for creating any of the types of portals that I've discussed. Think of it like a web application that's hosted on a web server of your choice. It supports many servers in the market because it complies strictly with standards.

Liferay provides a complete development environment you can use to create a portal. It provides a runtime environment for hosting Java-based portal applications, also known as *portlets*. It offers a container where you assemble the portlets, configure them, and set their look and feel.

A typical portal page running in a Liferay portal is shown in Figure 1-13.

The Liferay web site shown in Figure 1-13 is itself based on the Liferay Portal product. As you can see, it resembles other web portals you've seen. Perhaps the next web portal you encounter will be running on Liferay.

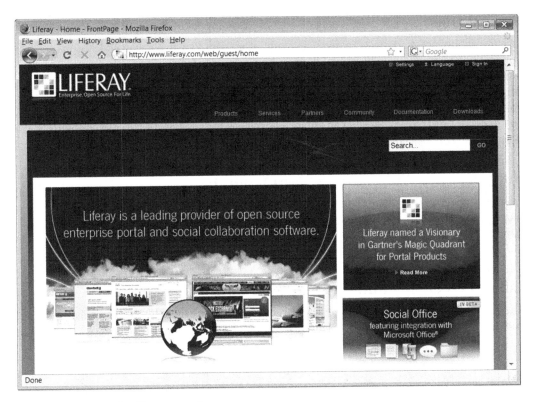

Figure 1-13. *A sample Liferay portal page*

Liferay Features

Liferay offers several benefits over similar frameworks in the market:

- Ease of use
- Support for a wide variety of applications
- Liberal licensing and open source code
- Extensibility
- Scalability
- Internationalization support
- Integration with other tools
- Adherence to industry standards

I will now discuss these features in more depth.

Ease of Use

Like the Yahoo! portal, portals created using Liferay are easy to use. You can add various applications to portal pages by using Liferay's drag-and-drop feature, and you can move them around by clicking and dragging. You can remove an existing application from the page with a single click on the close icon, and you can easily change the page layout by applying a different page template. You can also change the look and feel of a page by applying a theme provided by Liferay or third parties. So you can create a portal easily and allow the user to configure it as desired. You can take advantage of all these features without writing a single line of code.

Support for a Wide Variety of Applications

Liferay provides a wide range of applications or portlets that you can use, including wikis, blogs, chat, and discussion forums, to name a few. In addition to these, you can incorporate applications made available by user communities. You will be using several of these applications as you work through the examples in this book.

Liberal Licensing and Open Source Code

The use of Liferay on your servers is entirely free. The company has a liberal licensing policy: you don't need a license to use the product, even for commercial purposes.

Note Liferay Inc. earns its revenue by selling support and providing training.

Plus, Liferay has made the portal's entire source code available to the developer community. The ability to modify the source has the following implications:

- You can add features to your portals by modifying the code.
- Contributors can improve Liferay itself.
- Developers can add features to Liferay by creating plugins.

Extensibility

Liferay is easily extensible. You can add new features to it without making any changes to the source code. This makes it easy to migrate to newer versions of Liferay upon their release.

Scalability

Liferay is highly scalable. It can handle a large user base.

Internationalization Support

Liferay provides excellent support for internationalization. If your portal boasts many users from non-English-speaking countries, you can extend it to use other languages. You do not need to do any coding to accomplish this; you simply use the appropriate resource bundles. You can easily support languages such as German, Spanish, French, Italian, Japanese, and many more.

Integration with Other Tools

Liferay integrates easily with many third-party tools. For example, Liferay has its own content management system (CMS), but it also supports the more powerful Alfresco (http://www.alfresco.com). Liferay can also integrate with third-party Lightweight Directory Access Protocol (LDAP) servers. You'll find this integration useful when your existing data is stored in LDAP. In addition, Liferay supports several popular databases such as Oracle, IBM DB2, Apache Derby, MySQL, Informix, SQL Server, Sybase, and others.

Adherence to Industry Standards

Liferay is based on standard technologies, so it easily integrates with other standards-based technologies. For example, it easily integrates with the following:

- *Apache ServiceMix*: A popular open source ESB (Enterprise Service Bus)
- *Mule*: A lightweight messaging framework and highly distributable object broker
- *Ehcache*: A distributed cache for general-purpose caching
- *Hibernate*: A relational persistence service for Java and .NET
- *ICEfaces*: An open source Asynchronous JavaScript Technology and XML (Ajax) framework
- *jBPM*: A platform for executable process languages ranging from business process management (BPM) over workflow to service orchestration
- *Intalio/BPP*: Open source BPM and SOA (service-oriented architecture) software
- *JGroups*: A toolkit for reliable multicast communication
- *jQuery*: A JavaScript library that simplifies HTML document traversing, event handling, animating, and Ajax interactions for rapid web development
- *Apache Lucene*: A full-featured text search engine library written entirely in Java
- *PHP*: A general-purpose scripting language especially suited for web development; you can embed it into HTML
- *Ruby*: A dynamic, open source programming language
- *JBoss Seam*: An application framework for building next-generation Web 2.0 applications by unifying and integrating technologies such as Ajax, JSF (JavaServer Faces), EJB3 (Enterprise JavaBeans), Java portlets, and BPM
- *Spring and aspect-oriented programming (AOP)*: A leading Java/J2EE application framework
- *Apache Tapestry*: An open source framework for creating dynamic, scalable web applications in Java
- *FreeMarker*: A generic tool to generate text output based on templates

In addition to its integration with the preceding technologies, Liferay itself is written entirely in Java, a standard programming language. So you can easily modify, extend, and maintain Liferay.

Now let's look at Liferay's internals.

Under the Hood

Before you install Liferay, look under the hood to see how it works. A web portal consists of several web pages, also known as portal pages. Each portal page has a header and footer, and can also contain some menus and a logo. Between the header and footer, you'll see several applications that have been arranged via a predefined template. These applications are essentially the portlets.

A portlet, as I mentioned earlier, is an application that delivers content to the user. The underlying portlet code can generate the content dynamically. A portal page includes one or more portlets, and a portlet *container* manages the portlets.

The portlet container is responsible for persisting the user's preferences for each portlet and providing a runtime environment for each. Plus, a portlet container manages the interactions and communications among the hosted portlets. Thus, the container handles user requests made on the portal and forwards them to the appropriate portlets. The container displays the aggregated output of all its portlets to the user.

Page Internal Structure

The internals of a typical portal page are illustrated in Figure 1-14.

As Figure 1-14 shows, a portal page runs a portlet container that embeds several portlets. Each portlet has its own decoration and controls. Using these controls, you can customize the corresponding portlet. For example, you can easily change a portlet's look and feel by setting its border and background colors, width, text style, window title, margins, and so on. You will explore several of these features as you read the book and develop your own portals.

With the configuration control, you can set permissions on each individual portlet so that only designated users are authorized to use it. You can import or export data, and you can even share the entire portlet by giving its code to other users.

You can customize the location of each portlet on the displayed page by applying a template to change the layout. You can also create your own custom layouts and apply them to your pages. You can add and remove portlets to and from a web page at any time.

Portlets can communicate with other portlets on the same page, irrespective of the technologies they're using. The portlet container is responsible for providing all the features I just described.

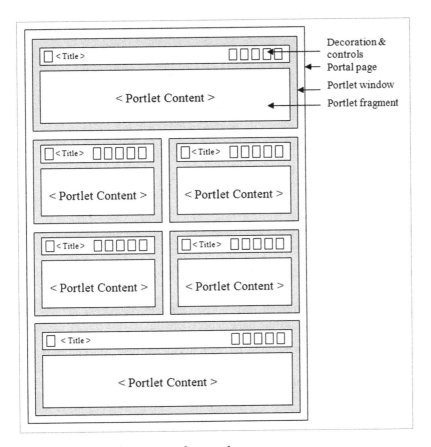

Figure 1-14. *Internal structure of a portal page*

Page Creation Process

When you display a portal page in your browser, certain activities take place in the portal server and container. These are illustrated in Figure 1-15.

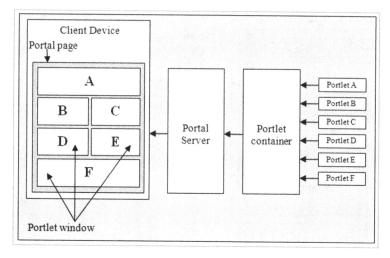

Figure 1-15. *How a portal page gets generated*

Assume that the portal page is to be rendered as six portlets embedded on the page (see Figure 1-15). Here's the process that occurs during page generation:

1. Each portlet—A, B, C, D, E, and F—generates the contents for the user. The contents might be static or generated dynamically, depending on the logic of the portlet application. Note that each portlet is basically a Java application that runs some code when activated.

2. The container receives the contents generated by several portlets.

3. The container hands over the contents to the portal server.

4. The portal server creates the portal page, which is essentially a sequence of HTML code that the browser can use. During page creation, the portal server applies the designated page layouts to place each portlet at the appropriate location.

5. The server sends the created page to the client device (the browser).

6. The browser displays the contents to the user.

At this stage, the portal is ready for further interactions with the user. The user looks at the presented contents and can decide to fetch further information by clicking one of the items on the displayed page. Let's examine what actions take place in the portal server and portlet container when a user requests additional data.

Request Handling

Examining the sequence (object interaction) diagram of a typical user action is the best way to understand the actions that take place in the portal server, portlet container, and portlets in response to a user request.

Tip A sequence diagram is one of the standard diagrams drawn during the object-oriented analysis and design (OOAD) of a software system. It describes the interactions among the various objects in the system and the order in which these interactions occur. You can obtain more information on sequence diagrams at http://en.wikipedia.org/wiki/Sequence_diagram.

Suppose the portal page contains three portlets: A, B, and C. The user initiates an action on the portal page that requires the contents of portlets A, B, and C to be modified. The events that take place during this interaction are illustrated in the sequence diagram presented in Figure 1-16.

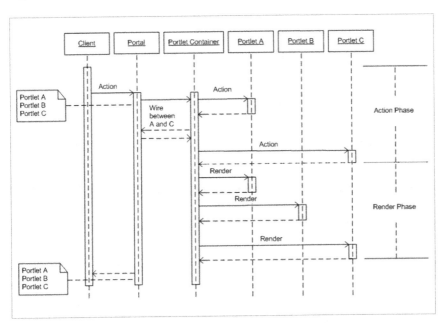

Figure 1-16. *Sequence diagram for user request*

Here are the events in the order they take place:

1. The user requests a data update by clicking the portal page.

2. The user request generates an action event on the portal server.

3. The portal server generates an event on the portlet container.

4. The container determines that the user request requires data in portlets A and C to be updated.

5. The container makes an Action request to portlet A to perform the data update.

6. Portlet A performs the requested action and returns the result, if any, to the container.

7. The container makes an Action request to portlet C.

8. Portlet C performs the action and sends the result, if any, to the container.

9. At this stage, the `Action` phase of the user request is completed. The container has all the data that it needs to render the page for the user.

10. The rendering phase of the user request starts.

11. The container fires a `Render` event to all three portlets—either sequentially or in parallel.

12. The container gathers the responses of all three portlets.

13. The container returns the updated page to the server.

14. The server displays the page on the user's browser.

15. At this stage, the user request is fully processed.

16. The server now awaits another interaction from the user.

You've now studied Liferay's internal architecture. It's time to install Liferay on your machine and run your first portal.

Installing Liferay

Installing Liferay on your machine is easy. The Liferay portal comes bundled with many popular web and application servers that are free for distribution. Liferay also supports many commercial servers, which you would have to obtain separately. If you are using any of the commercial servers, you will need to install and configure Liferay for these servers by following the instructions in the Liferay installation guide.

Note The installation guide comes bundled with the downloaded software.

Some of the popular free servers bundled with Liferay are:

- Geronimo
- GlassFish
- JBoss
- Jetty
- JOnAS
- Pramati
- Resin
- Tomcat

It is easy to set up a bundled installation. Liferay recommends the use of Tomcat as a bundled option because it's lightweight and popular among developers. We'll use Tomcat for the examples in this book.

Note After you create a portal using the server of your choice, you can port it without changes to any other server that supports portlets (the JSR 168 and JSR 286 specifications).

Downloading Liferay

You can download the Liferay installation from the official Liferay site (`http://www.liferay.com/web/guest/downloads`). On this page, you will find several bundles for download. Under "Liferay Portal Standard Edition," download Liferay Portal Bundled with Tomcat 6.0 (at press time, the current Liferay version was 5.1.2 and the current Tomcat version was 6.0).

After you select the Tomcat 6.0 option, the browser redirects to Sourceforge.net and begins the download automatically. The name of your downloaded file is `liferay-portal-tomcat-6.0-5.1.2.zip`.

Setting Up J2SE

Before you set up Liferay, you need to download and install Java on your machine. If you have Java 2 Platform, Standard Edition (J2SE) 1.5 or above already installed, you can skip this step. You can download the latest J2SE version from `http://java.sun.com/javase/downloads/index.jsp` (Java SE 6 Update 10 RC, at press time). The name of the downloaded file is `jre-6u10-rc2-bin-b31-windows-i586-p-05_sep_2008.exe`.

To set up Java on your machine, simply double-click the installer. The setup wizard guides you through the entire installation procedure. After the installation completes successfully, you will need to set the following environment variables.

Create a new system variable called `JAVA_HOME` and set its value to your installation folder. For example, if you selected `C:\Java\jdk1.6.0_02` as the installation folder, use this complete path as the value for the `JAVA_HOME` environment variable. You will then need to modify the system `PATH` variable. Add the value `%JAVA_HOME%\bin` to the beginning of the path.

Tip The preceding installation instructions are for the Windows platform. For Linux and other platforms, follow the appropriate procedures in the Java SE installation instructions.

Setting Up Liferay

Setting up Liferay on your machine is easy: simply extract the contents of the downloaded file to any folder on your machine. For the purposes of this book, I'll assume that the files are extracted to the root folder of the `C` partition. When you extract the files to `C:\`, you will notice that the installation creates a folder called `liferay-portal-tomcat-6.0-5.1.2` in `C:\`. That's all you need to do to set up Liferay.

If you examine the contents of the installation folder, you will find several subfolders. The `bin` subfolder contains the binaries for starting and stopping the server, whereas the `webapps` subfolder contains the installed web applications. The `lib` subfolder holds the various runtime libraries. You will be examining the contents of these folders when you deploy your custom-made themes and portlets for your portal. Even the third-party themes and portlets provided by Liferay user communities are deployed to these folders. You will need to navigate to the bin folder to start and stop the Tomcat server. When you start the Tomcat server, Liferay automatically starts and is ready to use.

Testing the Liferay Installation

To start Liferay, navigate to the c:\ liferay-portal-tomcat-6.0-5.1.2\bin folder and double-click the startup batch file. This opens a console window and starts Tomcat server. The server startup messages are displayed in the console window. When the server completes its startup, you are ready to use Liferay.

Open the browser and type the following URL:

http://localhost:8080

You will see the page shown in Figure 1-17 displayed in your browser.

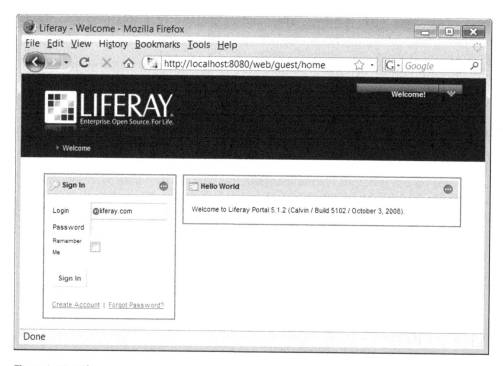

Figure 1-17. *Liferay startup page*

You can now log in to the portal using the following information:

Login: test@liferay.com
Password: test

Accept the Terms of Use on the next page. Upon logging in successfully, you will see the page shown in Figure 1-18.

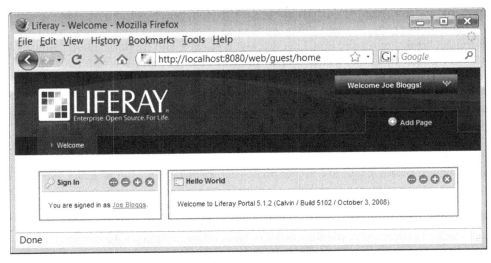

Figure 1-18. *Liferay portal page upon successful login*

Note the welcome message shown in the top-right corner. The default user for this portal is Joe Bloggs, whose name also appears in the *Sign In* portlet. The *Hello World* portlet shows another welcome message along with the current build version of the Liferay portal. At this stage, you have set up Liferay on your machine and are ready to explore further and create your own portals.

To shut down Liferay, you will have to shut down the Tomcat server. You can do so by running the shutdown batch file provided in the bin folder of the Liferay installation.

Summary

In this chapter, I first considered a few definitions of the term *portal*. A portal is essentially a gateway to a set of potentially dispersed Internet applications. It provides the aggregation of contents from several applications, offering uniform access and a consistent look and feel. You saw the workings of well-known portals Yahoo! and Google as examples, and you explored different categories of portals based on their content, such as personal, academic, regional portals, and more. This category list continues to grow.

In addition to its aggregation functionality, portals offer even more benefits than conventional web sites, such as support for user collaboration. A portal can facilitate group discussions, blogs, document sharing, and calendars.

I then discussed some of the resources for creating portals. Many vendors provide tools for creating and hosting portals, such as Liferay, which provides a portlet container for assembling portlets in a portal. It also provides several off-the-shelf portlets for your immediate use. You will be studying and using Liferay for this book's sample portal application. Portals created using Liferay must be hosted on an application server; Liferay supports many application servers, both commercial and free.

Liferay offers several benefits over other portal servers and portlet containers on the market. First, it is easy to use: creating a portal in most cases is a simple process of dragging and dropping portlet applications provided by Liferay and its user communities. Second, Liferay is open source and free. Third, it's extensible: you can extend it easily without making any changes to the source code. So when you upgrade to newer versions of Liferay, your existing portals will not break. Fourth and fifth, Liferay is highly scalable and supports internationalization. Sixth, it easily integrates with several existing products. Seventh, it is standards-based. So a portal created with Liferay can be hosted on any of the standards-compliant application servers without any code changes.

After looking at the benefits of Liferay, we turned to its architecture. A Liferay portal page runs under a container that aggregates several portlets. A user can add any number of portlets to the container, which manages the lifecycle of each portlet and provides for proper interaction among portlets. The container also handles user interactions.

A user request causes `Action` and `Render` phases to take place in the portal server. Whenever a user makes a request on a portal page, the server initiates actions on the container, which in turn brings about further actions on the embedded portlets. The portlets perform the requested actions and return the results to the container. The container then starts the `Render` phase in which all concerned portlets are asked to render their portions of the output. The aggregated page is then returned to the server, which finally renders the output page in the user's browser.

After studying the theory, you began some hands-on work. You downloaded and installed Liferay on your machine. After setting up Liferay, you tested the installation by running a sample portal provided with it.

In the next chapter, you will begin creating your own portal.

CHAPTER 2

■ ■ ■

Creating Portal Pages

In the first chapter, you installed and tested Liferay. In this chapter, you will begin the process of creating a Liferay portal. Our portal will include several features of a typical portal, including customizable web pages. You'll create a few web pages for the sample portal, which will be based on a practical case study that I'll describe shortly. After creating these pages, you'll customize their look and feel using Liferay's templates.

More specifically, in this chapter you will learn to

- Understand the case-study requirements

- Create a portal

- Add, delete, and edit pages

- Add child pages

- Set the tab order of pages

- Understand page themes and apply them to your pages

- Download and install additional themes

- Set page contents

- Understand the *Plugin Installer* application

- Set a home page

- Understand how to use the *Journal Content* application

- Use the *News* and *RSS* applications

- Use sign-in and navigation applications

- Change page layouts

- Navigate the created portal

But first, I'll describe the sample portal.

Defining the Securities Portal

Securities investors across the world will tell you that to make money in the securities market, you need easy access to a wealth of information. Without investment tips and timely information about market movement, one can lose money by investing in the wrong securities or investing at the wrong time. This is why we have securities advisory firms, which invest your money in the market and manage your funds in return for a fee. Some investors, however, prefer to trade directly and do not rely on advisory firms.

Before the days of online trading, the only way to invest in the market was through phone calls to your stockbroker. This was painful and time-consuming. Online trading has simplified investing so that even small-time investors can trade in the market at their convenience. Not surprisingly, recent days have seen a tremendous increase in the amount of securities investors. These new investors would benefit from a portal that can educate and advise them. Even seasoned investors could use the timely and correct information delivered by the portal in order to make money in securities trading.

You'll create such a portal in this book. I'll try to cover the requirements of a typical investor, but you should feel free to configure the portal to suit your individual needs.

Before we begin our portal development, let's try to assess a typical investor's requirements for such a portal. Generally, securities investors fall into two broad categories: fundamental analysts and technical analysts. A fundamental analyst looks at a company's fundamentals, such as its balance sheet, P&L (profit and loss) report, order books, cash flow, ROI (return on investment), and so on. Based on this fundamental data, the analyst would weigh the company's strength in the long run, forecast its growth in the next one to three years, and make decisions on investments accordingly.

A technical analyst creates short-term charts on a company's daily trading prices and long-term charts for the last five or more years' worth of data. She might also chart periods in between, such as one year, one month, or even one day. A one-day chart provides information about online trades, which helps investors who engage in day trading.

Whether an investor is a fundamental analyst or a technical analyst, she would generally require

- Access to critical and timely data
- Timely updates on both general and corporate news
- Trade data from stock exchanges
- Expert analysis
- Peer-to-peer collaboration

Let's look at these requirements in more depth.

Access to Critical and Timely Data

By law, any corporation or publicly traded company must publish its financial results on a timely basis each fiscal year. Such information is printed in the form of annual reports, and also usually available on company web sites. Access to this information is important for an investor.

Investors might also be interested in data that compares one corporation to another in the same industry. Many third-party organizations publish these comparative statistics on a company's fundamentals.

Our proposed portal should make such information easily accessible to the users. The portal should provide links to sites that publish fundamental data, comparative studies of a corporation's financial results, and so on.

Timely News Updates

The markets are often driven by world news. A new government policy announcement might boost market sentiments, whereas a tragedy such as 9/11 could have the opposite effect.

In addition to general news, corporate news plays an important role in the trading of a particular security. For example, Microsoft's announcement of a new operating system or a new data center might result in heavy trading of its stock on that particular day. Access to information about corporations' stock splits, issue of bonus shares, and the like is important to analysts—especially technical analysts.

So our portal should provide timely news updates on worldwide events as well as corporate announcements.

Trade Data from Stock Exchanges

The stock exchanges publish end-of-day (EOD) data about all the securities traded on the exchange that day. The EOD data consists mainly of the following:

- *Open price*: The price at which the first trade took place
- *Close price*: The last traded price
- *High price*: The highest trade price during the day
- *Low price*: The lowest trade price during the day
- *Volume*: The number of trades during the day

Stock exchanges provide even more EOD data than the items I've listed, all of which is important for a technical analyst. The analyst draws historic price charts such as open-high-low-close (OHLC) charts, candlestick charts, and moving-average charts based on this data. He can plot such charts for the long term or the short term, depending on the type of analysis being performed.

Stock exchanges can deliver data for each trade either through a live feed or a delayed feed. You have probably seen live data on TV channels such as CNBC and Bloomberg Television. Access to this information is vital for day traders who buy and sell the same stocks within a day.

Our portal should provide a gateway to sites that provide technical charts, historical data, and live data.

Expert Analysis

The financial analysts do live TV broadcasts of their opinions on the markets and stocks. They also publish their opinions and advice on their web sites. Our portal should allow users to watch such live broadcasts in a small window on the portal page during trading hours. Day traders who usually keep their televisions tuned to investment channels will appreciate this live-analysis feature of the portal.

Peer-to-Peer Collaboration

Investors often buy and sell stocks based on advice from their friends and relatives, so they could benefit from instant messaging (IM), mobile Short Message Service (SMS), and other communication methods. A retail investor also reads blogs by heavyweights in the markets and industries. New investors might need to understand certain market terms and definitions, so they might find it helpful to browse contributions on a wiki. Our portal should provide message boards, wikis, chats, e-mail, instant messaging, and other means of user collaboration.

Now that you've considered the type of content that an investor's portal should offer, you can start creating the portal.

Creating the Securities Portal

In Chapter 1 you installed and tested the Liferay installation on your machine. Now, open Liferay Portal by typing this URL into your web browser:

```
http://localhost:8080
```

You need to log in before you create your first portal page. At the top-right corner of the screen, you will find a *Welcome!* drop-down menu. Click the down arrow to see the list of menu choices, and select *Sign In* to pull up a sign-in screen (see Figure 2-1).

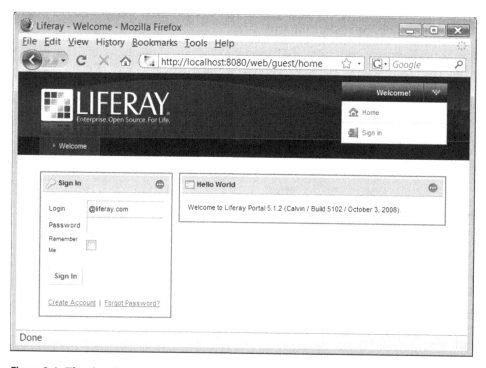

Figure 2-1. *The sign-in page*

Enter the following login information:

```
Login: test@liferay.com
Password: test
```

After successful login, Liferay displays the Terms of Use on your screen. If you tested your installation earlier (as described in Chapter 1), you will not get the Terms screen again. When you accept the terms, you will see the Welcome page.

You'll see a *Welcome* tab at the top-left corner of the page and an *Add Page* hyperlink at the top-right corner. You will use the latter to add pages to your portal.

Adding a Page

Clicking the *Add Page* menu adds a blank page to your portal and asks you to name the corresponding tab. Enter the name **Home** in the tab and click the *Save* button next to it. You now have a new page with the tab name *Home* (see Figure 2-2). Click this newly created tab to switch to your *Home* page, which is just a blank page right now. You need to add applications to it to make it meaningful.

Figure 2-2. *A blank Home page*

Deleting a Page

Before you add more pages to your web portal, you should understand how to delete a page from the portal. If you accidentally add a page that you don't want, deleting it is simple. To go through the process, you'll delete the newly created *Home* page. First deselect the *Home* page by selecting another page—the *Welcome* page, in this case. Now place the mouse cursor on the *Home* tab. You will notice that a red button appears on the top-right corner of it. This is the button for deleting the page.

Tip The delete button is small and easily missed. Look carefully at the top-right corner of the tab itself to locate a little red icon. This is the delete button.

When you click this button, both the *Home* tab and *Home* page disappear from your portal. Of course, before deleting the page, Liferay asks you for confirmation. The page is deleted from the portal only when you confirm that you want it removed.

Changing the Page Name

If you want to change the name of an existing page during portal development, you can simply click the tab name of the desired page. When you hover the mouse cursor over the name, the cursor becomes a text-insertion icon. Clicking the tab at this point pops up an edit box with the current tab name. You can now edit the displayed name. Click the *Save* button next to the edit box or simply hit the Enter key to save your changes. The new name now appears in the tab. If you decide to discard the changes, click any other tab to deselect the current page or hit the Esc key. Doing this discards your changes and retains the old name in the display tab.

Now that you've seen the process of creating and deleting a web page in your portal along with changing the name of an existing page, you should add several more pages.

Adding Multiple Pages

Because our portal will cater to the needs of both fundamental and technical analysts, you'll create portal pages to meet the requirements of both groups. The page for those who believe more in fundamental analysis will aggregate the corporations' fundamental information and provide analysis by experts. The page for technical analysts will contain technical information such as charts, tickers, and so on.

In addition to the fundamental and technical pages, you'll also create a page for community collaboration. You'll host several community-related activities on this page such as message boards, blogs, calendars, wikis, and so on.

Finally, you'll need a page for the portal administrator. So you'll create these new pages for your portal, following the previous instructions on adding pages:

- Home
- Fundamentals
- Technicals
- Community
- Admin

Adding Child Pages

So far you have created the portal's main pages, whose names appear in their page tabs. Most of the time you'll find it sufficient to create only the main pages, but in certain situations you might want to create child pages for the main pages. The user will access these child pages through submenus of the main pages' tab names. You'll now add a few child pages to the *Community* page.

To add a child page, click the *Welcome* drop-down box shown on the top-right corner of the screen. Select the *Manage Pages* menu option from the displayed list (see Figure 2-3).

Figure 2-3. *Menu options available under your login*

Clicking the *Manage Pages* menu option opens the application that lets you manage your web pages (see Figure 2-4).

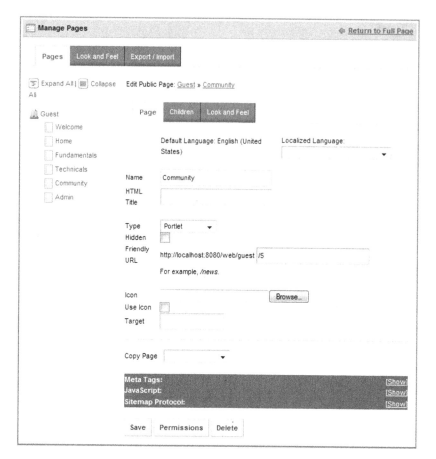

Figure 2-4. *The Manage Pages application screen*

Here, you will find options for editing a page, changing its look and feel, and exporting and importing page data. By default, the application opens in page-edit mode and displays the information on the currently selected page. On the left side of the page, you will see the hierarchy of all the pages currently defined in the portal.

To add a child page under the *Community* page, first click *Community* from the list of pages on the left and then click the *Children* tab. This changes the screen to child-page mode (see Figure 2-5).

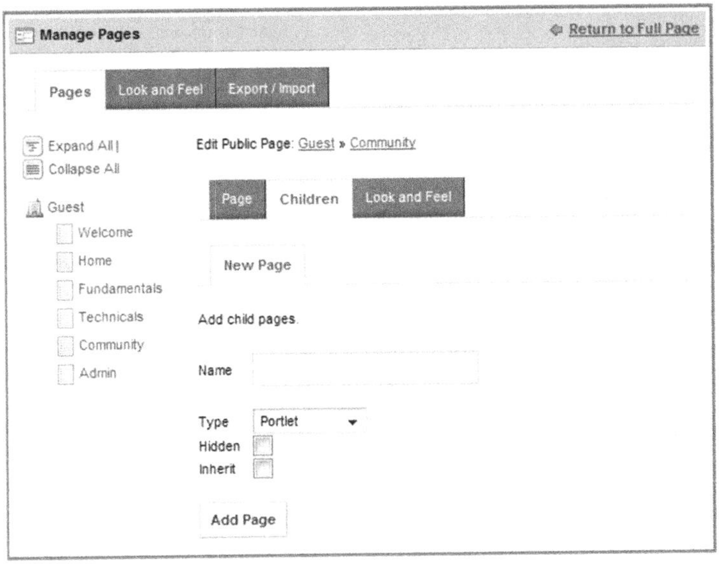

Figure 2-5. *Child-page entry screen*

Enter **Fundamental Analysts** as the name for the new page. Leave the other values as their defaults and click the *Add Page* button to add the page under the *Community* main page. Add two more child pages under the *Community* page with the names **Technical Analysts** and **General Investors**. Each time you add a child page, the hierarchy on the left side of the screen updates to show you the newly added page.

Note You will be required to expand the node hierarchy to see the child pages. Initially, before any child pages are defined, the nodes don't display expansion icons. Once you add child pages, you can access their nodes using the new expansion icons in the tree.

After you add the three child pages, your page hierarchy should look like the one shown in Figure 2-6.

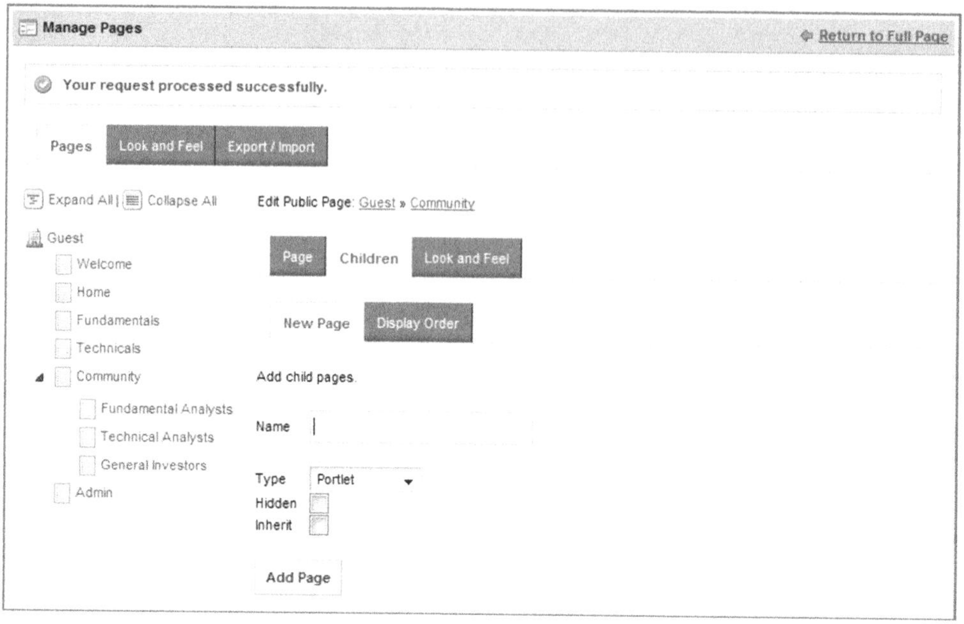

Figure 2-6. *The complete hierarchy of the main and child pages*

Now, return to the main screen by clicking the *Return to Full Page* link at the top-right corner of the screen.

Changing the Page's Display Order

So you've added several pages to your web portal. But perhaps you are not satisfied with the order in which the pages are arranged in the display tabs. To modify the order, click the *Pages* tab in the *Manage Pages* application and select the top node in the displayed list. Select the *Display Order* tab on the right side of the page to bring up the list of child pages in a list box.

Alongside the list box, you will find up and down arrow buttons. Select one of the child pages in the list box and use the arrow buttons to move it up or down in the list. Once you are satisfied with the new list order, click the *Update Display Order* button. Click *Return to Full Page* to examine your changes.

To set the display order of any other node's child pages, select the node in the tree hierarchy and follow the same steps. Figure 2-7 shows how the screen looks when you select the *Community* node and access the *Display Order* tab.

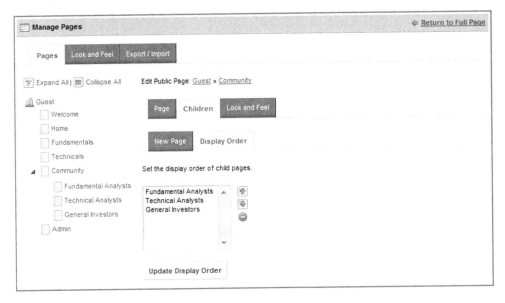

Figure 2-7. *Editing the page's display order*

Editing a Page

You can edit a page to change its tab name, HTML title, and so on. In the *Manage Pages* application, select the top-level *Pages* tab, then the *Page* tab underneath. Select the page you want to edit from the hierarchy; let's do the *Fundamentals* page first (see Figure 2-8).

If you wish to change the page name, type it in the *Name* edit box. In the *HTML Title* edit box, type the title for the page. Leave the type as *Portlet*. In the *Friendly URL* edit box, change the default URL to **/Fundamental**. By default, Liferay assigns a URL to every page that you create. It would be difficult to remember all the machine-generated URLs, so it's a good idea to assign a URL of your choice to each created page using the *Friendly URL* edit box.

You can set the page's icon using the *Browse* button to populate the *Icon* field. Once you are satisfied with your edits, click the *Save* button to save your changes.

Likewise, select other pages in the hierarchy to edit them. After you complete the edits on all the desired pages, click the *Return to Full Page* link to return to your portal and verify your changes.

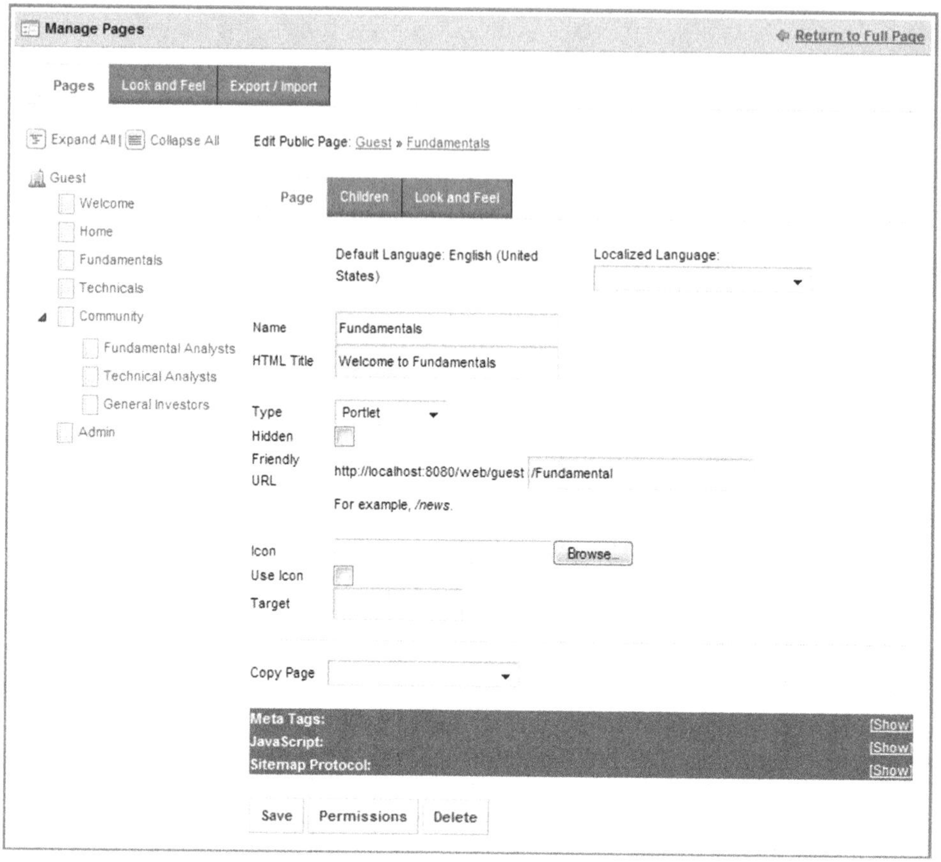

Figure 2-8. *Edit options for a page*

Applying Themes

So far, you have learned to add, delete, and customize pages in your portal. A page added to the portal is displayed in the tab list.

■**Note** Generally only the top-level pages are shown in the portal's tab list. The child pages appear in a drop-down list under the corresponding parent page tab. Not all page themes have this capability. If a chosen theme does not offer this capability, you will need to use sitemap or navigation portlets (discussed in the section "Using the Sign-In and Site-Navigation Portlets") to get a list of child pages.

Clicking any tab brings the corresponding page to the forefront. But how do you change the look of your entire portal? In other words, how do you change the header, footer, page logo, placement of tabbed menus, and so on? Liferay allows you to change the look and feel of your entire portal by providing themes. A theme basically defines the look of your web page. Liferay provides some default themes, and many more themes created by Liferay user communities are available to you.

You will now learn to apply a new theme to our web portal. Start the *Manage Pages* application and select the *Look and Feel* tab from the top-left corner of the page (see Figure 2-9). The changes you make here will apply to all the pages you have created.

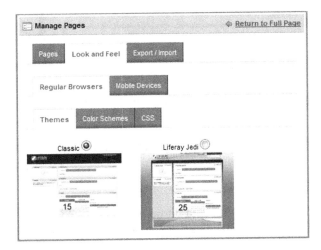

Figure 2-9. *Theme selection page*

On this screen, you will find a list of themes provided in the Liferay installation. Each item on the list also shows a thumbnail image of how your screen will look after applying the corresponding theme. The currently applied theme for our portal is *Classic*. Select the *Liferay Jedi* theme instead. Observe the changes by returning to full-page view and navigate to different pages to verify the application of the new theme.

The *Welcome* page of our web portal after the *Liferay Jedi* theme is applied is shown in Figure 2-10.

Figure 2-10. *The Liferay Jedi theme*

Individual Page Themes

It is also possible to apply a different theme to each page in your portal. To do so, once again start the *Manage Pages* application. Select the page to which you want to apply a new theme. You will see several options for editing the page; click the *Look and Feel* tab. You will see the list of available themes as you did when applying a theme to the entire portal. Select a different theme for the chosen page. Likewise, select different pages from the page hierarchy and apply a new theme to each one. Once you have completed the changes, return to the portal. Now view the pages by clicking their respective tabs. You will find that each displayed page has a different look depending on the applied theme.

■**Note** Changes made to individual pages override the global settings. Thus, once you set a theme for a particular page, any new theme applied globally would not affect the currently set theme for this particular page.

Installing New Themes

Liferay provides many themes beyond what's included in the basic product. You can download and install these themes from the web portal that you have created so far. The themes are packaged in .war files as web applications. You will need to download and deploy these on your web server using the *Plugin Installer* application that Liferay provides. As the name suggests, *Plugin Installer* allows you to install new themes, portlets, and layout templates. I'll show you how to add this application to the web portal's *Admin* page.

Click the *Admin* tab to activate the administration page. This page is currently blank; it does not contain any applications. To add an application to this page, select *Add Application* from the *Welcome* menu (see Figure 2-11).

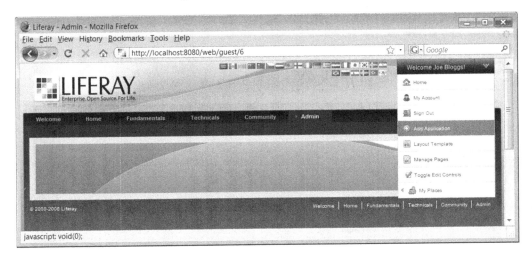

Figure 2-11. *Add Application menu choice*

Clicking the *Add Application* menu displays the list of available applications on the left side of the screen (see Figure 2-12).

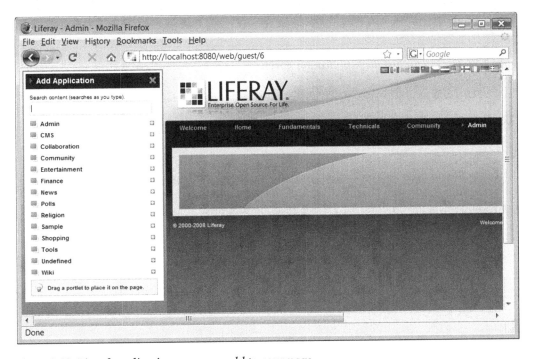

Figure 2-12. *List of applications you can add to your page*

The applications are arranged by category. Click the *Admin* menu item, select the *Plugin Installer* application, and click the *Add* button next to it. You will find that the application has been added to your *Admin* web page (see Figure 2-13).

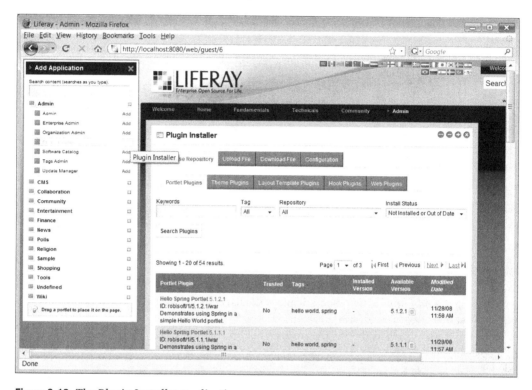

Figure 2-13. *The Plugin Installer application screen*

Caution You must be connected to the Internet while performing these steps.

In the *Plugin Installer* application, you will find theme plugins, portlet plugins, layout-template plugins, and web plugins. Click the *Theme Plugins* tab to see the list of available themes and select the *Envision 5.1.1.2* theme as an example.

Note These plugins change periodically. If you do not find the Envision theme listed on your screen, select any available theme for the purposes of this exercise.

Selecting the theme displays the product information on the next screen (see Figure 2-14).

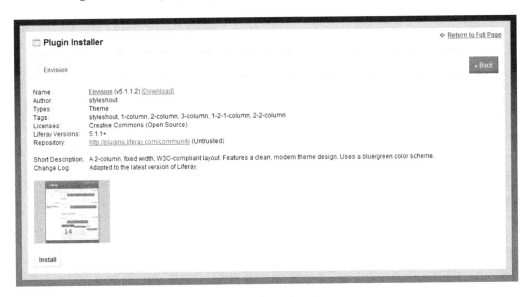

Figure 2-14. *Product information on the selected application*

Click the *Install* button to download and install the theme. After the theme downloads successfully, you will get a *Done* message at the bottom of the screen, after which Liferay performs the installation. It takes a few seconds to install the theme on the server; you can monitor the installation process on the web-server console. Once the theme has deployed successfully, return to the full-page view of your portal.

You can now apply the new theme to a page of your choice. When you drill down to the *Themes* option in your *Manage Pages* application, you will see the newly added theme as shown in Figure 2-15.

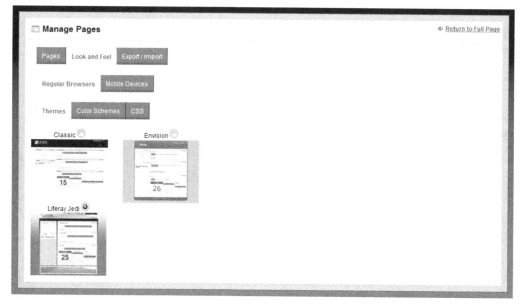

Figure 2-15. *Updated theme-selection page*

Select the new theme to apply it to your web page. If you're using the *Envision* theme, your page will look like the one shown in Figure 2-16.

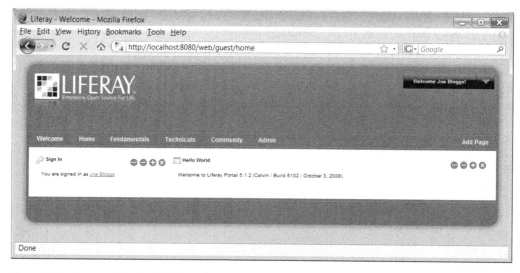

Figure 2-16. *A page with the Envision theme applied*

The *Plugin Installer* application makes it easy to download and install themes directly through your Liferay portal. But you'll need to follow a different process to use themes from Liferay's user communities. I'll discuss that next.

Downloading Community Themes

You can download the community themes from the Liferay web site (http://www.liferay.com). Under the *Downloads* menu option, you will find the *Official Plugins* and *Community Plugins* menu options. Select *Community Plugins* to display a product list that includes portlet plugins, layout-template plugins, and theme plugins. The list runs across multiple pages, but I've included a partial screenshot of one of the pages (see Figure 2-17).

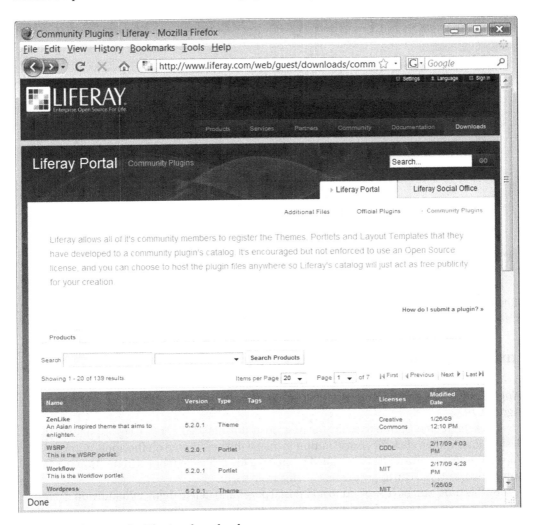

Figure 2-17. *Community Plugins download screen*

Scroll down the list on the first page and select the *Transparentia* theme for our portal. (If you do not find this theme listed on the first page by the time you read this book, use the search facility to locate it.) This takes you to the product description page as shown in Figure 2-18.

Figure 2-18. *Product description screen of a typical community plugin*

At the bottom of the screen, click the *Actions* button associated with the most recent version of the plugin. Then click *Direct Download* to start downloading the plugin's .war file. Save the file to a desired location.

Installing Community Themes

To install the *Transparentia* theme you just downloaded from the Liferay web site, start the *Plugin Installer* application and click the *Upload File* tab. You will see the screen shown in Figure 2-19.

Click the *Browse* button to select the previously downloaded .war file corresponding to the desired theme, then click the *Install* button to install the new theme on the application server. You can verify that the theme is installed by viewing the available themes in the *Manage Pages* application, and you can apply the new theme from there.

By this time, you have learned to add portal pages and delete them, edit individual pages, set page themes, and so on. Now for the most important part: adding content to your portal pages.

Figure 2-19. *Uploading a new theme to the server*

Aggregating Content

In this section, you will learn to add applications and aggregate their contents for display on a single page. You'll be aggregating Java portlets from Liferay and its community sites. In general, you should study the functionality of the available portlets to see whether they suit your portal's requirements. In this case, you'll initially focus on applications that fulfill the business requirements described in the section "Defining the Securities Portal."

Begin by customizing the *Home* page: activate the *Home* page on the portal by clicking the respective tab. To display the list of available applications, select the *Add Application* menu item from the *Welcome* drop-down list. (You saw this list earlier while adding the *Plugin Installer* to your *Admin* page.) Let's now examine the different categories and applications available for use:

- Admin
- CMS
- Collaboration
- Community
- Entertainment
- Finance
- News

- Polls
- Religion
- Sample
- Shopping
- Tools
- Undefined
- Wiki

Note The category names come from the installed portlets, so you might see new names in the list as more portlets are added to the official site.

I will now give you an overview of the applications available under each category. It would be impossible to describe each application in detail, so I'll consider only applications relevant to the portal's needs and some general-purpose applications that you might find useful in creating other portals.

Admin

Under the *Admin* category, you will find many applications concerned with portal administration. For example, the *Admin* application gives you information on server uptime and statistics. It tells you about installed plugins such as portlets, themes, and layout templates. It allows you to install more plugins from the web.

The *Enterprise Admin* application allows you to create user groups, roles, password policies, and so on. In general, if you are creating an intranet portal for your enterprise that is distributed worldwide, this application will help you define the organizational structure. The *Organization Admin* application provides a subset of the *Enterprise Admin* application's functionality. The *Admin* category also contains the *Plugin Installer* application that you've already used. The *Update Manager* application allows you to uninstall themes.

CMS

The *CMS* category provides several services for content management. You can use the applications in this category to create journals and journal articles and search through them. You can create libraries and display documents stored in the libraries. You can create and view images from the galleries, display a list of recently viewed documents, view a map of the entire site, and navigate the site.

Collaboration

Under this category, you will find applications that allow you to manage blogs, calendars, message boards, wikis, and SMS messaging. This category has several applications that will help you incorporate peer-to-peer collaboration, which I discussed in the section "Defining the Securities Portal." We will be using most of these applications in our portal, so later chapters will cover them in more detail.

Communities

As the category name suggests, here you will find many applications related to communities. Using the *Communities* application under this group, you will be able to list your current communities, discover new communities, and even create your own communities. The *Invitation* application lets you invite friends to join the communities you have created. Using the *Directory* application, you can search for specific users, organizations, and user groups.

The *Bookmarks* application helps you set bookmark entries on the portal, and the *Page Comments* application lets you add and view the comments on the current portal page. You will be able to view the page's ratings using the *Page Ratings* application.

Entertainment

You'll find two entertainment applications under this category: *Reverend Fun* and *Words*. *Reverend Fun* offers humorous cartoons, and *Words* scrambles and unscrambles a word that the user submits.

Finance

Under the *Finance* category, you will find three finance-related tools: *Currency Converter*, *Loan Calculator*, and *Stocks*.

The *Currency Converter* application converts and displays the input amount to several currencies simultaneously. A user can select from most of the world's currencies through the application's *Preferences* option.

The *Loan Calculator* application computes and displays the EMI (Equated Monthly Installment) when given a loan amount, an interest rate, and a term period. It also displays the total interest paid over the loan tenure and the grand total paid (the sum of principal plus total interest).

The *Stocks* application displays the current stock prices of the selected securities, along with the percentage change in price. It shows you the *OHLC* (open-high-low-close) price chart along with the *Volume* chart of any security for which data is available. As you can do with other applications, you will be able to set your own preferences for the stock symbols using the *Preferences* menu option.

Because our portal is related to stocks and finance, we will be using these and many other third-party finance applications.

News

Like *Finance*, the *News* category is important for our portal. It provides an application, also called *News*, that allows you to add live news to your portal. Similarly, the *RSS* application allows you to add an RSS feed to your portal pages. You can select the feed source for both *News* and *RSS* applications.

In addition to these applications, the *News* category provides two more applications: *Alerts* and *Announcements*. As the names suggest, you can set and manage alerts using the *Alerts* application and make announcements on your site using the *Announcements* application. I'll show you how to use these applications in the portal.

Polls

Under the *Polls* category, you will find two applications: *Polls* and *Polls Display*. Using the *Polls* application, you can set up polls to which the users can respond. You can then display the results using the *Polls Display* application.

Religion

The *Religion* category contains the subcategory *Christianity*. Under this are four applications related to Bible, Global Prayers, and so on. We won't be using this category in our investor's portal, but its applications might prove useful in the creation of a religion-related portal.

Sample

The two most important applications to a portal developer under the *Sample* category are *IFrame* and *Web Proxy*. These applications provide a gateway to other sites.

Shopping

Under the *Shopping* category you will find two applications. The *Shopping* application provides a shopping cart and the *Amazon Rankings* application displays Amazon.com sales-rank information.

Tools

Under the *Tools* category, you will find a list of several useful portlets such as dictionary, language settings, network utilities, password generator, quick notes, search, and so on.

Undefined

The *Undefined* category contains portlets whose categories have not been defined by the portlet developers.

Wiki

The *Wiki* category contains the *Wiki* application, which allows you to set up a wiki on your portal, and the *Workflow* application, which allows you to create and manage workflows.

Setting Up the Home Page

Now that you've gotten a brief overview of Liferay's official applications and you've become acquainted with the process of adding an application to a portal page, you can start setting up the contents for the *Home* page of our securities portal. The *Home* page will include descriptive information about our portal, site navigation, and current news. You'll also include the login application, which will request login information from a user and display it to a user who has already logged in.

To add introductory text to the portal, you'll use the application called *Journal Content*.

Adding an Introduction

To put a portal introduction on the *Home* page, add the *Journal Content* application from the *CMS* category. After you've done this, your screen should look like the one shown in Figure 2-20.

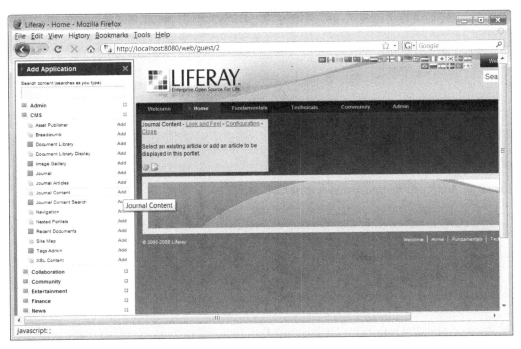

Figure 2-20. *The Journal Content application screen*

At the top of the application screen, you will find links that allow you to set the look and feel and to configure the application. Next to the *Configuration* link, you will find the *Close* link. Clicking this link removes the application from the web page (after you confirm you'd like to delete it, of course). At the bottom of the application screen, you will find two icons: one allows you to select an existing article for display; the other allows you to add a new article. You don't have any articles yet, so select the option to create a new one.

Creating an Article

Click the *Add Article* icon to bring up the screen shown in Figure 2-21. Here, you will be able to create a new article for display.

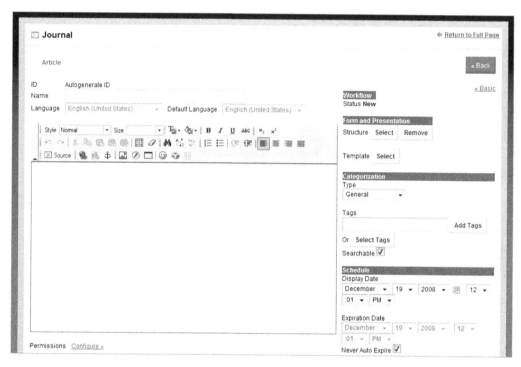

Figure 2-21. *Adding contents to a new journal article*

In the article editor, enter the following information:

Welcome to

Inernational Security Investors Portal

Are you a small investor or a big investor? Do you invest in domestic markets or world markets? Are you a short-term investor or a long-term investor? Do you trust technical analysis or fundamental analysis? It doesn't matter. As long as you trade in securities, this portal is for you.

After entering the information, select and format the text as you wish. (I'll show you some typical sample output later in this section.) After you are done with the text editing, enter the article name as **Welcome Journal** and click the *Save and Approve* button at the bottom of the screen. This returns you to the portal *Home* page, where you'll be able to see the journal-article entry as you formatted it.

Adding an Image

You will now add an image to the journal article. Open the main *Journal Content* application screen to display your article list. Select an article and click the *Edit Article* icon to open it in the editor. Place the cursor at the top-left corner of the article where you would like to add the image, and click the *Insert/Edit Image* icon in the editor toolbox to open the *Image Properties* dialog (see Figure 2-22).

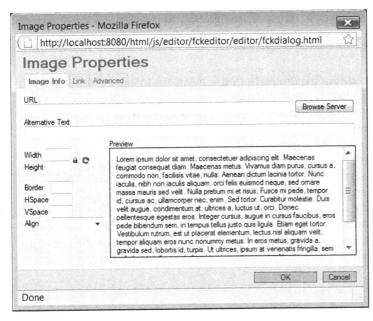

Figure 2-22. *Selecting an image for the journal article*

In the *Image Properties* dialog, you need to enter the URL of your image. You haven't loaded the image on the server yet, so click the *Browse Server* button to see the list of available servers. Select the Guest folder and create a new subfolder called Images where you will store your uploaded image documents. The corresponding screenshot is shown in Figure 2-23.

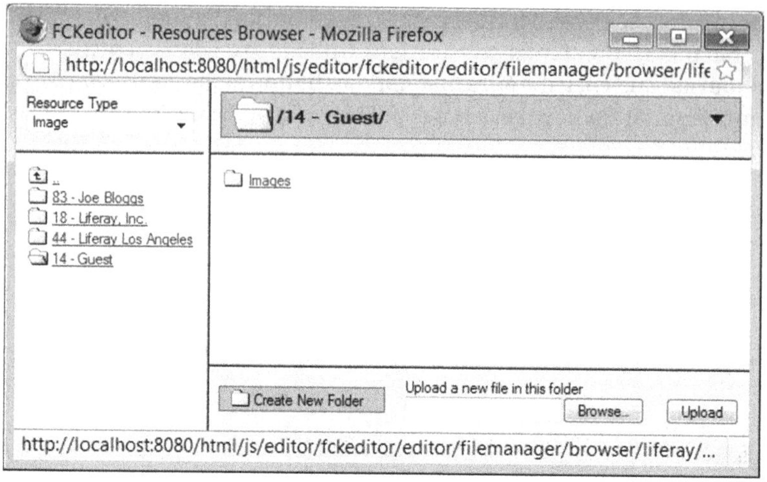

Figure 2-23. *Selecting a folder for uploading images*

Select the Images folder and click the *Browse* button to locate the image file you want to upload. After selecting the file, click the *Upload* button to upload the image file to the server. After the image is uploaded, you will return to the *Browse Server* screen where you can select the recently uploaded file. The URL of the file now appears in the edit box in front of the *Browse Server* button on the *Image Properties* screen.

Stay in the *Image Properties* screen and enter some *Alternative Text* in the corresponding edit box, such as **ISI Logo**. When you hover the mouse cursor over the image, the alternative text you just entered will appear as a tool tip. At this stage, you should be able to see the image along with the rest of the text in your Image Properties window. Click the *OK* button in the image-selection dialog, then click the *Save* button in the editor window to return to the *Home* page and view the changes. You should be able to see both the text and image in the journal entry.

Setting Look and Feel

You will now add some design elements to the article. Click the *Configuration* button (the first button on the left in the group of four buttons displayed in the right-hand corner) and select the *Look and Feel* menu item from the displayed list. You will see the configuration dialog as shown in Figure 2-24.

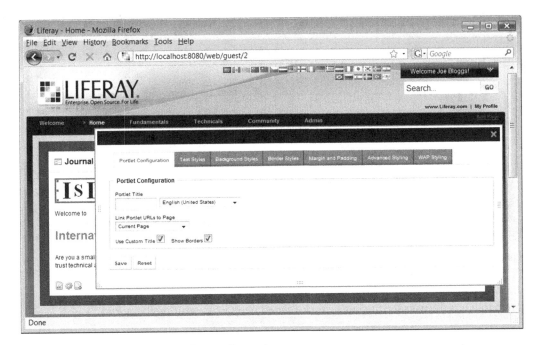

Figure 2-24. *Journal Content portlet-configuration screen*

Here, you will be able to set the text, background, border styles, margins, and paddings. Click the *Background Styles* tab to set the background color for the article (select blue, in this case).

Now set the margins and paddings using the *Margin and Padding* tab. Set the *Padding* to *20 px* and leave the *Margin* setting as is. Now set the portlet title by clicking the *Portlet Configuration* tab. You'll opt for a blank title, so remove any contents from the *Portlet Title* edit box. Check the *Use Custom Title* check box and uncheck the *Show Borders* check box next to it. The latter action will remove the application border when it is displayed on the portal page.

Click the *Save* button to save all the changes you have made to the *Journal Content* portlet. Close the dialog to return to the *Home* page, where all your changes should be reflected in the displayed journal entry. At this stage, your *Home* page should look similar to the one shown in Figure 2-25. (The appearance might differ, depending on the colors you chose and the picture you uploaded.)

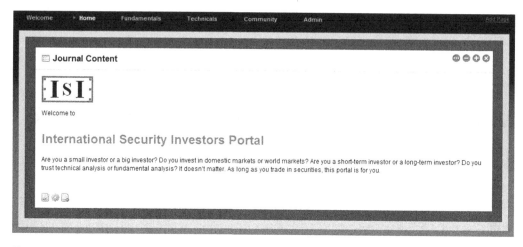

Figure 2-25. *The customized Home page*

Now you'll add a few more applications to your *Home* page, starting with the *News* application that lets the user see the latest stock-related news when visiting the portal.

Adding News

Liferay provides a portal application for an online news feed. You will find this *News* portlet listed under the *News* category of the *Add Application* list. Add this *News* application to your *Home* page and view the changes (see Figure 2-26).

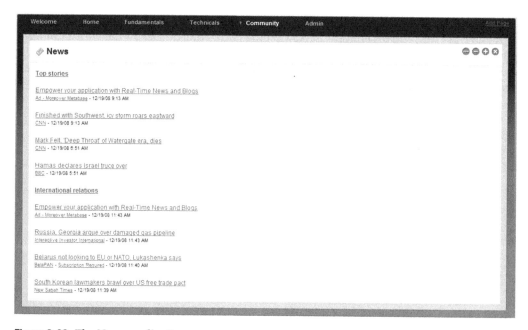

Figure 2-26. *The News application*

As in the case of the *Journal Content* application, you will find icons for setting the look and feel of the application and configuring it. In addition to these two icons, you will find two new icons called *Preferences* and *Guest Preferences*, which let you set the news feed. Use the *Preferences* option to get news related to equities markets. After clicking the *Preferences* icon, you will find the *News Selections* dialog with several news categories displayed in it. By default, two news feeds are already selected for you:

- *International relations* under the *Society* category

- *Top stories* under the *Top Stories* category

Deselect these default options by clicking their respective links and unchecking the corresponding check boxes. Click the *Save* button to persist your changes and the *Back* button to go back to the previous screen. Now click the *Finance* category to see its various news feeds (see Figure 2-27).

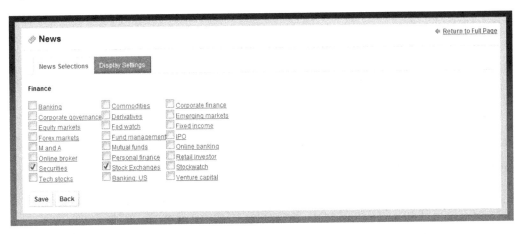

Figure 2-27. *News feeds available under the Finance category*

Select the *Securities* and *Stock Exchanges* options. Save your changes and return to full-screen mode. You will find that the news related to the selected choices is displayed in the *News* portlet. You can select different news feeds by returning to the *Preferences* dialog.

Adding an RSS Feed

Now you'll add an RSS feed to your *Home* page. You will find the *RSS* application listed in the *News* category of the *Add Applications* menu list. Add this application to your *Home* page. As you did with the *News* application, you will need to customize this application by selecting the source for the RSS feed. To select a new URL for the RSS feed, click the *Configuration* icon. You will find three URL sources listed on this page. Remove these sources by clicking the delete icon next to each one. Add these two new URLs by clicking the URL icon and entering the following information in the URL text boxes:

```
http://www.nyse.com/audience/systemstatus/TraderUpdates.xml
http://www.nyse.com/audience/systemstatus/flooralerts.xml
```

After you make the changes, your screen should look like the one shown in Figure 2-28.

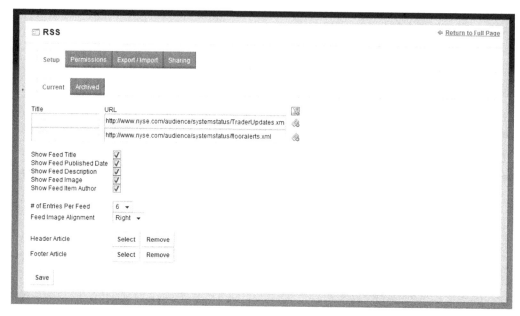

Figure 2-28. *Setting the RSS feed source*

These URLs provide news on the NYSE (New York Stock Exchange). Feel free to add any RSS feed of your choice. You can add multiple URLs for different RSS feeds. Once you complete your edits, save your changes and return to the *Home* page. You will find the news related to your selected topics displayed in the RSS portlet on your *Home* page.

Using the Sign-In and Site-Navigation Portlets

Finally, you will add two more applications to your *Home* page: *Sign In* and *Site Map*. The *Sign In* portlet, listed under the *Tools* category, allows the user to log in to the portal and displays the user information after she logs in. The *Site Map* application, listed under the *CMS* category, displays the map of the entire portal site and allows the user to navigate to any page easily. Add both applications to your *Home* page. The use of these applications is self-explanatory.

As an alternative to the *Site Map* portlet, you can use the *Breadcrumb* portlet or the *Navigation* portlet under the *CMS* category to display site-location information on your page. The *Navigation* portlet allows you to set the display and bullet styles for the displayed map path, whereas the *Breadcrumb* portlet allows you to set only the display style. These two portlets are also context-sensitive. For instance, the *Navigation* portlet shows only navigation options to child pages of the page where it is being shown. The *Breadcrumb* portlet allows you to view a context-sensitive list of your navigation history.

Now that you have added a few applications to the *Home* page, you'll rearrange their positions on the page to get the look you want and improve usability as a result.

Changing Page Layouts

Liferay provides several templates you can use to customize your page layouts. To apply a new template to your page, select the *Layout Template* menu option under the *Welcome* drop-down menu. You'll see a dialog box displaying several layout options (see Figure 2-29).

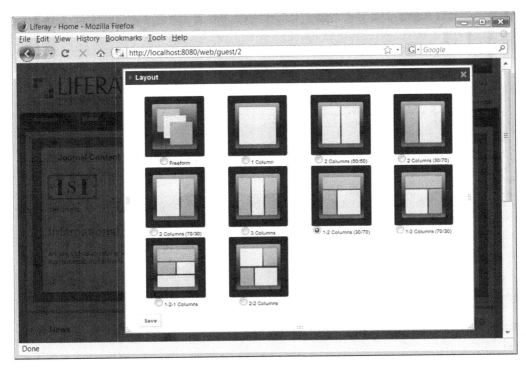

Figure 2-29. *Layout-selection dialog*

Here, you will find several layouts containing different combinations of columns and rows. If you apply the *Freeform* template to your page, for example, you will be able to set the absolute position for each application on the page. But for the time being, select the *1-2 Columns (30/70)* layout template for the *Home* page. Saving your selection returns you to the *Home* page with the new template applied to it. Now, you will need to rearrange your applications based on this template.

To move an application to a new location on the page, move the cursor to the application's title bar. Notice the pointer changes into a hand-like icon. Click and drag the application to the desired location. As you drag the application on the screen, Liferay displays the layout screen in the background. This makes it easy for you to identify and set the new position for your application. The application width automatically adjusts to the new width of your layout row or column.

Move all the applications to rearrange the page in a way that is most convenient for your use. A typical layout result is shown in Figure 2-30.

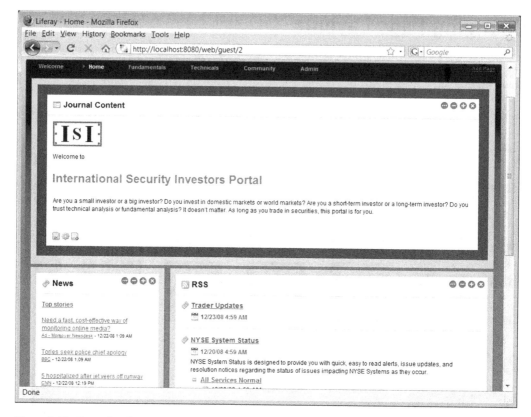

Figure 2-30. *Completed Home page*

■**Note** You can apply a different template to each portal page to give it an individual look.

If you are not satisfied with Liferay's official layouts, you can always download third-party layouts from the community-downloads section of the Liferay site. The procedure for downloading and installing the additional layouts is similar to the process for downloading and installing themes, as described earlier. When you download and install a layout, it gets added to the layout-selection dialog automatically. Simply select the new layout of your choice to apply it to your page.

Summary

This chapter started with a description of the portal that you'll be creating as you read this book: a portal for securities investors. I described the requirements for such a portal, such as access to widespread information on a timely basis; fundamental and technical analysis; expert advice; and peer-to-peer interaction.

After gathering the portal requirements, you learned how to create and manage pages on the portal. You now know how to add, delete, and modify a page. You can create a hierarchy of pages and manage their display order.

You also learned to set the look and feel of a page by applying a theme; you can apply a single theme to the entire portal, or individual themes to individual pages. You added the *Plugin Installer* application to your portal page to install new themes. You also learned how to download, install, and apply the third-party plugins created by Liferay user communities.

After learning to create portal pages, you learned how to add contents to a page. A portal page essentially consists of many applications called *portlets* or *plugins*. Liferay provides many "official" plugins, which are categorized based on their application and use. You'll be using several official applications on the portal described in this book.

You then started creating your first portal page. You set up the *Home* page and added some introductory text to it using the *Journal Content* application. You customized the introduction's look and feel by displaying both text and images and by setting the background color. You added *News* and *RSS* applications, setting the data source for both using the application-customization options. You also added site-navigation applications to your web pages.

Then you learned to modify the page's default display by setting a new page layout. You can apply a layout template to your entire portal, or to individual pages. Liferay provides several page layouts for you to use, and you can download additional layouts from the community-downloads area of Liferay's web site.

In the next chapter, you will learn to set up the organization and its users.

CHAPTER 3

■ ■ ■

Managing Portal Users

Portals are always created, owned, and managed by specific organizations, and the portal we created in the last chapter should be no exception to this rule. So now you'll learn to define an organization within your portal and manage the users within that organization. More specifically, you will learn to

- Create an organization, establish its details, and add multiple locations to it
- Create users, user groups, and a user with administrator privileges
- Set password policies and user-authentication options
- Set mail hosts and notification-mail templates
- Edit the settings of the default plugins available to users
- Create user communities and associate users with those communities

Setting Up an Organization

We'll call our portal *International Security Investors* (ISI), and we'll define an organization with the same name. We'll assume that ISI has acquired the domain isi.com, and that it's based in the United States with offices in other countries (see Table 3-1).

Table 3-1. *Proposed Organizational Map of ISI*

Country	Locations
USA	ISI-Illinois ISI-New York ISI-California ISI-Florida
India	ISI-Mumbai ISI-Delhi ISI-Kolkata
UK	ISI-London ISI-Birmingham
China	ISI-Shanghai ISI-Beijing

We'll create locations for the cities listed in Table 3-1, and user groups for the locations with large user bases. You'll learn to add user groups, assign users to those user groups, and assign roles to those users. You'll also accommodate guest users, who will have restricted rights on our portal.

You will use Liferay's *Enterprise Admin* application to define an organization and perform other user-management tasks. The *Enterprise Admin* application allows you to create user groups, roles, password policies, and so on. In general, if you are creating an intranet portal for your enterprise that is distributed worldwide, this application will help you define the organizational structure. Use the *Add Application* menu to add the *Enterprise Admin* application to the *Welcome* page or any other portal page you'd like. (See Chapter 2 for details on creating portal pages.)

Creating a New Organization

To define a new organization, click the *Organizations* tab in the *Enterprise Admin* application. You will see a screen similar to the one shown in Figure 3-1.

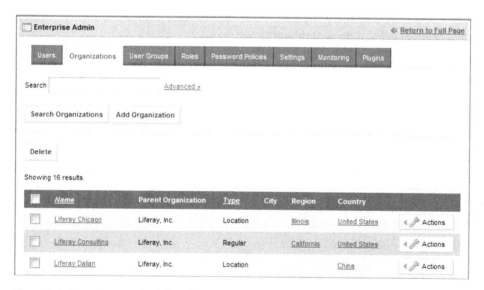

Figure 3-1. *List of currently defined organizations*

Here, you will find several organizations already defined in your installation. The *Search* option in the upper portion of the dialog allows you to search for an organization with a particular name. If you perform a search, all the organizations matching that search criterion will appear in the bottom portion of the screen.

Alongside the *Search Organizations* button, you will find a button entitled *Add Organization*. Click this button to pull up a dialog box for creating a new organization (see Figure 3-2).

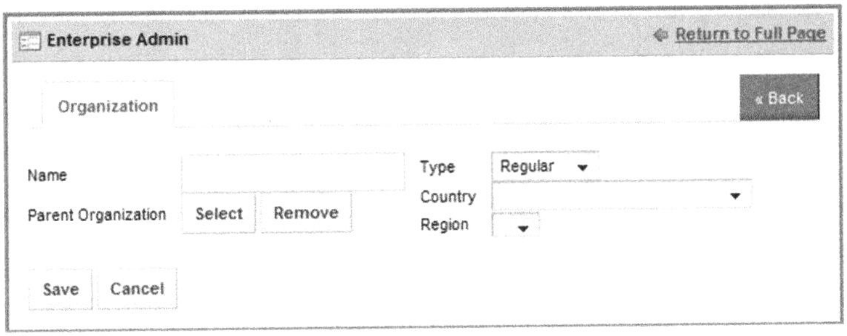

Figure 3-2. *Defining a new organization*

On this screen, enter **ISI** in the *Name* edit box and select *Regular* from the *Type* drop-down box. You have two choices for the *Type* setting: *Regular* and *Location*. You should assign *Regular* to the organization's headquarters and *Location* to any of its satellite offices. Select *United States* as the *Country* and *Illinois* as the *Region*. Don't worry about assigning the organization a unique ID; Liferay automatically does that for you.

The *Select* button near the *Parent Organization* label allows you to define the parent organization for the organization being created. Because our ISI organization is itself a parent organization, do not click this button. After entering the information, click the *Save* button to save your changes. This creates the ISI organization in your Liferay portal installation. Next, you will add some other organization details.

Adding Organization Details

After your request for creating a new organization is processed successfully, Liferay opens a dialog asking you to enter further details about the newly created organization. It displays three sections for adding addresses, services, and comments underneath the organization definition (see Figure 3-3).

Every organization has e-mail and snail-mail addresses, web sites, phone numbers, and so on. Under the *Save* button, you will find four tabs:

- *Email Addresses*
- *Addresses*
- *Websites*
- *Phone Numbers*

You use these tabs to add the corresponding details to the organization.

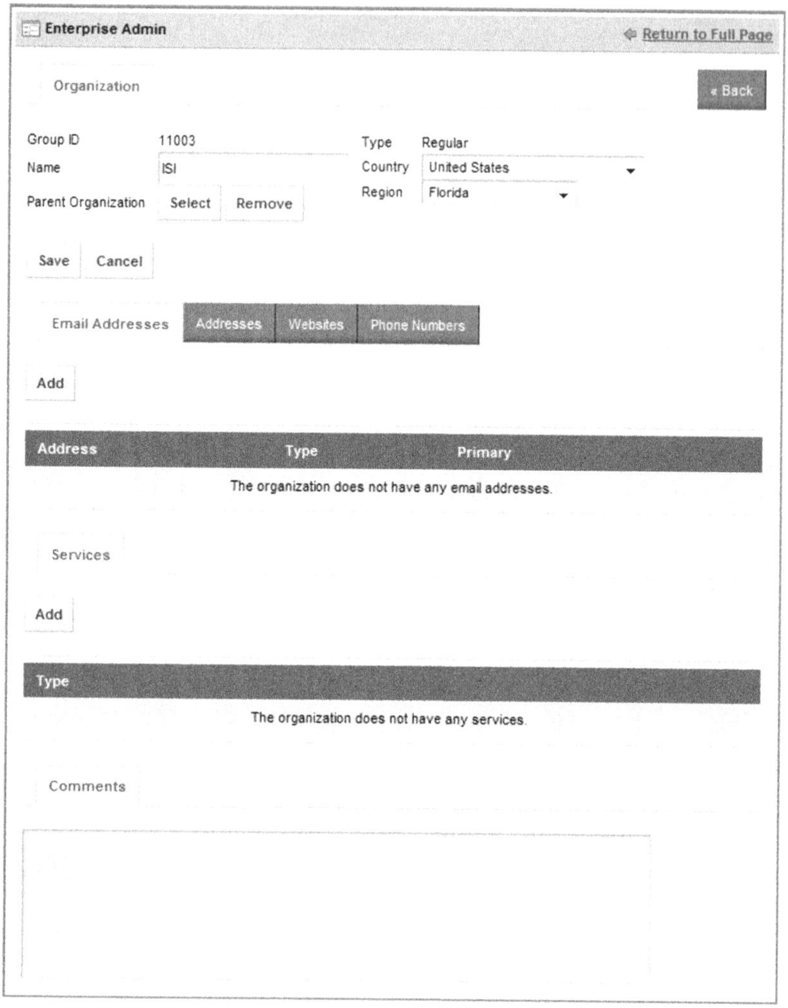

Figure 3-3. *Dialog for entering organization details*

Email Addresses

To add the organization's e-mail addresses, select the *Email Addresses* tab and click the *Add* button shown underneath. You will see the screen shown in Figure 3-4.

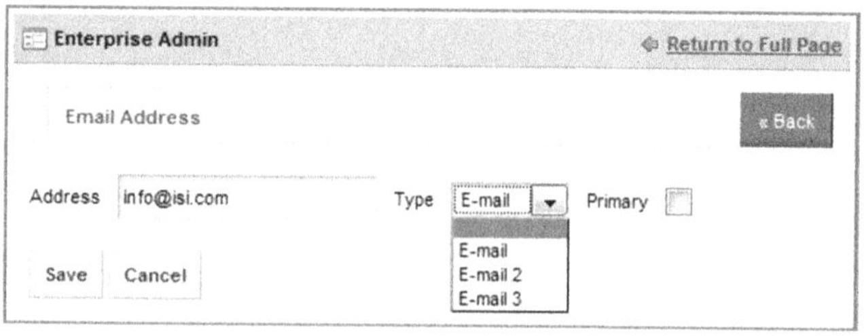

Figure 3-4. *Setting up the organization's e-mail addresses*

You'll see an *Address* text box and a *Type* drop-down list box. You have three *Type* choices: *E-mail*, *E-mail 2*, and *E-mail 3*. Enter **info@isi.com** as the e-mail address and set its type to *E-mail*; make it a primary e-mail address by marking the corresponding check box. You can add as many addresses as you'd like, but note that you can have only one primary address. After entering an address and its type, save your edits by clicking the *Save* button.

Addresses

Next, you will enter the snail-mail address of our organization. Select the *Addresses* tab and click the *Add* button. In the resulting dialog, enter your organization's street address and specify whether it will serve as your mailing address and/or your primary address by selecting the corresponding check boxes. After entering the details, save your changes. The details you entered will appear immediately on the *Organization* screen under the *Addresses* tab. If you wish to edit or delete a listed address, click the *Actions* button next to it and choose the appropriate option (see Figure 3-5).

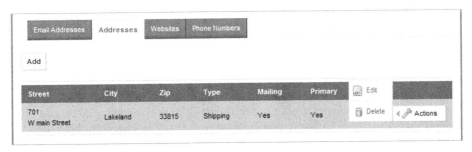

Figure 3-5. *Edit and Delete options for modifying organization details*

Web Sites and Phone Numbers

To enter the web site for our ISI organization, select the *Websites* tab, click the *Add* button, and enter the URL http://www.isi.com in the resulting dialog. Select its type as *Public*. (The other option for the type is *Intranet*.) Mark the *Primary* check box.

To add phone numbers for your organization, select the *Phone Numbers* tab and click the *Add* button. In the resulting dialog, add the number, the extension, the type, and whether it is a primary contact number. You can choose from several predefined types, such as fax, local, toll-free, and so on. You can enter multiple phone numbers and change them any time by going into the *Edit* option of the *Actions* menu.

Services and Comments

After adding the organization's primary details, you can add a list of services that it offers. You will find the *Services* tab underneath the series of tabs for contact information. Click the *Add* button to pull up the screen for adding services offered by your organization (see Figure 3-6).

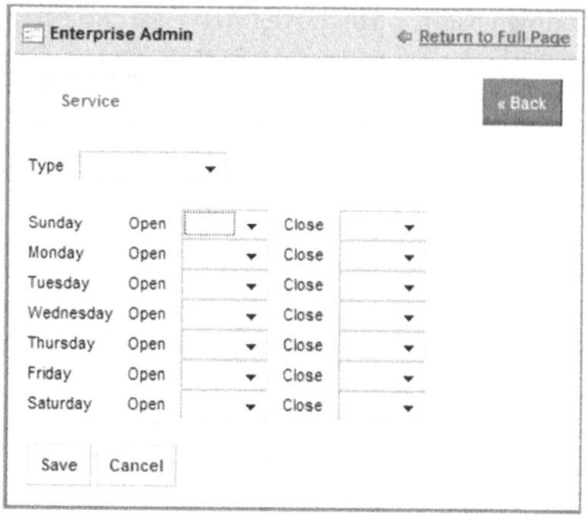

Figure 3-6. *Setting the organization's service details*

The *Type* drop-down box lists several predefined services such as *Administrative, Contract, Training*, and so on. You can add multiple services for your organization. For each service, you can specify the hours of availability for different days of the week. Because we are creating a portal that will be available to our users around the clock, we will not list any services for our organization.

Lastly, you can add any comments to your organization definition in the multiline edit control at the bottom of the *Organization* screen. Save all your changes. This completes the organization definition.

Defining the Organization's Locations

We will now add the information about our organization's worldwide locations (see Table 3-1). Each ISI location will have its own organization that's a child of the parent ISI organization. I'll show you how to create the locations for the offices in India: Mumbai (formerly known as Bombay), New Delhi, and Kolkata (formerly called Calcutta).

To create a new child organization, click the *Add Organization* button in the *Enterprise Admin* application. Enter **ISI-Mumbai** as the organization name, select *Location* (rather than *Regular*) as the type, and enter **India** as the country (see Figure 3-2). Now you need to select the parent organization. Click the *Select* button next to the *Parent Organization* label, then select *ISI* from the resulting list. Save your changes by clicking the *Save* button and return to the organization definition screen. Here you can add details specific to the *ISI-Mumbai* organization as you did for the main *ISI* organization.

Add two more organizations called *ISI-Delhi* and *ISI-Kolkata* under the main *ISI* organization. Make sure that you enter the relevant details for each organization under its organization definition.

Creating Users

Now we will add users to our organization. Select the *Users* tab in the *Enterprise Admin* application screen and click the *Add User* button to get the screen shown in Figure 3-7.

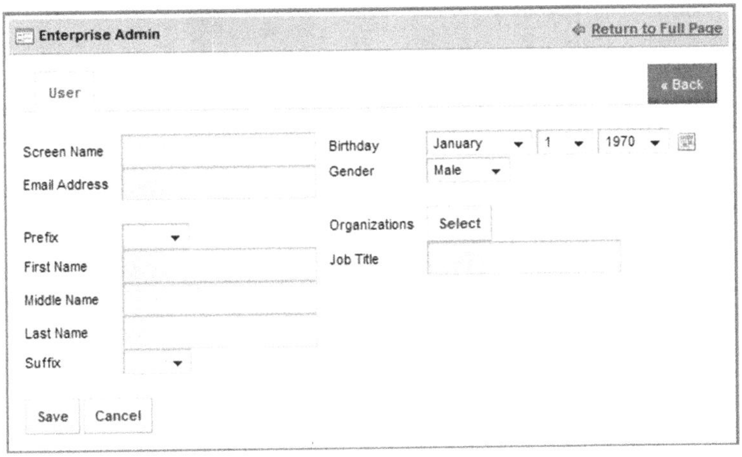

Figure 3-7. *Creating a new user*

You'll first create the *Admin* user to whom we will assign the administrative rights for managing our entire portal. Provide the following information for the *Admin* user:

1. *Screen Name*: Enter **Admin**.

2. *Email Address*: Enter **admin@india.isi.com**.

3. *Prefix*: Enter **Ms.**

4. *First Name*: Enter **Anita**.

5. *Last Name*: Enter **Thomas**.

6. *Birthday*: Provide the birthday of your choice using the drop-down boxes.

7. *Gender*: Choose *Female*.

8. Organizations: Click the *Select* button and choose *ISI*.

9. Job Title: Enter **Administrator**.

Save your edits. You now have a new user in your ISI organization. After you save the changes, you'll get a screen that lets you enter further details (see Figure 3-8).

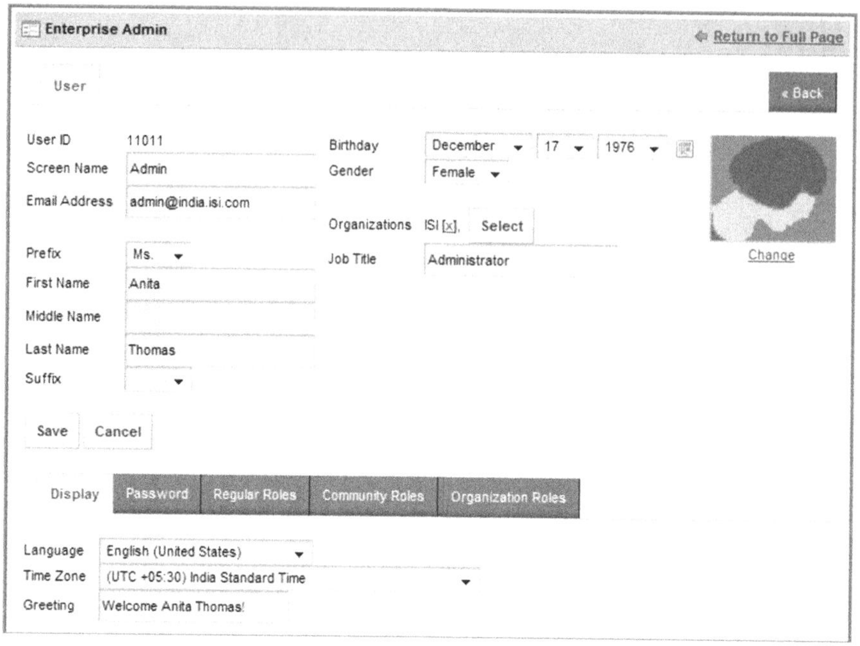

Figure 3-8. *Entering user details*

Note that the image displayed in Figure 3-8 is not set automatically. I created this picture and uploaded it for this *Admin* user. You can easily change the picture by clicking the *Change* link under the picture and selecting the desired image file.

■**Note** You probably noticed the "Welcome Joe Bloggs!" message with a drop-down menu on your portal. This text comes from the welcome message created in the *User* screen's *Display* tab (see the following "Display Options" section). For our *Admin* user Anita, **Welcome Anita Thomas!** appears in the *Greeting* field automatically. So whenever she logs in to the portal with her account, she'll see "Welcome Anita Thomas!" instead of "Welcome Joe Bloggs!"

From the *User* screen shown in Figure 3-8, you can set various details including the user's welcome message, password, and roles. Let us look at these options one by one.

Display Options

Under the *Display* tab, you can set the user's default language, time zone, and greeting message (see Figure 3-8). Select the default language from the *Language* drop-down list and the time zone from the *Time Zone* list. We will set this to *UTC +05:30* for our *Admin* user Anita, who resides in India. In the *Greeting* message, Liferay has already added a welcome message incorporating the username you entered while creating the user on the previous screen. Do not forget to save your edits by clicking the *Save* button.

Password Settings

Select the *Password* tab to set the password for the newly created user—enter **admin** as the password, in this case. Note that you'll need this password the next time you sign in using the *Admin* account. If you mark the *Password Reset Required* check box on this screen, the user will be required to change the password during the first login. Remember to save your changes by clicking the *Save* button.

User Roles

Each user assumes a particular role while using the portal. Depending on the role, the user will be assigned a certain set of permissions. The three predefined roles are:

- *Regular Roles*
- *Community Roles*
- *Organization Roles*

Click the *Regular Roles* tab and locate the *Assign Regular Roles* button. Below the button, you will find the two default roles that Liferay has already assigned: *Power User* and *User*. If you want to assign an additional role, click the *Assign Regular Roles* button. This opens up a screen that displays the list of current roles. Click the *Available* tab to get a list of all available roles (see Figure 3-9).

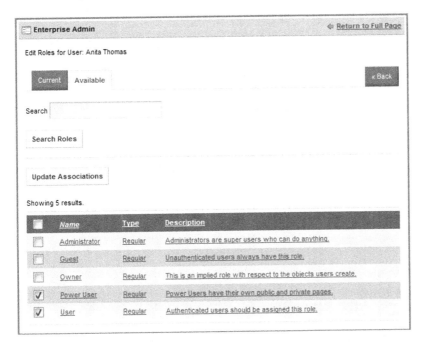

Figure 3-9. *Assigning roles to a user*

Because we are creating an *Admin* user with administrator privileges, you should assign the *Administrator* role. Mark the check box near the *Administrator* role and click the *Update*

Associations button above the role names. This associates the new role with the current user. Now go to the *Current* tab to verify that our *Admin* user now has three roles listed onscreen: *Administrator*, *Power User*, and *User*. After logging in to her account, Anita Thomas will now enjoy administrator privileges as Joe Bloggs does. So we don't need to log in to Joe's account from now on. We can log in to Anita's account to create and manage our ISI portal.

■**Tip** You can now delete the default *Welcome* page that Liferay provided in your portal. From this point forward, you can use the *Admin* account to create new pages and manage the entire site.

In addition to the *Regular* roles, you can set the user's *Community* and *Organization* roles. In fact, Liferay allows you to create new roles under these categories and assign them to any user. Click the *Back* button to see the tabs for *Community Roles* and *Organization Roles*. Clicking these tabs will enable you to assign the respective roles.

User Addresses

Underneath the *Display* tab on the *User* screen, you will find a list of tabs that allow you to set the various types of addresses for the user:

- *Email Addresses*
- *Addresses*
- *Websites*

These tabs allow you to enter a user's e-mail and snail-mail addresses, as well as a URL. The default address is the organization address. The screen for entering these details resembles the screen for entering the details for your new organization.

Phone Numbers and IDs

Under the *Addresses* section of the *User* screen, you will find a tabbed page with options for entering several IDs and phone numbers for the created user. Here are the options you can work with:

- *Phone Numbers*
- *OpenID*
- *SMS Messenger ID*
- *Instant Messenger IDs*
- *Social Network IDs*
- *Alerts and Announcements*

Adding a user phone number is similar to adding a phone number for the organization. (The default number is the organization phone number.) Likewise, adding the *OpenID* and *SMS Messenger ID* is straightforward. Just click the respective tabs and enter the requested information.

The *Instant Messenger IDs* screen allows you to add several IDs pertaining to different IM (Instant Messenger) service providers. These are AIM, ICQ, Jabber, MSN, Skype, and Yahoo! Messenger. Under the *Social Network IDs*, you can enter the user IDs for Facebook, MySpace, and Twitter.

Finally, under the *Alerts and Announcements* tab, you will find the delivery-mode options for different types of alerts and announcements (see Figure 3-10). You can choose from e-mail delivery, SMS delivery, and web-site delivery, the latter of which is the default. You can opt for one delivery mode or multiple delivery modes for each type of message—*General*, *News*, or *Test*.

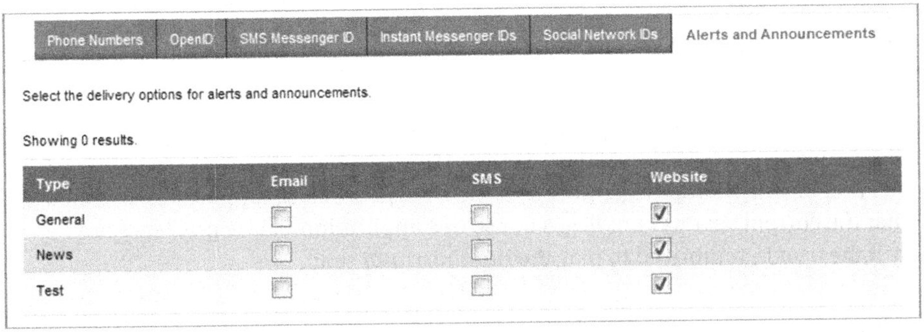

| Phone Numbers | OpenID | SMS Messenger ID | Instant Messenger IDs | Social Network IDs | Alerts and Announcements |

Select the delivery options for alerts and announcements.

Showing 0 results.

Type	Email	SMS	Website
General	☐	☐	☑
News	☐	☐	☑
Test	☐	☐	☑

Figure 3-10. *Setting delivery options for alerts and announcements*

Signing In As an Administrator

In the previous section, you created an *Admin* user with administrator privileges. Now you will log off from the current test user and sign in using the new *Admin* user account. Go to the *Welcome* menu and click *Sign Out* to sign off from the test-user account. Click the *Sign In* menu to log on using the new account. Enter the following username and password:

Login: **admin@india.isi.com**

Password: **admin**

If you set the user correctly in the previous section, your login will succeed and you will see the message with "Anita Thomas" displayed in the *Sign In* application of the *Welcome* page (see Figure 3-11). Of course, the first time you sign in, you will need to accept the terms of use.

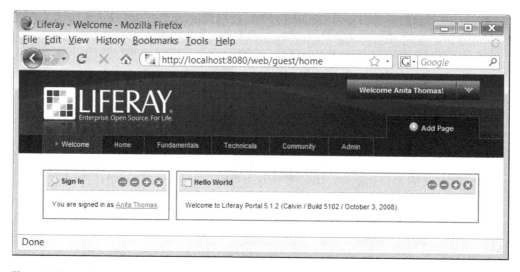

Figure 3-11. *Welcome screen for the new Admin user*

If you didn't already do so in the section "Setting Up an Organization," add the *Enterprise Admin* application to your *Admin* page. Note that the *Enterprise Admin* application is enabled, indicating that the current user has privileges to use this application. These privileges are granted only if the user is authorized to play the *Administrator* role.

Adding More Users

Using your *Admin* account, you will now add a few users to the portal. The process of creating an additional user is the same as creating the *Admin* user (see the "Creating Users" section).

Under the *Users* tab in the *Enterprise Admin* application, click on the *Add User* button to add a new user. As you did with the *Admin* user, enter the appropriate details and select the appropriate organization. Then you'll be prompted to enter the additional information about phone numbers, addresses, and IDs.

You can use the default roles for the new users, or assign some of them only the *Guest* role. Later on, you will be able set the privileges for each role to control which pages and applications are available to a given user under a certain role. For the time being, create a few users at different organizational locations. (Read more about roles and permissions in the section "Setting Permissions over a User" under "Performing Actions on Users.")

For this example, let's create users with usernames consisting of two letters followed by four numbers. The first letter designates the user's location: *m* for Mumbai, *d* for Delhi, or *k* for Kolkata. The second letter designates whether the user is a fundamental analyst (*f*) or a technical analyst (*t*); later we'll assign those users to corresponding groups. The four-digit number indicates the order in which the user was created. So your first few fundamental analysts in Mumbai would be named *mf0001*, *mf0002*, and so on. Your first few technical analysts in Kolkata would be *kt0001*, *kt0002*, and so on.

Creating User Groups

Now, we will create two user groups: the *Fundamental Analysts* and the *Technical Analysts*. Select the *User Groups* tab in the *Enterprise Admin* application screen; you'll have the option to search for an existing user group or to create a new user group. Click the *Add User Group* button to create a new user group. Your screen should look like the one shown in Figure 3-12.

Figure 3-12. *Defining a new user group*

On this screen, enter the name and description of the user group you want to create. For the first group, enter the name **Fundamental Analysts** and this description: **This group meets the requirements of fundamental analysts**. For the second group, enter the name **Technical Analysts** and this description: **This group meets the requirements of technical analysts**.

Saving your edits brings you back to the *Enterprise Admin* screen, where you will find the newly added groups listed at the bottom.

Assigning Members to User Groups

Your next task is to assign members to the user groups you just created. Select the *User Groups* tab in the *Enterprise Admin* application again. You will see a list of available user groups. Click the *Actions* button associated with the group to which you wish to add members. You'll see a menu that shows the different actions you can perform on the selected group (see Figure 3-13).

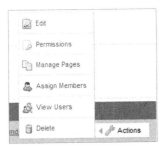

Figure 3-13. *Permitted actions on user groups*

Click the *Assign Members* option. The resulting screen shows a list of currently assigned members, which in our case is empty. Click the *Available* tab to see which users are available to add to the list (see Figure 3-14).

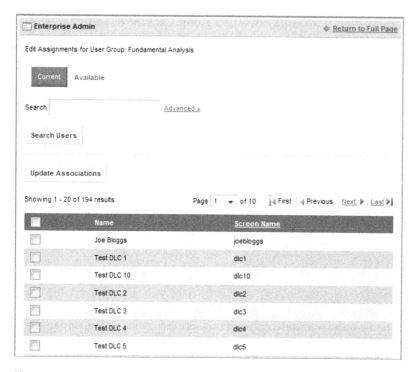

Figure 3-14. *List of users available for assignment*

Select users such as *kf0001*, *mf0001*, and *mf0002* by marking the corresponding check boxes in the list. Or you could use the *Search Users* facility to locate the desired users. Click the *Update Associations* button to add these users to the currently selected group. If you now select the *View Users* option under the group's *Actions* menu, you will see all members of the group.

The other actions you can take on a user group include setting permissions by assigning roles, managing pages belonging to a group, editing the group information, and deleting the group itself. Some of these options closely resemble the actions you can perform on individual users, which we'll discuss in the "Performing Actions on Users" section.

Organization Structure

If you have followed all the steps for creating the ISI organization, creating users, defining user groups, and assigning members to those groups, your organization structure should look like the one shown in Table 3-2.

Table 3-2. *ISI Organization Structure*

Organization	ISI (International Security Investors)					
Location	**ISI-Mumbai**		**ISI-Delhi**		**ISI-Kolkata**	
User Group	**Fundamental Analysts**	**Technical Analysts**	**Fundamental Analysts**	**Technical Analysts**	**Fundamental Analysts**	**Technical Analysts**
User	mf0001	mt0001	df0001	dt0001	kf0001	kt0001
	mf0002	mt0002	df0002	dt0002	kf0002	kt0002
	....	....	....	....	....	....
	....	....	....	....	....	....
	....	....	....	....	....	....

Performing Actions on Users

Clicking the *Actions* button associated with an individual user on the *Enterprise Admin* application's *Users* screen yields these options:

- *Edit*
- *Permissions*
- *Manage Pages*
- *Impersonate User*
- *Deactivate*

You will now study each of these options.

Note If you click the *Actions* button associated with your own login name, you will see only the first three of the preceding options. This is expected, because impersonating yourself and deactivating your own account do not make sense.

Editing User Information

If you select the *Edit* action on a user, you can edit the user's details in the same screen that you used to create the user. You can assign new values to the fields *Screen Name*, *Email Address*, *First Name*, *Last Name*, and so on. In addition to the basic details, you can also edit the password settings, roles, addresses, and web sites, phone numbers, SMS IDs, and IM IDs. Save your changes when you're done.

Setting Permissions over a User

With the *Permissions* option in the actions menu, you can assign various permissions regarding how *other* users can manipulate a selected user's account. For example, you can determine whether other users can view a selected user's details. You can also remove a user's ability to delete his own account or edit his own details.

To work with the permissions over a user, click the *Available* tab under *Regular Roles*. An edit-permissions screen for a typical user is shown in Figure 3-15.

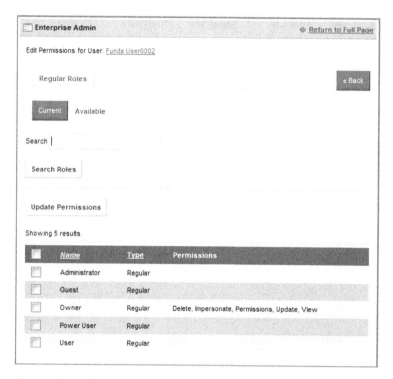

Figure 3-15. *Assigning permissions to a user*

Select the *Power User* role and click the *Update Permissions* button. You will see the screen shown in Figure 3-16.

On this screen, you will see the various privileges available to the *Power User* role over the selected user. The list on the left displays what users under that role *can* do with the selected user's account; the list on the right displays what those users *can't* do. Using the two arrow buttons shown between the lists, move the actions from one list to another to achieve the desired permissions. After completing the changes, click the *Finished* button to return to the edit-permissions screen. You will find the new set of permissions listed to the right of the selected role.

When a user in this role signs on to the portal, she will have the permissions over the selected user as you defined on this edit-permissions screen.

Note The *Administrator* role always has all permissions over a user, so there is no need to set up the *Administrator* role in any user account.

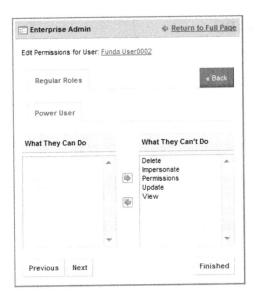

Figure 3-16. *Updating permissions for the Power User role*

Managing Pages

The *Manage Pages* option in the actions menu allows you to manage a list of pages for the selected user. You can add new pages, arrange their hierarchy, set the display order, apply different page templates, and so on. These options are the same as the ones offered by Liferay's *Manage Pages* menu option that we discussed in Chapter 2.

Impersonating a User

With the *Impersonate User* option, you can impersonate the selected user. So if you have currently logged in as our administrator, Anita Thomas, and if you select this menu option on another user named *Funda User0002*, you will find yourself logged in as *Funda User0002* in a new browser window. You'll also see a message that clearly states you are impersonating another user. The message displays a link allowing you to return to your own user account (see Figure 3-17).

Figure 3-17. *Impersonating a user*

Deactivating a User

Clicking the *Deactivate* option deactivates the selected user (after you confirm the deactivation, of course). After the user is deactivated, he will be removed from the list of users.

Establishing Password Policies

By this time, you have created an organization and added several users to it. Each of these users will log on to our portal using the username and password supplied by the administrator. It is important that the user set her own password—she shouldn't use the administrator-assigned password forever. In fact, you saw earlier (in the "Password Settings" section under "Creating Users") that the administrator can force the user to change her password during her first login. However, we need better password policies than this to ensure the safety and security of our portal. Liferay provides a default password policy and also allows you to create your own policies for securing your portal.

To edit the existing password policy or to create a new policy, select the *Password Policies* tab in the *Enterprise Admin* application. You will find the *Default Password Policy* in the list of available policies. By default, this is the only policy available to you, so you will now create a policy of your own. To do so, click the *Add Password Policy* button to open the screen shown in Figure 3-18.

Figure 3-18. *Creating a new password policy*

Enter a name and description of your choice for this new policy. If you want a forced change on the password, enable the *Changeable* check box. Also mark the *Change Required* check box and select the *Minimum Age* to one of the values displayed in the drop-down list. Your users will now be forced to wait until the indicated time period elapses before they are allowed to change their password.

In addition to a forced change in password, you can set several features on your password policy:

- *Syntax Checking Enabled*: If this option is enabled, the entered password would be checked for its length and/or compared against certain words.

- *History Enabled*: If this is enabled, the portal maintains a history of passwords and prevents the user from repeating previous passwords.

- *Expiration Enabled*: When this is enabled, the user's password expires after the specified time period elapses.

- *Lockout Enabled*: When this option is selected, the portal automatically locks out the user after a certain number of login failures.

When you select any of the preceding options, the application displays further options that allow you to fine-tune the selected feature (see Figure 3-19).

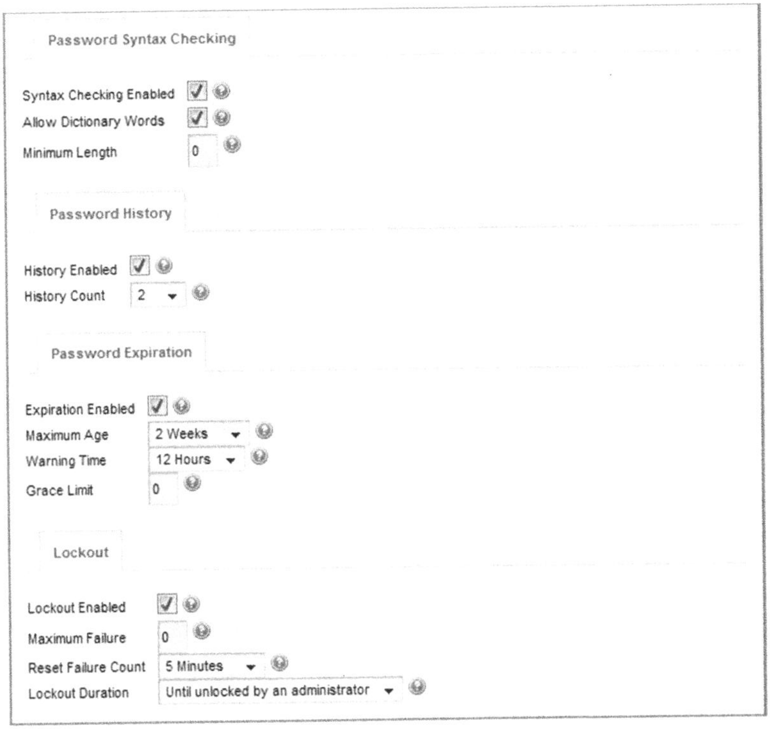

Figure 3-19. *Available options for a new password policy*

Changing Default Settings

In the process of creating an organization, defining its structure, and adding users, you probably noticed that Liferay assigns default values to several fields. You can actually change these default settings and assign your own values to certain fields. Here are the settings you can change:

- *General Settings*: You can specify name, ticker symbol, mail server, and so on.

- *Authentication*: You can control how a user is authenticated on the portal.

- *Default User Associations*: You can set the default communities, roles, and user groups.

- *Reserve Screen Names*: You can reserve screen names and e-mail IDs so that nobody else can use them.

- *Mail Host Names*: You can set the mail-host names.

- *Email Notifications*: You can set the default e-mail addresses and templates for notification messages.

You will now study each of these options in detail.

General Settings

The *General* settings screen is shown in Figure 3-20.

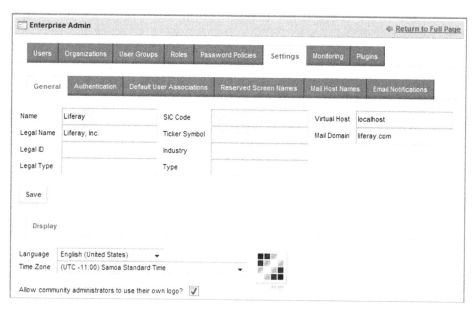

Figure 3-20. *Default general settings*

You will change the default values and use values specific to the organization. Enter the following information in the *General* settings dialog:

- *Name*: **ISI**

- *Legal Name*: **ISI Ltd.**

- *Ticker Symbol*: **ISI**

- *Industry*: **Finance**

- *Type*: **Securities**

- *Mail Domain*: **isi.com**

- *Time Zone*: **EST**

Leave the rest of the fields at their default values. Save your edits by clicking the *Save* button.

In the *Display* subscreen, you will find the Liferay logo. You will now set your own logo here. Click the *Change* link underneath the displayed logo. In the file-selection dialog, enter the path and file name of the ISI enterprise logo. Save your changes. The modified screen is shown in Figure 3-21.

Figure 3-21. *Modifying general settings*

When you return to full-page view, you will find the new logo displayed on the page.

Note Not all page themes display the logo. Figure 3-21 uses the *Classic* theme, which displays the logo, but themes such as *Jedi* and *Transparentia* do not.

Authentication

On the *Authentication* screen, you will find several settings pertaining to different types of authentication:

- *General*

- *LDAP*

- *CAS*

- *NTLM*

- *OpenID*

- *Open SSO*

- *SiteMinder*

General Settings

The *General* settings screen for authentication is displayed in Figure 3-22.

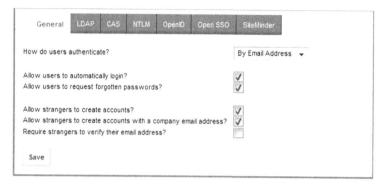

Figure 3-22. *General settings for authenticating a user*

Here, you can select the mode of authentication. This can be any of the following three values:

- *By Email Address*
- *By Screen Name*
- *By User ID*

Depending on this value, the user will be required to enter her e-mail address, screen name, or user ID while logging in to the portal. You can then mark the desired check boxes to change other authentication settings. For example, you can allow the user to log in automatically using her previously entered credentials. And if the user forgets her password, she can request the password by e-mail. You can also allow strangers to create accounts.

LDAP

Liferay supports several LDAP servers for user authentication. On the *LDAP* settings dialog, you will find a list of several servers:

- *Apache Directory Server*
- *Fedora Directory Server*
- *Microsoft Active Directory Server*
- *Novell eDirectory*
- *OpenLDAP*
- *Other Directory Server*

Select the directory server that your organization is using and enter its relevant details (see Figure 3-23).

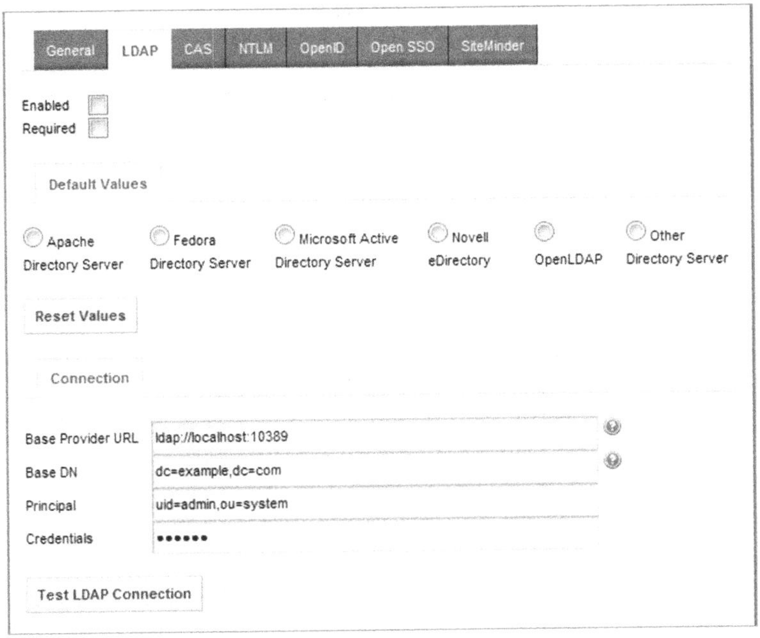

Figure 3-23. *Directory-server settings*

Here, you will be required to enter the server-connection details, specify search filters for user authentication and mappings, specify search filters for groups and their mappings, select the password policy, and so on. Note that these details depend on the particular server and its installation. Liferay facilitates the verification of details by providing several test buttons on this screen.

Others

Other tabs listed on the *Authentication* screen include *CAS, NTLM, OpenID, Open SSO,* and *SiteMinder.*

On the *CAS* settings screen, you will have to enter the login/logout URLs, the server name, the service URL, and other details. On the *NTLM* settings screen, enter the IP for the domain controller and the domain name. On the *OpenID* screen, there are no additional settings. You simply need to enable this option by marking the *Enabled* check box. On the *Open SSO* screen, enter information such as the login/logout URLs and service URL, as well as attributes for screen name, e-mail address, first name, and last name.

Default User Associations

You can set the default associations for the newly created users in the *Default User Associations* screen under the top-level *Settings* tab in the *Enterprise Admin* application (see Figure 3-24).

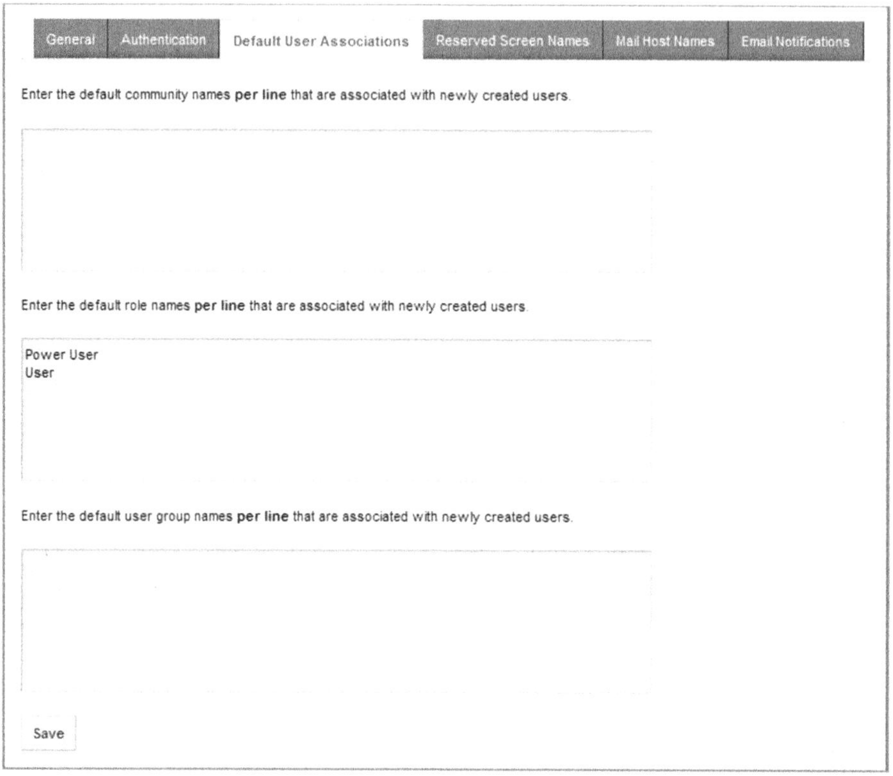

Figure 3-24. *Setting default associations for a new user*

Here, you can enter the default community names in the top multiline edit control. In the case of multiple community associations, you enter each community name on a separate line. The newly created users will be automatically associated with the communities listed here.

In the second multiline edit control, enter the roles to be associated with the newly created user. The two default roles are *Power User* and *User*. You also saw two Liferay-defined roles, *Administrator* and *Guest*; you can add these roles here if you wish to associate them with the new user.

In the third multiline edit control, enter the names of the groups that a new user will belong to.

Reserved Screen Names

On the *Reserved Screen Names* screen, you can reserve one or more screen names and e-mail addresses to prevent new users from setting up accounts with those values.

Mail Host Names

Click the *Mail Host Names* tab to list additional mail-host names. Note that you already set the main *Mail Domain* in the *General* subscreen within the *Settings* screen (see Figure 3-20).

Email Notifications

The *Email Notifications* screen has three subscreens: *General, Account Created Notification,* and *Password Changed Notification.* Click the *General* tab to set the sender's name and e-mail address for account-related messages generated by your portal. In the other two subscreens, you'll find Liferay's default notification templates for messages confirming that a user has created an account or changed a password. The *Account Created* mail-notification template is shown in Figure 3-25. You can modify the message using the various terms defined underneath the text editor.

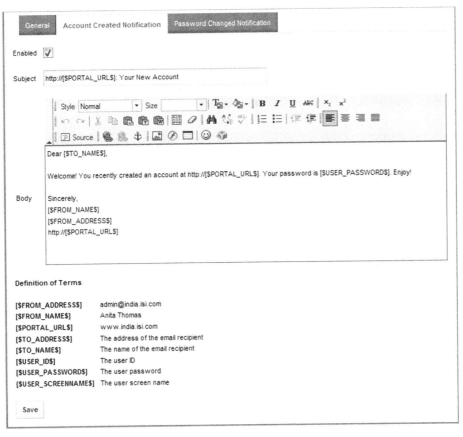

Figure 3-25. *E-mail template for Account Created notification*

Suppose that our administrator, Anita, creates a new user. That user will receive an e-mail notification as shown in Figure 3-26. You can modify the *Password Changed* template in a similar manner.

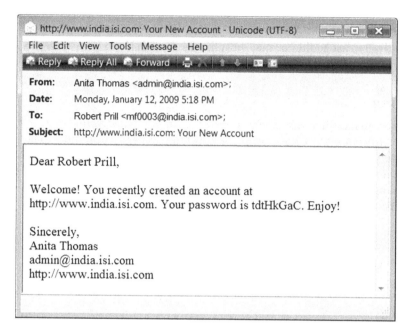

Figure 3-26. *E-mail notification message about a new account*

Tip If your machine has an SMTP server running locally, the default portal configuration will use it. If you wish to use a different server to send the e-mail messages, then you must edit the `ROOT.xml` file located inside your portal installation under `conf/Catalina/localhost` and register your server there.

Editing Settings for Default Plugins

Finally, you can configure the default plugins that will be available to your portal users. Remember that plugins are basically the portlet applications that the user can install on her pages. Using the *Plugins* tab, you can configure what portlets, themes, layout templates, and other plugins your portal users are allowed to use depending on their roles. Here, for example, you can determine that power users can access only certain themes and add only certain portlets to their pages.

Under the *Enterprise Admin* application's *Plugins* tab, you have five secondary tabs:

- *Portlet Plugins*
- *Theme Plugins*
- *Layout Template Plugins*
- *Hook Plugins*
- *Web Plugins*

The *Portlet Plugins* subscreen is shown in Figure 3-27.

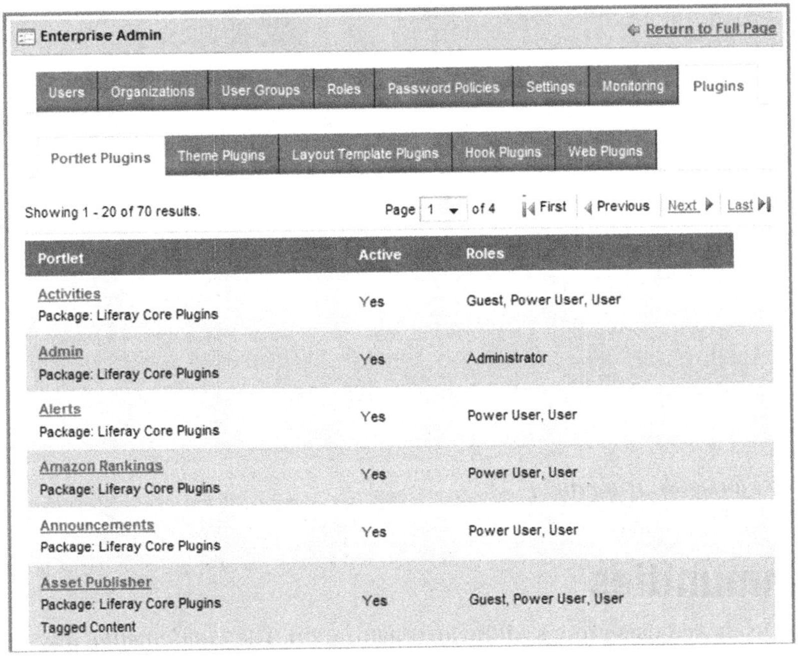

Figure 3-27. *List of default portlet plugins*

Here, you will find a list of portlet plugins arranged alphabetically. These are *Liferay Core Plugins*, so you should leave them as *Active*. However, you can set the roles under which these applications will be made available to our users; these roles are listed in the third column of the table. Click a plugin name to access a screen that lets you change the plugin's default settings. For example, when you click the *Activities* portlet link, you will see the screen shown in Figure 3-28.

In the multiline edit control, you will find the list of roles under which this plugin is available. Change this list to meet your requirements. To deactivate the plugin, uncheck the *Active* check box.

Similarly, you can repeat this same process to change the default settings for other types of plugins such as themes and layout templates.

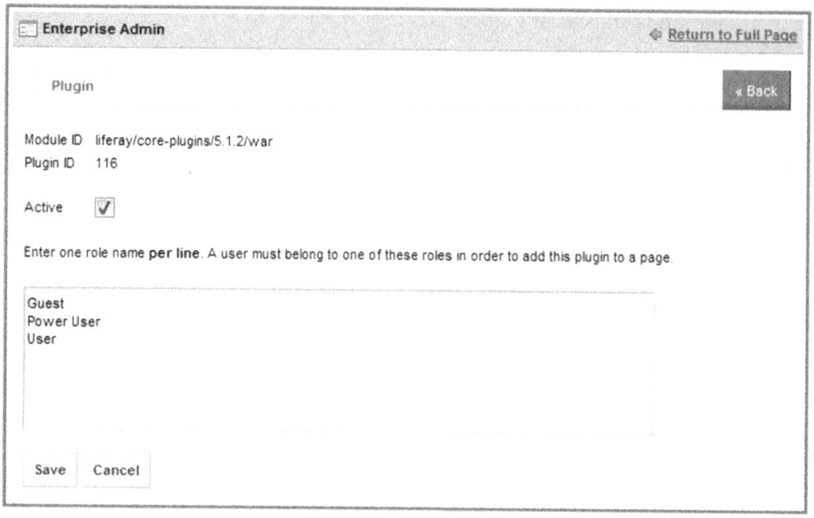

Figure 3-28. *Assigning roles for access to a plugin*

Creating Communities

So far, you have created users and user groups within an organization. The *Fundamental Analysts* and *Technical Analysts* user groups are classified according to the respective users' area of interest. But the portal administrator controls user-group membership. If you want to create a different kind of group that the users themselves can control, you should create a *community*. A community can be of three different types:

- Open
- Restricted
- Private

An open community allows the user to join and leave at any time. In the case of a restricted community, an administrator must admit the user requesting a membership. A private community is equivalent to a restricted community, but it's not listed in the *Communities* portlet, which you use to create and manage communities. I'll discuss this portlet next.

Installing the Communities Portlet

To install the *Communities* application on your portal page, follow these steps:

1. Navigate to the portal page where you wish to add the *Communities* application.

2. Select the *Add Application* menu from the *Welcome* drop-down list.

3. Locate the *Communities* application under the *Community* category.

4. Add the application to the portal page. Your screen at this stage should look like the one shown in Figure 3-29.

Figure 3-29. *Adding the Communities application*

You will now create a new community called *Fundamental Analysts*.

Creating a Community

To create a new community, follow the steps listed here:

1. Click the *Add Community* button in the *Communities* portlet.

2. Perform these steps in the resulting screen:

   a. *Name*: Enter **Fundamental Analysts**.

   b. *Description*: Enter **A community for fundamental analysts**.

   c. *Type*: Select the *Open* category.

   d. *Active*: Leave this box checked.

3. Save your edits by clicking the *Save* button.

Repeat those steps to create another community called *Technical Analysts*. Now that you've created two communities, you'll need to associate users with them.

Tip Users can become members of a community by locating it in the *Communities* portlet and clicking the *Join* option. They can also leave a community they joined previously by using the *Leave* option.

Associating Users with Communities

Individual users, users belonging to an organization, and users who are part of a user group can also be associated with any community. To associate a user with a community, follow these steps:

1. Click the *Available Communities* tab on the *Communities* application's main screen. You will see the list of all available communities (see Figure 3-30).

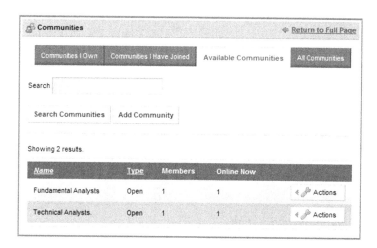

Figure 3-30. *Displaying available communities*

2. Click the *Actions* button associated with the *Fundamental Analysts* community.

3. Select the *Assign Members* menu option.

4. Select the *Available* tab under the *Users* main tab to see a list of all available members. Members already associated with the specified community have a checked box displayed near their usernames.

5. Mark the check boxes associated with the users whom you wish to add to the community.

6. Click the *Update Associations* button to associate the selected users with the specified community.

7. If you wish to add all the members of an organization to a community, click the *Organizations* main tab and click the *Available* tab underneath it to see the list of available organizations. If you want to skip this step, proceed to step 10.

8. Select the organizations that you wish to associate with the specified community.

9. Click the *Update Associations* button to create the new associations.

10. To associate an entire user group with a community, click the *User Groups* main tab, click the *Available* tab underneath it, select the desired group(s), and click the *Update Associations* button.

You will be using these communities in later chapters to perform certain common tasks.

Summary

In this chapter, you learned to use Liferay's *Enterprise Admin* and *Communities* applications to manage your portal's users. *Enterprise Admin* allows you to create organizations, users and user groups, roles, password policies, and so on. *Communities* allows you to create user communities and associate users with those communities.

First, you defined a multinational organization as owner of the International Security Investors (ISI) portal and established details including its e-mail addresses, snail-mail addresses, web sites, phone numbers, services, and worldwide locations.

Then you learned to create users, user groups, and a user with administrator privileges. For individual users, you entered their passwords, addresses, phone numbers, and roles. A user with an administrator role can create additional users, grant user permissions, and even impersonate another user.

Finally, you learned to perform other user-management tasks such as setting password policies and user-authentication options, setting mail hosts and notification-mail templates, and configuring the default plugins available to users.

In the next chapter, you will learn to create discussion forums so your portal's users can discuss matters of interest.

CHAPTER 4

Creating Discussion Forums

In the previous chapter, you created an organization and added a few users to the securities portal. Because these users will be investing in stock markets, they will likely seek information from informal discussions in user communities, including recommendations from investors and others. Our portal certainly needs a facility where users can come together and discuss their ideas, stories, findings, and recommendations. You can achieve this goal with the help of a discussion forum.

You have probably experienced discussion forums on the Internet. Such forums have several logical categories of discussions, and under each you might find multiple threads started by different community users. Users post messages to these threads and others post their replies.

Liferay provides all these features through its *Message Boards* application. In this chapter, you will learn to use this application to set up the discussion forum for the portal's users. In particular, you will learn the following:

- Creating discussion forums
- Creating and managing discussion categories
- Subscribing and unsubscribing to categories, threads, and feeds
- Setting user permissions
- Creating threads
- Posting messages and replies
- Managing message boards
- Checking posts and subscriptions
- Listing recent posts
- Examining statistics
- Banning unwanted users
- Tagging contents
- Configuring message boards

Setting Up a Forum

The *Message Boards* application that you'll use to set up the portal's discussion forum is listed in the *Collaboration* category. To use this application, first set up a new page for the discussion forum:

1. Log in to our ISI portal using the *Admin* account.

2. Add a new page called *Forum* in the *Fundamental Analysts* community.

3. Use the *Add Application* menu to add the *Message Boards* application to the *Forum* page.

The screenshot for adding *Message Boards* is shown in Figure 4-1.

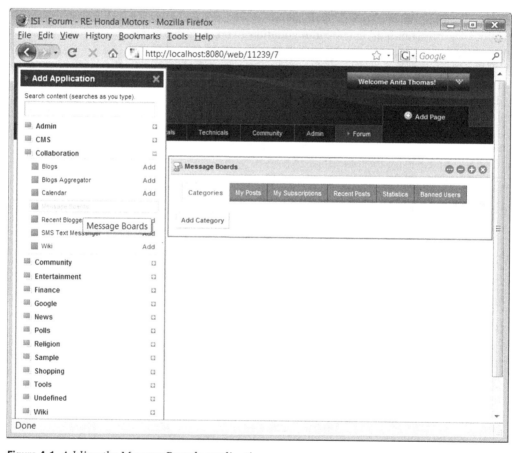

Figure 4-1. *Adding the Message Boards application*

The *Message Boards* application provides these tabbed menus:

- *Categories*
- *My Posts*
- *My Subscriptions*
- *Recent Posts*
- *Statistics*
- *Banned Users*

The *Categories* menu option allows you to define new categories and manage existing categories. Generally, a discussion forum contains categories associated with different topics or types of users. For example, in the securities portal you might want two categories: one for fundamental analysts and the other for technical analysts. Offering discussion-forum categories makes it easier for users to find and focus on what they want.

As a user, you might be posting messages to the forum. The *My Posts* menu option lets you view all your posts, monitor them, and edit them.

You can also offer your users the ability to subscribe to a particular discussion on the forum. A subscribed user receives notification whenever new messages are posted or new changes are made on the given topic. The *My Subscriptions* menu option allows you to view and monitor all your subscriptions.

The *Recent Posts* menu option displays all recent posts. This saves you the trouble of sorting the posts by date and listing all the latest ones.

The *Statistics* menu option provides information on the number of categories, posts, and participants in the forum, including a list of the top posters. These statistics help you understand how users are participating in your discussion forum.

Finally, the *Banned Users* menu option gives you details about users who have been banned from participating in the discussion forum. Administrators or users with appropriate rights are allowed to ban any unwanted user; they can later unban that user so the user can resume participation in the discussion forum.

You'll now study these various menu options in depth to understand how to set up, monitor, and administer a discussion forum.

Defining Categories

The first thing you need to do while setting up a discussion forum is create categories and set access rights to them. For the securities portal, you'll initially create two discussion categories: Fundamental Message Bulletin and Technical Message Bulletin. Click the *Add Category* button in the *Categories* menu option to create these categories. You should see the screen shown in Figure 4-2.

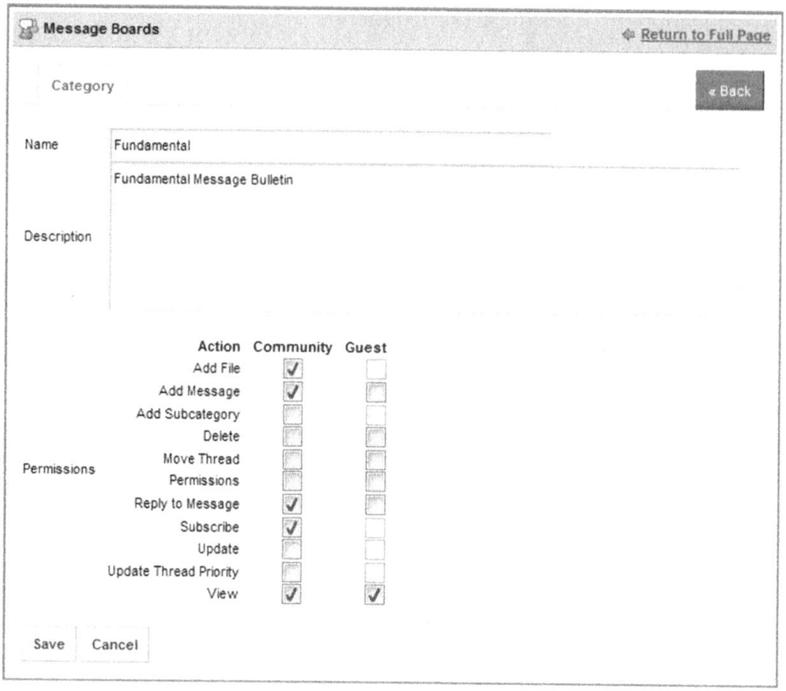

Figure 4-2. *Adding a new category*

Here, you will enter the category name and its description. To create the *Fundamental* category, enter **Fundamental** in the *Name* box and **Fundamental Message Bulletin** in the *Description* box.

Before you save the new category, you might want to set permissions on it. You can assign different permissions depending on the user type. Generally, there are two types of users: community and guest.

Note In Chapter 3, you learned to create communities. You created two communities: the *Fundamental Analysts* community and the *Technical Analysts* community. You can assign rights to the users in these communities that differ from the rights of a guest user.

You can set the permissions for each type of user in the check boxes on the *Category* screen (see Figure 4-2). For each category you create, you can enable or restrict a user's rights by specifying the actions they are allowed to perform. By default, a community user is granted permission to add a file, add a message, reply to a message, subscribe to a discussion, or view posts. A guest user, on the other hand, only has the right to view posts. (I'll delve further into permissions in the "Permissions" section under "Category Actions," and in the "Permissions on Categories" section after that.)

After assigning the desired rights to the two kinds of users, click the *Save* button. You'll see the screen shown in Figure 4-3 if your request processed successfully.

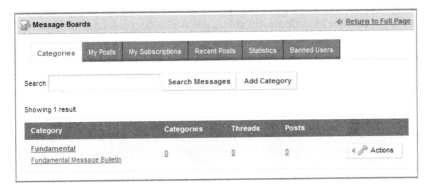

Figure 4-3. *Listing all categories*

You can now see the newly added *Fundamental* category in the list of categories. Likewise, you can add another discussion category called *Technical* (for the technical analysts); you will see this second category appear below the *Fundamental* category in the list.

Category Actions

After adding categories, you might want to perform certain actions on them before making them available to the forum users. Click the *Actions* button that appears on the right side of the category name to pull up the following choices:

- *Edit*
- *Permissions*
- *RSS*
- *Subscribe*
- *Delete*

Edit

Under the *Edit* option, you can modify the name and description of your category. Plus, you can select the category's parent category and even merge any category with its parent.

Note You can create a parent-child hierarchy by creating subcategories in a category. I'll discuss sub-category creation later in the chapter.

Permissions

Under this option, you can add roles and permissions. As I mentioned when I discussed the check boxes in the *Category* screen, you can assign certain allowed activities to community users and guest users. Such activities include adding messages to the discussion forum, deleting messages, replying to messages, and so on. A community user, who enjoys more privileges than a guest user, can be classified as an administrator, a member, or an owner.

A user who creates a community is the owner of that community. The community owner can appoint a user as the community's administrator, and assign administrative rights to that user accordingly. All other users belonging to that community are classified as ordinary members.

The actions that a user is allowed to perform depend on his or her role in the community. You can control these permissions through the *Permissions* menu option; when you click it, you will see the screen shown in Figure 4-4.

Figure 4-4. *Updating user rights*

You'll see two tabs onscreen: *Regular Roles* and *Community Roles*. I've already listed the possible community roles: owner, administrator, and ordinary member. A guest user is classified as a regular role. Other regular roles are ordinary user, power user, owner, and administrator. For each type of user, you can assign different rights that allow various actions on the created category.

Figure 4-4 displays a list of currently assigned permissions under *Regular Roles*. Note that our guest user has only the *View* permission. If you want to change a guest user's permissions, mark the check box in front of the *Guest* user listing and click the *Update Permissions* button. You'll see the screen shown in Figure 4-5.

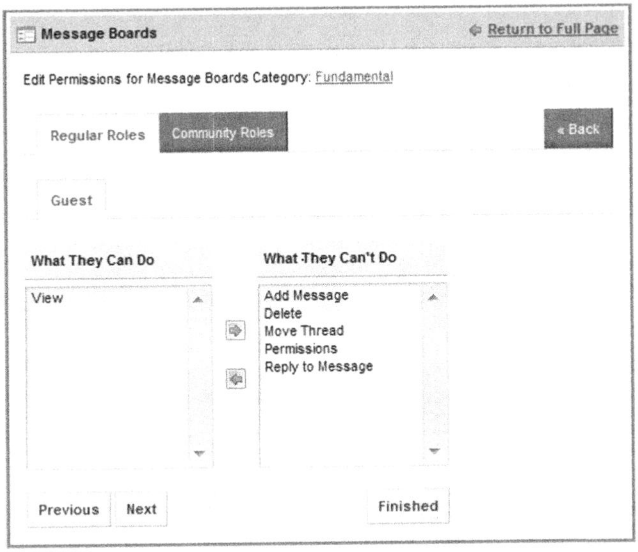

Figure 4-5. *Selecting permissions for assignment*

The actions that a guest can perform are shown in the list on the left, and the actions a guest cannot perform are shown in the list on the right. Using the two arrow buttons, you can move these actions into the desired lists. After you complete your changes, click the *Finished* button to see the assigned actions on the main permissions screen. You can go through this process for the community-role users as well as the regular-role users.

Note I'll delve more deeply into the various permissions and their implications in the next section, "Permissions on Categories."

RSS

Here's another thing you might want to do to a discussion-forum category before making it available on your portal: generate an RSS feed based on posts to that category. An RSS feed proves useful in several situations, especially ones in which the feed is dynamic. The RSS view of our *Honda Motors* thread[1] in the *Automotive Industry* category is shown in Figure 4-6, as seen in IE (Internet Explorer).

---

1 You will be creating this thread later in the chapter. I have mentioned this here just to show you what the RSS output looks like.

Note I show Mozilla's Firefox browser throughout this book, but I'm using IE to show the RSS feed application because it provides somewhat more functionality than Firefox. Once you learn how to exploit IE's functionality, learning Firefox's functionality is trivial. The functionality provided by other browsers might differ substantially from the capabilities of IE and Firefox.

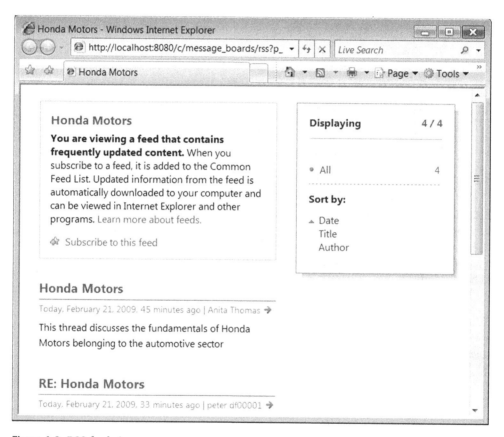

Figure 4-6. *RSS feed view*

You can sort the feed output by date, title, or author. You and your users can subscribe to this feed by clicking the *Subscribe to this feed* link (see Figure 4-7).

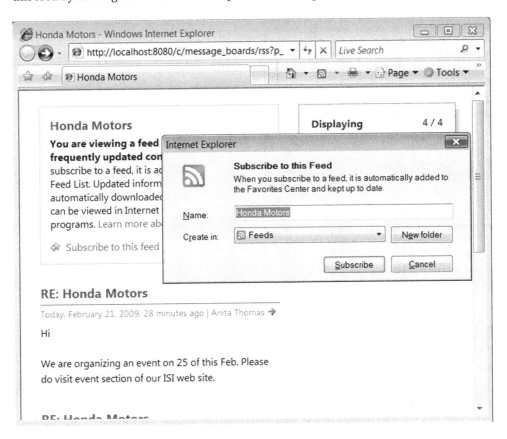

Figure 4-7. *Subscribing to a live feed*

You need to enter the name and the folder for the feed. Once you subscribe to a feed, the portal displays a confirmation message. Clicking the *View my feeds* hyperlink that appears on the next screen displays a list of all your subscribed feeds. You can then select any displayed feed and set its properties by clicking the *View feed properties* link. The resulting *Feed Properties* screen is shown in Figure 4-8.

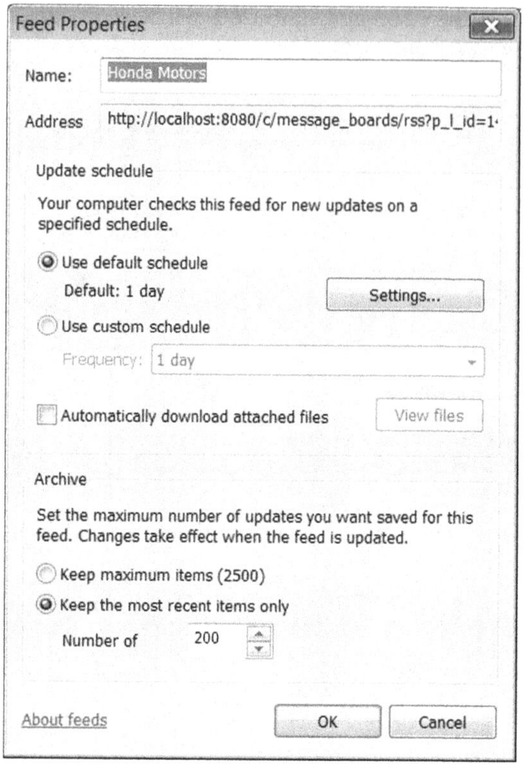

Figure 4-8. *Setting feed properties*

On this screen, you can set the feed's update frequency. The default schedule is one update per day, but you can modify this setting to receive updates as often as every 15 minutes or as rarely as once a week. (You can even specify that you never want updates.) Modify the schedule by selecting the *Use custom schedule* radio button and choosing the desired frequency from the drop-down list. You can also choose to automatically download the attached files by marking the corresponding check box. In the *Archive* section of the screen, you can restrict the number of feed entries to be archived if you want to save valuable real estate on your hard drive. You can keep a maximum of 2,500 items or specify your own limit; the portal will archive only the most recent entries up to that limit.

Subscribe

Yet another action you can perform on a discussion-forum category is allowing your users to subscribe and unsubscribe to it. After users subscribe, they will be notified of posts and changes made by other members. Members who are already subscribed to a category have the option of unsubscribing through the *Actions* button, as the *Subscribe* menu option automatically changes to *Unsubscribe* as appropriate.

Delete

Access the *Delete* option through the *Actions* button to delete the currently selected discussion category. You'll be asked to confirm before the entry is actually deleted.

Permissions on Categories

As I mentioned in the "Category Actions" section, you can use the *Permissions* action menu to set the various permissions for different types of users. Now I'll provide details about the various permissions that you can assign or deny to users:

- Add File
- Add Message
- Add Subcategory
- Delete
- Move Thread
- Permissions
- Reply to Message
- Subscribe
- Update
- Update Thread Priority
- View

■**Note** The available set of permissions depends on the user's role. The preceding list is comprehensive; it consists of all the available permissions that you can apply to a user.

Add File

If you grant the Add File permission to your users, they will be able to attach files while posting messages or replies (see Figure 4-9).

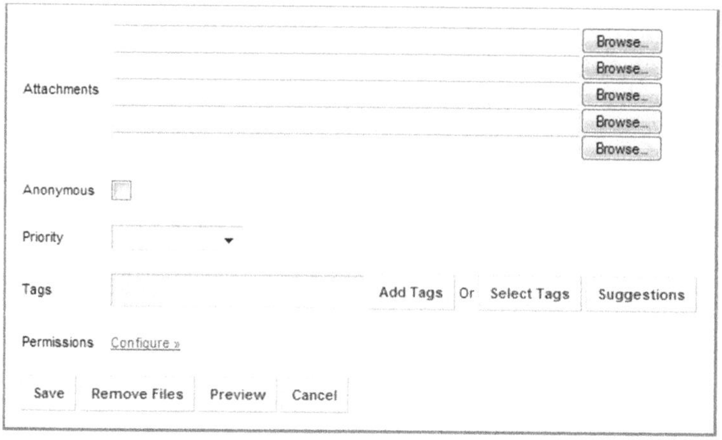

Figure 4-9. *Attaching files to a message*

A user can attach as many as five files to a reply. If the user changes her mind before posting the reply, she can remove the list of all selected files by clicking the *Remove Files* button.

Add Message

Posting messages to the forum is allowed only if the user has been granted the Add Message permission. Users with only the View permission will not be able to contribute to the forum.

Add Subcategory

I'll discuss subcategories further in the next section. But for now, suffice it to say that the Add Subcategory permission allows a user to add subcategories under the existing categories. Creating categories and subcategories helps organize discussion threads logically and makes it easy for users to search, locate, and read only the threads of interest to them.

Delete

With the Delete permission, a user can delete existing categories and subcategories. Over time, some discussion threads will become stale or will have only historical importance. Deleting categories containing those threads will improve the forum experience for new readers, who might not be interested in viewing those threads.

Move Thread

The Move Thread permission allows a user to move a discussion thread from one category to another. This again helps organize threads into logical units. I'll discuss how to move a thread in the more detailed "Moving Threads" section later in this chapter.

Permissions

The Permissions permission lets a user set the various permissions described in this section. Generally, only the owner and administrators will have this permission because they are the only ones who should have the ability to grant or deny rights to other users.

Reply to Message

A community user will have the Reply to Message permission granted by default. With it, the user can reply to any message on the forum. A guest user will not have this permission granted by default, and thus will only be able to view messages without replying. Generally, you'll want to trace who has posted replies on the forum, so you don't want to grant this permission to a guest user.

Subscribe

With the Subscribe permission, a user can subscribe to the feeds of his choice.

Update

The Update permission allows a user to modify a message.

Update Thread Priority

With the Update Thread Priority permission, a user can modify the priority assigned to a thread within the current category.

View

With the View permission, a user can view messages posted by all users.

Subcategories

So far you have created two discussion categories: *Fundamental* and *Technical*. You will now learn to create subcategories under these categories so you can organize your information in logical units. For this example, you'll create a subcategory called *Automotive Industry* under the *Fundamental* category. (You were briefly introduced to this subcategory when I discussed RSS feeds earlier in the chapter.) All the discussion threads pertaining to the automobile industry will appear under this subcategory in the forum.

To create a subcategory under *Fundamental*, click the category in the list displayed on the *Categories* screen of the *Message Boards* application. Your screen will show the full path to the *Fundamental* category along with a button to add a subcategory. Click this button to bring up the familiar category-addition screen. Here, you can enter the subcategory's name and description, and also set permissions. After you have finished making changes, click the *Save* button to create the subcategory and add it under the *Fundamental* category.

You can create as many subcategories as you wish to organize all the discussions into logical units.

Note You can also merge categories to remove unwanted categories without losing their corresponding threads, as discussed earlier in the "Edit" section under "Category Actions."

Exploring Threads

A forum thread starts when an authorized user posts a message to initiate a discussion. Users then reply to the post, followed by other users, and so on. In this manner, a thread can grow quite large. Here's how to create a thread.

Creating a Thread

You'll create a thread under our *Automotive Industry* subcategory to open a discussion about the fundamentals of the corporations in the automotive sector. Click the *Post New Thread* button in the *Threads* tab to pull up a screen similar to the one shown in Figure 4-10.

Figure 4-10. *Creating a new thread*

Do the following for the various fields:

- *Subject*: Enter **Honda Motors**.

- *Body*: Enter **This thread discusses the fundamentals of Honda Motors**.

- *Anonymous*: Leave this unchecked.

- *Priority*: Select *Announcement* from the drop-down list.

- *Tags*: Leave this blank for now.

- *Permissions*: You can configure permissions as discussed earlier or leave this field untouched.

Before saving your changes, you might want to set the look and feel of the body contents. You can set the font, color, text alignment, and so on using the various buttons at the top of the editor. Once you are satisfied with the design, click the *Save* button. This saves your changes and posts your message to the thread. Your newly posted thread should look like the one shown in Figure 4-11.

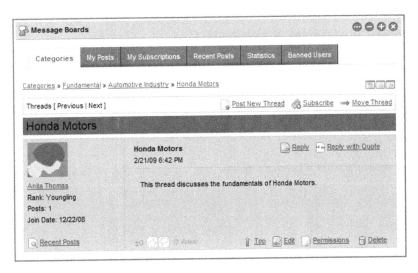

Figure 4-11. *A typical message post*

Actions on Posts

After you have posted a message to a thread that you started, you can perform various actions on it:

- *Edit*: This option allows you to modify your post's subject, body text, priority, tags, and so on. You edit existing posts with the editor you used to create the post.

- *Permissions*: While creating the category, you set up the permissions for users in regular and community roles. You can edit any of these permissions using this menu option.

- *Delete*: This simply allows you to delete the current post (you'll first be asked to confirm).

- *Reply*: This option allows you to post a reply—yes, you can reply to your own message. Sometimes you might want to a post a reply rather than edit the message itself to draw other users' attention to your changes. When you post a reply, the new reply message appears under the original message, so that others can see your remarks on the existing message. You create the reply message in a screen similar to the one you used to create a new post.

- *Reply with Quote*: This option puts the original message body in quote tags.

All your messages and replies appear in a hierarchy at the top of the screen that displays the threads. Using the links in the hierarchy, you can jump to any post to edit it or reply to it. A typical message hierarchy is shown in Figure 4-12.

Figure 4-12. *Hierarchy of posted messages*

Subscribing to a Category or Thread

So far you have learned to create categories and threads. How do you know when somebody posts a message to a thread? To get an automatic update when new posts are made or existing posts are modified, you need to subscribe to the desired category or thread.

To subscribe to a particular category, perform the following steps:

1. Click the *Categories* tab and locate the desired category in the displayed list.

2. Click the *Actions* button.

3. In the displayed menu, click the *Subscribe* option.

You are now subscribed to the currently selected category. The menu changes accordingly, showing an *Unsubscribe* option instead.

To subscribe to a particular thread, follow the steps listed here:

1. Select the appropriate category to which the desired thread belongs.

2. Locate the desired thread in the list of displayed threads for the selected category.

3. Click the *Actions* button.

4. Click the *Subscribe* menu option.

You are now subscribed to the currently selected thread. The menu changes accordingly, showing an *Unsubscribe* option that you can use to terminate your subscription to the current thread.

The purpose of subscribing to a category or thread is to receive notifications whenever changes or new posts are made. Liferay sends such notifications to all the subscribers through e-mail. The notification messages are automatically generated and dispatched. As an administrator, you get an opportunity to set up the format and the text of these notification messages. You will learn to set up these notification messages in the "Configuring Message Boards" section later in this chapter.

Tip You can view all your subscriptions by clicking the *My Subscriptions* tabbed menu. I'll discuss this feature in the "Managing Message Boards" section later in the chapter.

Moving Threads

Sometimes you'll want to reorganize discussion threads by moving them from one category to another. To do this, first navigate to the desired category to get a list of its threads (see Figure 4-13) and then select the thread that you want to move.

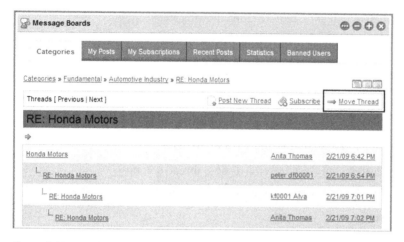

Figure 4-13. *Moving a thread to another category*

At the top-right corner of the screen, you will notice the *Move Thread* button. Click this button to get the *Category* selection screen as shown in Figure 4-14.

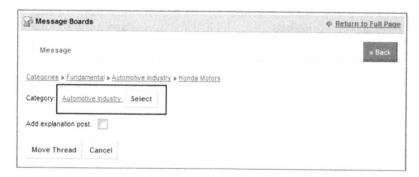

Figure 4-14. *Selecting a destination for your thread*

Click the *Select* button to get a list of categories and choose the category where you want to move your thread. The selected category name appears after the *Category* label. Click the *Move Thread* button to complete the move operation. You will see the moved thread under the new category.

Managing Message Boards

Let's revisit the main tabbed menus in Liferay's *Message Boards* application: *Categories, My Posts, My Subscriptions, Recent Posts, Statistics*, and *Banned Users*. You have already studied the *Categories* menu option in depth, but I'd like to discuss one more action that it enables you to perform: searching the forum for messages containing specific words. On the *Categories* screen shown in Figure 4-15, you will notice the *Search Messages* button.

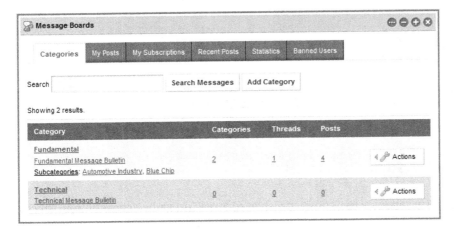

Figure 4-15. *Searching for posts*

To the left of the *Search Messages* button, you'll see an edit box where you can enter search terms. When you click the button, the application searches all the messages in the forum for the search terms and displays the results. You can navigate to a particular message from that display.

Note The application searches the messages by category. To narrow the search scope, navigate to the desired level in the category hierarchy and perform your search from there.

Now you'll explore the other menu options in Liferay's *Message Boards* application to see how they help you manage your message boards.

My Posts

When you select the *My Posts* menu option, you will see a list of all your posts. This list consists of all the threads you started as well as your posts to threads that other users started. For each thread, the application displays the identity of the thread's originator, the number of posts, and the number of views, in addition to the date, time, and author of the most recent post. A typical output screen displaying the list of posts for our administrator Anita is shown in Figure 4-16.

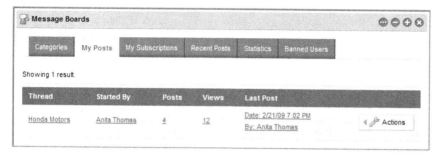

Figure 4-16. *Viewing your posts*

You can perform various actions on each displayed thread using the *Actions* button, which I discussed toward the beginning of the chapter in the "Category Actions" section. To recap, such actions include editing, setting permissions, subscribing to the thread, viewing it in RSS format, and deleting the thread. The actions available to you depend on the permissions you've been granted for the selected thread.

My Subscriptions

The *My Subscriptions* menu option allows you to view all your subscriptions to various categories and threads (see Figure 4-17). You can perform actions on your subscriptions using the *Actions* button, just as you did with threads in the *My Posts* screen.

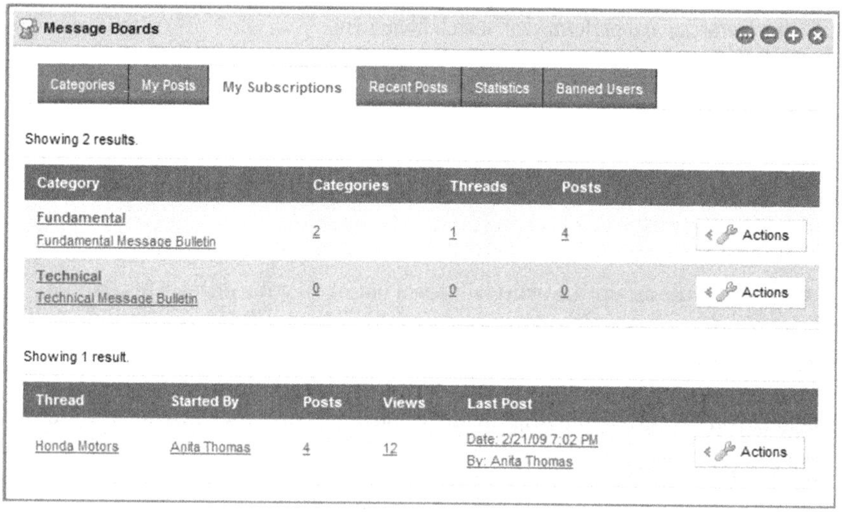

Figure 4-17. *Viewing all your subscriptions*

Recent Posts

The *Recent Posts* option allows you to view all the recent posts made by various users. It provides information on each thread, including the date and author of the last post made to it (see Figure 4-18).

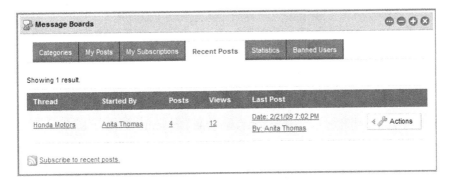

Figure 4-18. *Listing all recent posts*

You can take advantage of the *Actions* button here as well, and you also get a choice to subscribe to recent posts through an RSS feed.

Statistics

The *Statistics* option shows you statistics on the discussion-forum posts. It gives you both general statistics and statistics about the forum's top posters. General statistics include the forum's number of categories, number of posts, and number of participants. This statistical data helps you better monitor and manage your forum. Statistics about top posters include the number of posts they have made, their joining date, and the date when they last posted to the forum. You might find it useful to know who your most active users are.

Banned Users

You might find occasion to ban a user from your forum. The *Banned Users* menu option displays information on all the users who are no longer allowed to participate. The screen displays the user ID of the banned user, the name of the administrator who implemented the ban, and the date the ban started (see Figure 4-19). You'll also notice that the date on which a user can be unbanned is displayed in the list. Liferay will automatically unban the user on the given date unless an administrator manually specifies otherwise.

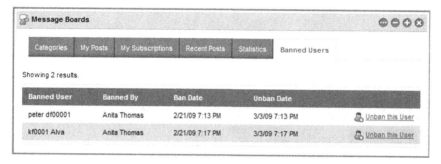

Figure 4-19. *List of banned users*

To ban a user, first display a list of posts through the *Categories* tab or the *Recent Posts* tab. Then navigate to the post that has violated the rules of your forum. Under the author's name, you will find a link to ban the user (see Figure 4-20).

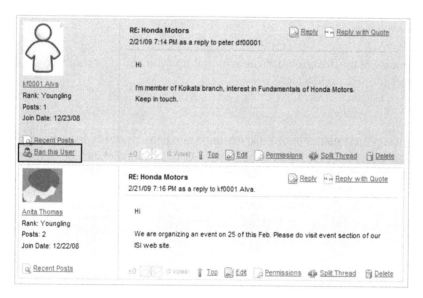

Figure 4-20. *Banning a user*

Clicking this link will prevent the user from posting to the forum. Also, observe that the link has changed to *Unban this User*. Clicking this would unban the user so that she can resume posting to the forum.

Working with Tags

As the number of your forum's community users increases, searching through their posts might become strenuous. The use of tags proves handy in such circumstances. You can give users the ability to tag their postings with important keywords. You can then search the entire forum for tagged keywords.

Tagging Contents

Tagging the contents is an easy task. When creating a message earlier, you might have noticed the *Tags* edit box at the bottom of the message-editor dialog (see Figure 4-21).

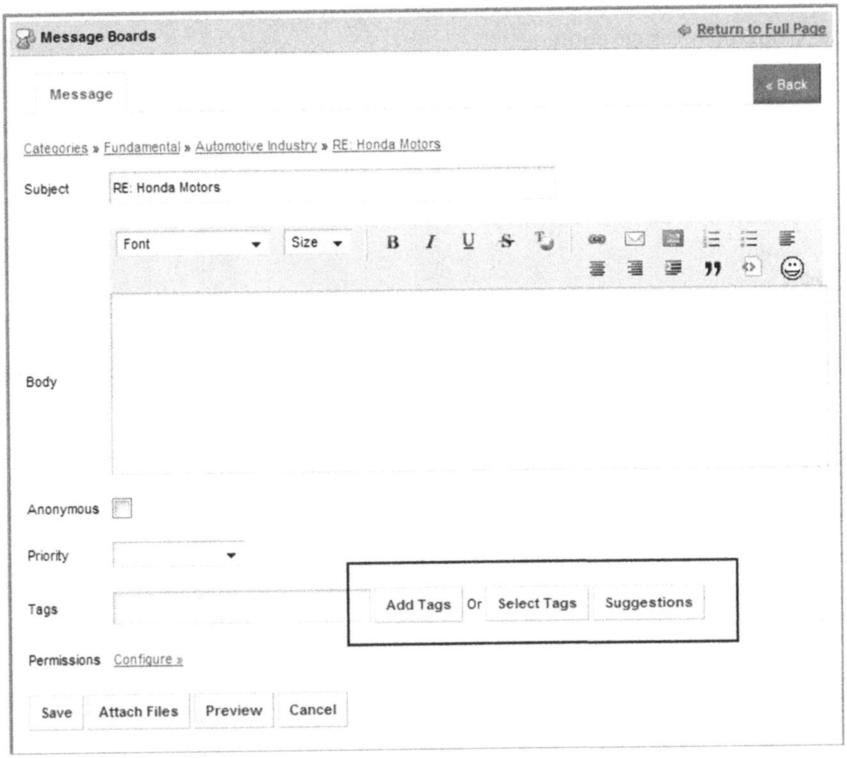

Figure 4-21. *Tagging messages*

In this dialog, you get an option either to select an existing tag or to create a new tag.

Adding Tags

To add new tags, use the following steps:

1. Type the desired tag name in the *Tags* edit box.

2. As soon as you type one or more characters, you'll see a list of existing tags that start with those letters.

3. You can select the tag name from the displayed list or enter a new name.

4. Click the *Add Tags* button.

5. The tag name will appear above the *Tags* label.

Tag Suggestions

If you can't decide on the tag names for the message, Liferay provides help by suggesting some. To get the suggestions, follow these steps:

1. Click the *Suggestions* button. A list of names will be displayed onscreen; Liferay gets these names from the message contents.

2. Mark all the names you want to add to your list using the corresponding check boxes.

3. Click the *Save* button. This adds all selected tag names to the list of tags.

4. Note that the tags also appear above the *Tags* label indicating that the current message is tagged with these keywords.

Removing Tags

Sometimes, you might wish to remove a tag applied to a message. To remove a tag, simply click the "x" displayed in front of the tag name. The selected keyword will disappear from the tag list.

Selecting Tags

Follow these steps to tag the current message with a preexisting tag:

1. Click the *Select Tags* button to pull up a list of existing tags. (I'm assuming you have already added a few tags.)

2. Select the desired tag for the message. You can select multiple tags.

3. Click the *Save* button.

4. The selected tag(s) appear above the *Tags* label.

■**Tip** Liferay supports metatags: a tagging system that you can use not only for messages, but also for blogs, documents, wikis, images, journal articles, and so on.

Configuring Message Boards

In previous chapters, you learned to configure the portlet applications that you added to your portal pages. Similarly, you can configure the *Message Boards* application by creating some of the application's default settings. When you click the configuration icon in the *Message Boards* application, you will see these tabbed options onscreen:

- *Email From*
- *Message Added Email*
- *Message Updated Email*
- *Thread Priorities*

- *User Ranks*

- *RSS*

- *Anonymous Postings*

- *Ratings*

Let us now look at these options in depth.

Email From

The *Email From* option allows you to configure the e-mail settings of your notification messages. The corresponding tabbed screen is shown in Figure 4-22.

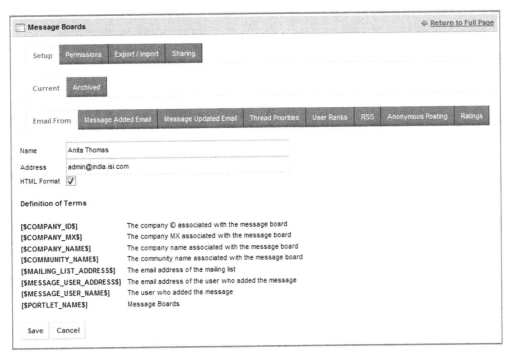

Figure 4-22. *Configuring the e-mail format for the Email From notification*

Here, you need to enter the name and e-mail address of the message sender. Mark the *HTML Format* check box if you want to format the message in HTML. The screen also displays the list of definitions used in your message.

Message Added Email

The *Message Added Email* option allows you to set the default format for the notification message that goes to subscribers when a new message is posted to the forum.

You can define the *Subject, Body,* and *Signature* for the message. Liferay offers some predefined terms you can use for these three fields, but you can choose to exclude them from your custom-formatted message. You can also type arbitrary text around the defined terms to further customize the message.

Message Updated Email

The *Message Updated Email* option functions like the *Message Added Email* option. It allows you to set the default format for the notification message that goes to subscribers when an existing forum message has been updated.

Thread Priorities

The *Message Boards* application defines three priorities in the *Thread Priorities* screen: *Urgent*, *Sticky*, and *Announcement* (see Figure 4-23).

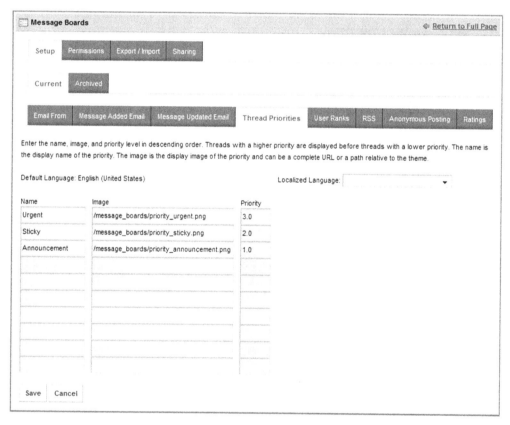

Figure 4-23. *Setting priority levels for threads*

Depending on importance, priority levels are set from 1 to 3. *Urgent* is assigned the highest priority level (3.0) while *Announcement* has the lowest priority level (1.0). For each priority name, a URL for an image is assigned. This image gives users a visual clue regarding the message priority.

You are free to redefine these priority levels. For example, you might decide to create more priority levels ranging from 1 to 5, or even 1 to 10. Edit the displayed boxes to modify the predefined priority levels and to add new ones. You can also select the localized language of your choice from the drop-down list and perform the additional step of translating the text for the thread-priority levels into that language.

Once you are done with your editing, click the *Save* button to save your changes. You and your users will then be able to apply these priorities to newly created messages.

User Ranks

It is always a good practice to rank the users who post to your forum. Such ranking is typically assigned based on the number of postings made by the user.

The *Message Boards* application provides a set of predefined ranks, which include these:

- Youngling=0

- Padawan=25

- Jedi Knight=100

- Jedi Master=250

Each rank name is listed with the number of postings required to achieve that rank. For example, a newbie is assigned the *Youngling* rank. When a user makes 25 postings to the forum, he achieves the *Padawan* rank. After 100 postings, the *Jedi Knight* rank is assigned, and so on. You can modify the rank names as well as the number of required postings to create your own ranking system. You can also add more ranking levels of your own.

In addition to the ranks for community users, *Message Boards* also supplies several predefined ranks for forum moderators. As you can do with thread priorities, you can select a localized language and translate the ranking text into this newly selected language.

RSS

In the "Category Actions" section toward the beginning of this chapter, you saw that it was possible to view forum postings in RSS format. The *RSS* tabbed menu allows you to set defaults for your RSS feed, such as the maximum number of items to display, the display style, and the format.

You can display between 1 and 100 items in your RSS feed by making the appropriate selection from the drop-down list. The numbers initially increment by a factor of 1, then by 5, and finally by 10.

For your RSS-feed display style, you have three choices: full content, abstract, and title. If you decide to use a small number as your maximum, you'll have space to display full content in the feed. If you use a large number, you might want to display the title only. For in-between cases, display the abstract.

Finally, you have three choices for the feed format: RSS 1.0, RSS 2.0, and Atom 1.0.

Tip If you are interested, you can read more about RSS formats in Wikipedia.

Anonymous Postings

The *Anonymous Postings* option lets you specify whether to allow anonymous postings to your forum. Enabling anonymous postings will allow users to post messages without signing on to the forum. If you wish to associate each post with the identity of the post's author, uncheck the check box on this screen.

Ratings

The *Ratings* option lets you enable or disable message ratings for the forum via a single check box.

Summary

In this chapter you studied Liferay's *Message Boards*, an important application that lets you create a feature on your portal to facilitate discussion among your user communities. You learned to create discussion threads as well as categories to better organize those threads. You learned to manage these categories and set permissions for them depending on the user type. Such permissions include attaching files to messages, adding or deleting messages, adding subcategories, and moving threads.

In addition to managing discussion categories, you also learned to manage other forum elements such as posts and subscriptions. Displaying recent posts and vital statistics on posts is easy. Regarding subscriptions, you can allow a user to subscribe to particular types of messages, to set the frequency of message delivery, and to view that information in a browser as an RSS feed.

You also learned how to ban users who violate the rules of your forum. You can easily display and manage the list of banned users, and you can unban users when you want to reinstate their ability to participate.

You learned to manage forum growth by allowing users to tag their messages with keywords, making targeted searches easier. Posters can use keywords provided by the *Message Boards* application or keywords they create themselves.

Finally, you learned how to configure the *Message Boards* application itself. You now can set up e-mail notifications, define thread priorities, implement a user-ranking system, configure RSS-feed formats, enable or disable anonymous message postings, and allow message ratings.

CHAPTER 5

■ ■ ■

Facilitating Collaboration

In the previous chapter, you set up discussion forums to let your portal users collaborate with one another by participating in different discussion threads. You can think of this collaboration method as "offline" in that users might not get responses to their postings immediately. You can facilitate several other kinds of collaboration in your portal. Some of these allow real-time communication, meaning the users would be able to participate in live discussions. I'll discuss several different forms of collaboration in this chapter. In particular, you will learn the following:

- Setting up the mail-client application on your portal
- Popping up e-mail from your Gmail accounts and your Internet Message Access Protocol (IMAP) accounts
- Sending mail
- Setting up an SMS application and sending SMS messages
- Setting up a live-chat application and using it for multiple concurrent users
- Searching and locating users, organizations, and user groups
- Inviting users to participate in discussions

The first application that we'll consider is Liferay's *Mail* application.

Integrating Mail

Almost all computer users rely on e-mail as their primary means of communication, so you'll integrate a mail client into your portal. Through Liferay's *Mail* application, you will be able to retrieve your mail without leaving the portal and e-mail other people from the application itself. This lets you go on working in the same environment and helps you avoid the overhead of switching to another mail client.

Adding the Mail Client

Liferay version 5.1.1 comes with the *Mail* application, but version 5.1.2 (the current version at the time of this writing) does not. So you'll need to download this mail-client application from the Liferay web site.

Note Refer to Chapter 2 for the steps to download a portlet from Liferay's site and install it on your server.

To add the *Mail* application, follow these steps:

1. Log in as *Administrator* to your ISI portal.

2. Create a new page called *Collaboration*. You'll use this page to add and test all the applications I'll discuss in this chapter.

Tip When you create an actual portal that other members will use, you will create the appropriate community (as discussed in Chapter 3), create community public pages, and add the required collaboration applications to them.

3. Select the *Add Application* menu from the *Welcome* drop-down list.

4. Locate the *Mail* application under *Collaboration*.

5. Add the application.

You will see the screen shown in Figure 5-1 after adding the application to the *Collaboration* page.

The *Mail* application serves as a client to both your regular IMAP accounts and your Gmail accounts. You need to configure the client for each type of e-mail account that you wish to use on your portal. Click the *Configure email accounts* link to configure the accounts. You will see the two choices displayed in Figure 5-2.

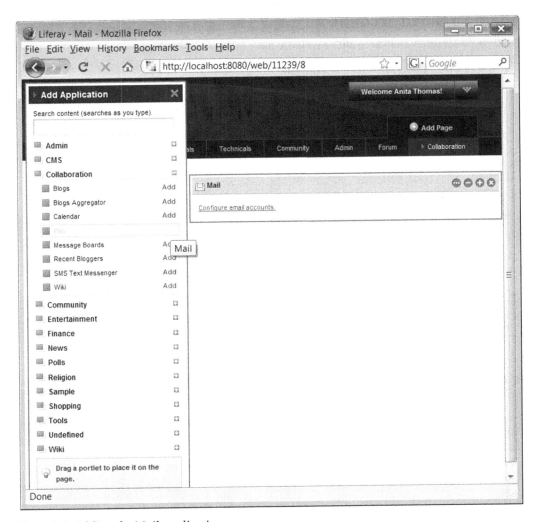

Figure 5-1. *Adding the Mail application*

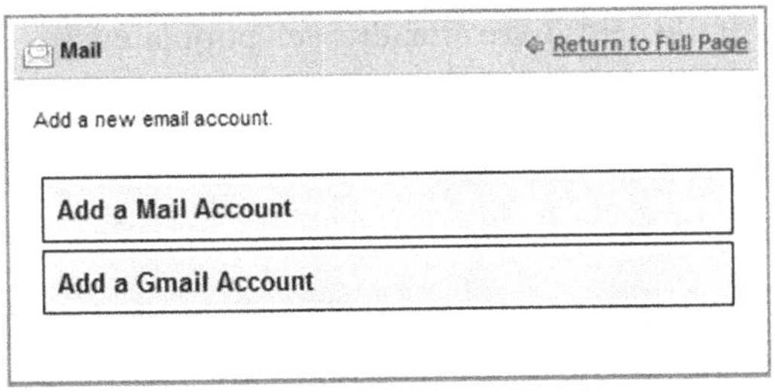

Figure 5-2. *Configuring e-mail accounts in the Mail application*

Adding a Gmail Account

First, you'll set up a Gmail account (see Figure 5-3):

1. Click the *Add a Gmail Account* button.

2. Enter your e-mail ID in the *User Name* edit box.

3. Enter the password in the *Password* field.

4. Click the *Save* button.

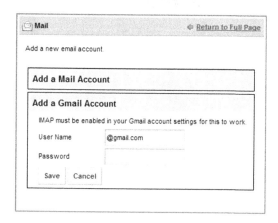

Figure 5-3. *Adding a Gmail account in the Mail client*

After you save your changes, the *Mail* application attempts to connect to the Gmail server to validate the entered account information. If all goes well, you'll see a message indicating that the connection is successful and that your account will be ready for use in a few minutes. You now need to set up the information for incoming- and outgoing-mail servers in the configuration screen that automatically pops up on your screen.

Adjusting Gmail Settings

You'll need to enter your Gmail account ID and password in the *User Name* and *Password* fields on this screen (see Figure 5-4), but the rest of the fields have already been populated by the application:

- *Incoming IMAP Server*: **imap.gmail.com**

- *Incoming Port*: **993**

- *use-secure-incoming-connection*: Checked

- *Outgoing SMTP Server*: **smtp.gmail.com**

- *Outgoing Port*: **465**

- *use-secure-outgoing-connection*: Checked

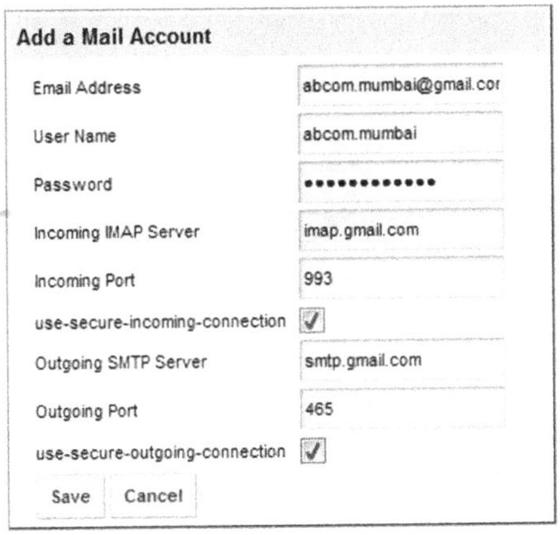

Add a Mail Account

Email Address	abcom.mumbai@gmail.con
User Name	abcom.mumbai
Password	••••••••••••
Incoming IMAP Server	imap.gmail.com
Incoming Port	993
use-secure-incoming-connection	☑
Outgoing SMTP Server	smtp.gmail.com
Outgoing Port	465
use-secure-outgoing-connection	☑

Save   Cancel

Figure 5-4. *Gmail account settings for incoming- and outgoing-mail servers*

Click the *Save* button to save your settings. If you make any errors while entering the configuration, click the *Configure email accounts* link on the *Mail* application's main page to re-enter or modify the required fields.

Tip If you have multiple Gmail accounts, you can set up the client to operate all of them. Use the same procedure as discussed in this section to add more accounts. The first added account becomes the default. To use another account at any time, select it from the list displayed in the drop-down combo box.

Retrieving Mail

After you configure and save the settings for your Gmail accounts, you will see the screen shown in Figure 5-5.

Figure 5-5. *Mail application screen after setting up e-mail accounts successfully*

At this time, you are all ready to use your Gmail accounts. First, we will look at how to retrieve your mail in the *Mail* client application.

Click the *Check your email* link. The mail from the default account will be retrieved and displayed in the client area. This screen (see Figure 5-6) resembles your regular Gmail account's inbox screen.

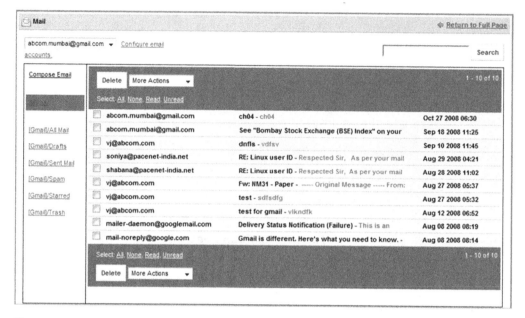

Figure 5-6. *Gmail inbox display in Liferay's Mail app*

Caution At the time of writing, the *Mail* portlet was version 5.1.1. Although this version deploys on Liferay 5.1.2, in some installations the Gmail mail did not pop up as explained in this section. In such situations, you might need to use the portlet on Liferay 5.1.1 where it works as expected, or await a newer version of the portlet.

On the left side of the client, you will see the usual menu options for navigating to different folders such as *Drafts*, *Sent Mail*, and so on. In the center of the screen you will see a list of all retrieved mail in your inbox. When you click the desired folder on the left, the mail from the selected folder will appear in the center. You can perform other operations as you can with your Gmail account in your browser: you can click any of the message headers to view the message body, you can mark and delete messages, and so on.

Sending E-mail

Just as you can retrieve your mail without leaving the portal, you can send mail without leaving the portal. To compose and send mail to others through the *Mail* application, click the *Compose Email* link. You will see the familiar screen for composing a new message (see Figure 5-7).

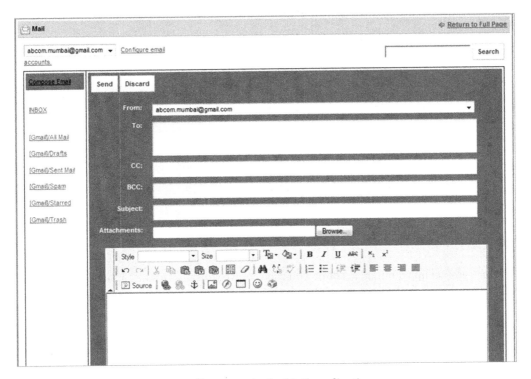

Figure 5-7. *Composing a new e-mail message in the Mail application*

Enter the appropriate information in the *From*, *To*, *CC*, *BCC*, *Subject*, and body-text fields, and include an attachment if desired. Once you are satisfied with the composed message, click the *Send* button to send it. The Gmail outgoing-mail server will dispatch the message.

Setting Up IMAP Accounts

As I mentioned in the section "Adding the Mail Client," the *Mail* application allows you to set up mail accounts other than Gmail. To set up your other mail accounts, follow these steps:

1. On the main screen of the *Mail* application, click the *Configure email accounts* link.

2. Click the *Add a Mail Account* button.

3. Enter the requested details of your mail account (see Figure 5-8), as you did with your Gmail account.

4. Save your changes.

Figure 5-8. *Configuring your IMAP mail account*

Once you set up your mail account, you can retrieve your mail in the client area or even compose and send mail, just as you did for your Gmail account.

■**Caution** Your incoming-mail server must support the IMAP protocol for the *Mail* application to work.

Extending Mail Functionality to Other Members

Note that what you've done so far applies only to a portal administrator—remember that you logged in as an administrator while adding the *Mail* application to your portal page. Now I'll show you how to extend this functionality to other members of your portal. You'll learn how to assign rights to other community members so that each member can set up her own e-mail client using her private mail configuration.

Follow these steps to extend the *Mail* application to other portal members:

1. Add a new public page under the desired community. (Adding pages is discussed in Chapter 2 and creating communities is discussed in Chapter 3.)

2. Add the *Mail* application to the public page you created in the previous step.

3. Click the *Configuration* button to set permissions. You will see the screen shown in Figure 5-9.

4. Select the *Power User* role from the *Available* tab and click the *Update Permissions* button. You will see the screen shown in Figure 5-10.

5. Assign all three displayed permissions to the *Power User* role: *Configuration, Preferences,* and *View.*

6. Click the *Finished* button to save your changes. Note that the *Power User* role now has the newly added permissions displayed in the roles listing.

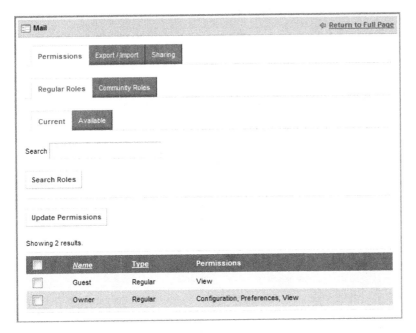

Figure 5-9. *Setting permissions in the Mail application*

Figure 5-10. *Setting permissions for the power-user role*

You have now successfully set the public page for the community users. When a community user logs on to her account and opens this public page, she will be able to configure the mail-client application with her own private e-mail configuration.

Using SMS

E-mail messages are asynchronous, which means the recipient might not see them immediately. With the advent of mobile phones, many people prefer SMS (Short Message Service) messaging because they can often get quicker responses to their messages. Liferay provides an application called *SMS Text Messenger* that allows you to send SMS messages.

You'll find *SMS Text Messenger* under Liferay Portal's *Collaboration* category. Add this application to your *Collaboration* page. After successfully installing the application, you can send SMS messages to your friends. In the application's client area, enter the *To, Subject,* and *Message* information (see Figure 5-11). Note that your message cannot contain more than 500 characters.

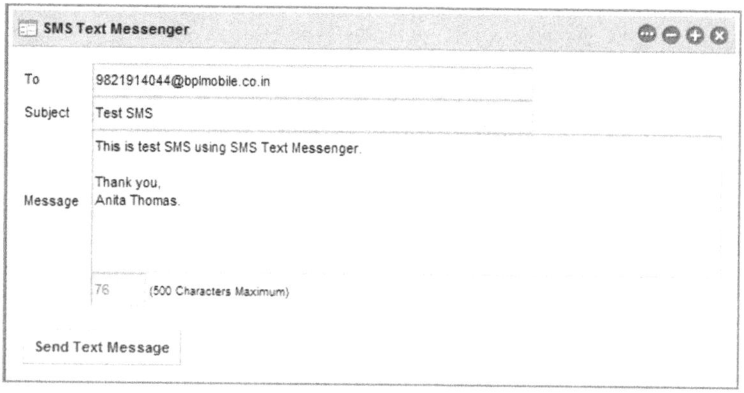

Figure 5-11. *Sending SMS messages through the SMS Text Messenger application*

After you populate the fields, click the *Send Text Message* button. The screen displays an appropriate message if the transmission was successful.

So far, you've seen methods of collaboration in which the communication between the users might not be live. Now you'll look at a Liferay application that allows live communication between users.

Adding Chat Functionality

Liferay provides a *Chat* portlet that facilitates instant communication among users who are live on the portal. In the case of discussion forums and e-mail applications, the sender never knows whether the recipient is currently online until he sees her reply to his message.

With the *Chat* application, every logged-in user knows which other portal members are currently online. All live users can intercommunicate through the *Chat* application.

Installing the Chat Application

The *Chat* application, although supplied by Liferay, does not come in the installation package. You must download the application from the official-plugins area of the Liferay web site and install it on your machine. Accomplish this by following these steps:

1. First add the *Plugin Installer* application to your *Admin* page (or any other page you'd like).

2. Select the *Portlet Plugins* tab.

3. Type **chat** in the *Keywords* text box and click the *Search Plugins* button. The output screen of the search result is shown in Figure 5-12.

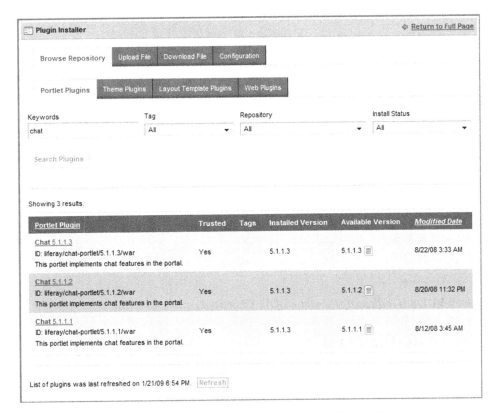

Figure 5-12. *Searching for the Chat portlet in the Plugin Installer application*

4. Select *Chat 5.1.1.3* from the displayed list of applications.

Note Chat 5.1.1.3 was the current version at the time of writing.

---

5. The *Plugin Installer* app now displays the application information for the selected *Chat* application (see Figure 5-13).

6. Click the *Install* button to install the application on your machine. After a while, you should see a success message.

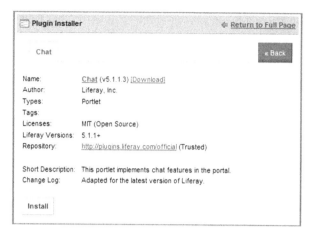

Figure 5-13. *Chat application information*

If you check out the bottom-right corner of the portal screen, you will notice a small label that reads *Chat (0)*. This indicates that the *Chat* application is currently active and has zero online users (see Figure 5-14).

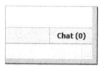

Figure 5-14. *Label indicating the status of the Chat application*

Testing the Chat App

As *Chat* obviously requires more than one participant, you will not be able to test the application until another user logs on to the portal. For testing, you will need to use another machine connected in the same network as your portal-server machine.

To test your *Chat* application, take the following steps:

■**Caution** At the time of writing, Liferay version 5.1.2 had a few bugs in the *Chat* application, which were brought up in Liferay's community forum. This entire section was tested on Liferay version 5.1.1.

---

1. Log in to your portal account on your machine.

2. Log in to another portal account on another machine.

Tip If you do not have multiple machines for testing the *Chat* application, open another browser (not another window of the same browser type) on your local machine. For example, if you're using Netscape, use Internet Explorer or Google Chrome for the second login. Now log on to the Liferay portal with some other account using this second browser. After you get connected to the portal, you will see that the number of *Chat* users has changed from zero to one.

3. Note that the label on the bottom-right corner of your screen now reads *Chat (1)*, indicating that one *Chat* user is online. This number will change as the number of live users grows and shrinks.

4. Click the *Chat* label to see who is currently online (see Figure 5-15). Again, the list will grow and shrink depending on who is logged in to the *Chat* application.

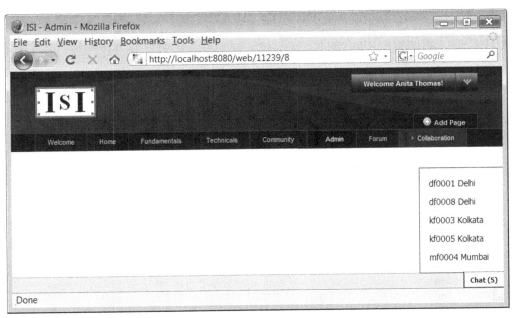

Figure 5-15. *The Chat application window showing the list of online users*

5. To initiate a chat with an online user, click the desired user name. A small window pops up on the top of the displayed user name (see Figure 5-16).

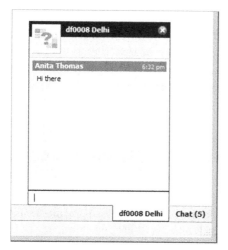

Figure 5-16. *Chatting with an online user*

6. Type a greeting into the edit box and press Enter. This delivers the message to the selected user.

7. Type a reply from the *other* machine where the selected user has logged in.

8. Go back to your own screen to see the reply from the other user in the text area (see Figure 5-17).

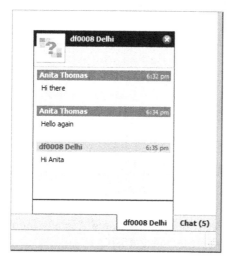

Figure 5-17. *A message and its reply in the chat window*

Chatting with Multiple Users

With the *Chat* application, you are allowed to chat with multiple online users concurrently. To chat with multiple users, click the desired user names. For each selected user, a new chat window pops up on your screen (see Figure 5-18).

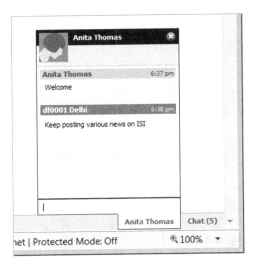

Figure 5-18. *Concurrent chatting with multiple users*

You can now send messages to multiple users in their respective chat windows, and receive messages from them as well.

Searching and Inviting

You have seen different ways to allow communication and collaboration among your portal users. In most of the cases shown so far, one user initiates a discussion and other users participate in it. But you might find occasion to invite certain users to join a discussion. Liferay provides applications that allow you to search the users in the entire portal directory and invite selected users to join discussions. In this section, you will study the two applications that offer search-and-invite functionality: *Directory* and *Invitation*.

Searching Users

The Liferay application that allows you to search the user database is called *Directory*. Follow these steps to set up the application:

1. Select the *Collaboration* page (or any other page where you'd like to add the new application).

2. Click the *Add Application* menu.

3. Select the *Directory* application under the *Community* category.

4. Add the *Directory* application to the page. The application screen should now look like the one shown in Figure 5-19.

Figure 5-19. *Directory application screen*

5. The application provides three tabs: *Users*, *Organizations*, and *User Groups*. As the names suggest, you can use these tabs to search for a desired user, organization, or user group.

6. In the *Search* edit box, enter the search criterion **funda**.

7. Click the *Search Users* button.

Caution You are currently logged in as an administrator and thus possess permissions to perform the various search operations described here. If you're not an administrator and you're using a preinstalled *Directory* application, you will be able to perform the various search operations only if the administrator has assigned you permissions to do so.

---

8. Note the resulting list of users matching your search criterion (see Figure 5-20). The first name, last name, screen name, job title, and organization are listed for each user.

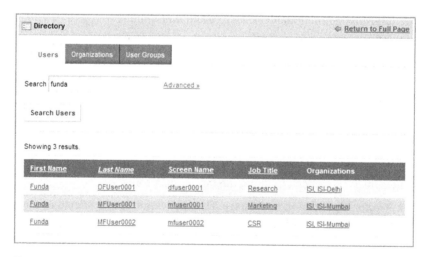

Figure 5-20. *Displaying the search results*

9. If the list is too large, you can narrow down your search by clicking the *Advanced* link to the right of the *Search* edit box. Clicking the *Advanced* link displays the screen shown in Figure 5-21.

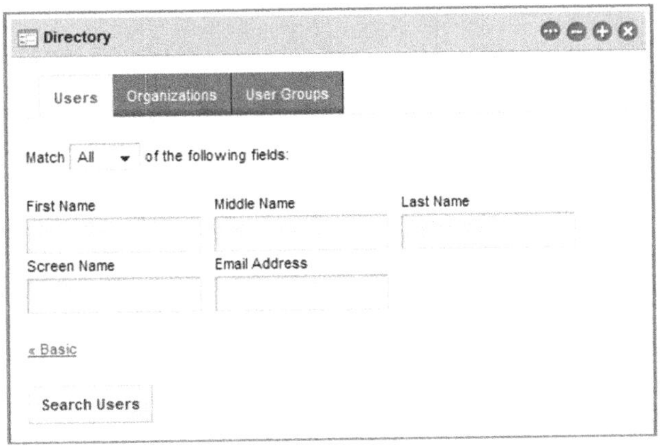

Figure 5-21. *Specifying advanced search criteria*

10. Here, you can enter one or more of the following search criteria: first name, middle name, last name, screen name, or e-mail address.

11. Select *All* or *Any* from the *Match* drop-down list.

12. Click the *Search Users* button to perform the directory search with the new search criteria.

Searching Organizations

In certain situations, you might want to invite members of certain organizations to participate in your discussions. In such cases, it is easier to search the portal directory for an organization rather than for individual users. To locate an organization that matches a particular criterion, perform the following steps:

1. Click the *Organizations* tab in the *Directory* application.

2. Enter your search criterion (**ISI**) in the *Search* edit box.

3. Click the *Search Organizations* button. You'll see the resulting list at the bottom (see Figure 5-22).

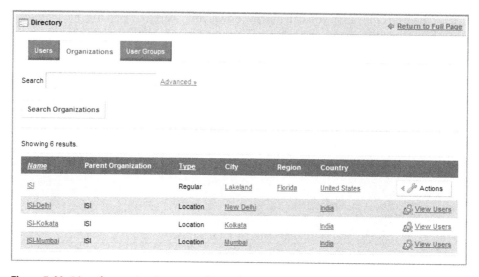

Figure 5-22. *List of organizations matching the search criterion*

4. Click the *View Users* link on the right side of each organization to see the list of users belonging to that organization.

5. If desired, perform an advanced search by clicking the *Advanced* link near the *Search* edit box (as you did when searching for individual users). You can fill in criteria such as the organization's name, address, type, country, and region.

6. You can choose to match all the entered search criteria or any of the entered fields by selecting the corresponding option in the *Match* drop-down list.

7. Clicking the *Search Organizations* button will display the list of organizations matching your search criteria.

Searching User Groups

In addition to searching individual users and organizations, you can also search user groups using the *Directory* application. To locate a desired user group, carry out the following steps:

1. Click the *User Groups* tab in the *Directory* application screen (see Figure 5-23).

2. Enter the search criterion in the *Search* edit box.

3. Click the *Search User Groups* button to perform the search. A list of matching user groups appears at the bottom.

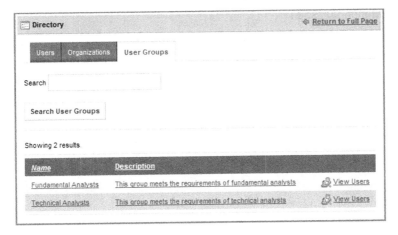

Figure 5-23. *List of selected user groups*

Note There is no advanced-search facility for user groups.

Inviting Friends

After you have searched and located the desired users, you can send them invitations to join your discussion forums or person-to-person discussions. Liferay provides an application called *Invitation* for this purpose.

Adding the Application

To add the *Invitation* application to your portal page, follow the steps listed here:

1. Select the *Collaboration* page (or any other page where you'd like to add the *Invitation* application).

2. Select the *Add Application* menu.

3. Select the *Invitation* application from the *Community* category. Adding the application brings up the screen shown in Figure 5-24.

Figure 5-24. *The Invitation application*

Configuring the Invitation Message

Before you send an invitation message to your friends, you must configure it first. To configure the message, follow these steps:

1. Click the *Configuration* icon in the *Invitation* application. You will see the screen shown in Figure 5-25.

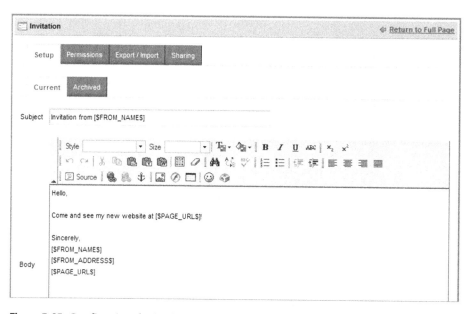

Figure 5-25. *Configuring the invitation-message format*

2. Compose your message by typing the desired *Subject* and *Body* text. (The various terms used in the *Subject* and *Body* text are explained right below the message body.)

3. Click the *Save* button to save your changes.

4. Click the *Archived* tab to archive the current message format for future use. You will see the screen shown in Figure 5-26.

5. Type the desired name for the current message format and click the *Save* button.

You will now be able to use the archived message format in the future by clicking the *Actions* button and selecting *Restore*.

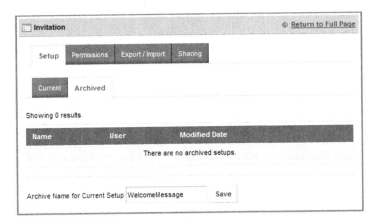

Figure 5-26. *Archiving the current message format*

Sending Invitations

After composing the delivery message, you can start sending the invitations to your friends. Here's how:

1. Click the *Invite Friends* link in the *Invitation* application. You will see the screen shown in Figure 5-27.

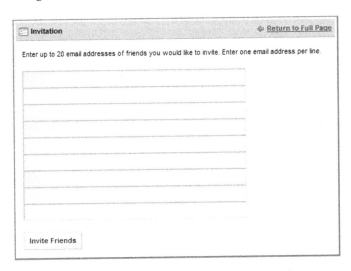

Figure 5-27. *Entering e-mail addresses to invite friends*

2. Enter the e-mail addresses of the desired friends in the displayed edit boxes.

3. Click the *Invite Friends* button.

You will see an onscreen message saying that the invitations have been dispatched to the friends you listed.

Summary

In Chapter 4, you learned how to set up discussion forums so that your portal users can collaborate with one another. You extended your collaboration repertoire in this chapter by delving into several more applications.

Liferay's mail-client application, called *Mail*, allows you to retrieve mail from your Gmail and IMAP mail accounts. You can also send mail to others using the same client application.

The *SMS Text Messenger* application allows you to send text messages to your friends' mobile devices, assuming your friends' mobile-service providers allow them to receive and display e-mail messages on the device.

Liferay's *Chat* application facilitates live chat among the users who are currently online. It allows a simultaneous chat between multiple users.

To initiate discussions with users, you first need to find them. The Liferay *Directory* application helps you easily search and locate desired users, organizations, and user groups. You can send invitations to the located users by using the *Invitation* application.

CHAPTER 6

■ ■ ■

Incorporating Blogs

In the last two chapters, you studied various ways of allowing collaboration among your portal users. In this chapter, you'll look at one more collaboration mechanism that's widely used in today's Internet world: blogging. You will learn to create and manage blogs, including how to

- Use Liferay's three blogging applications
- Create and manage blog entries
- Search blogs
- Post replies to blog entries and manage those replies
- Set user permissions on a blog entry
- Control the display of blog output
- Assign rights to users for various activities on the *Blogs* application

What Are Blogs?

Before we get started, let's review the nature of blogs. Blogging allows users to share their knowledge, experience, and opinions with others. It would be impossible for established publishers to circulate the views of millions of users by traditional means, so these companies have turned to web-based publishing, often in the form of blogging.

In addition to large organizations, smaller companies and individuals also create and manage sites that allow users to publish blogs. A user can register with such a site, create her own blog, and start publishing her views on the Internet. Other Internet users can visit and view the contents of this blog. Some of the popular blog sites run by large organizations, to name just a few, are http://www.blogger.com by Google, http://www.myyblog.com by Yahoo!, and http://blogs.msdn.com by Microsoft.

Blog Definition

Wikipedia defines a blog as follows:

> *A blog (a contraction of the term "Web log") is a Web site, usually maintained by an individual with regular entries of commentary, descriptions of events, or other material such as graphics or video. Entries are commonly displayed in reverse-chronological order.*

As the definition states, a blog is a web site maintained by an individual. How many individuals run blogs? The number easily reaches into the millions, with more than 100 million posts made in the last few years. Blogging has become so popular that nowadays you will find more than a million blog entries made every day.

These entries generally consist of plain text, but might also include graphics and video. The blogging software displays the blogged entries in reverse-chronological order, with the latest entry at the top of the list.

Why Blogging?

Bloggers are not a homogenous group. You'll find bloggers who share their views and ideas about personal issues, professional matters, corporate topics, and so on. Each blogs with a different purpose.

Bloggers can communicate via text, graphics, or even video, the latter of which allows more scope for expression than mere black-and-white text. Some people even use their blogs to earn money: if your blog is popular, you might consider putting advertisements on its page. The annual revenues from several of these blogs have exceeded $75,000.

So why shouldn't our International Security Investors (ISI) portal support blogging? The portal's goal involves bringing together general investors, fundamental analysts, and technical analysts, so blogs created by top-level analysts would certainly benefit the portal community.

We will now look at what facilities you can use to incorporate blogging on Liferay portals. Liferay provides three important applications to help you accomplish this: *Blogs*, *Recent Bloggers*, and *Blogs Aggregator*. You use all three of these to implement blogging in your portal.

Creating Blogs

The *Blogs* application allows you to add blogging functionality to your portal. To add blogging, follow the steps listed here:

1. Create a new public page called *Community* under the *Fundamental Analysts* community that you created in Chapter 3.

2. Select the *Add Application* menu.

3. Select the *Blogs* application under the *Collaboration* category.

Add the application to the currently selected portal page; you should see the screen shown in Figure 6-1.

Now that you have successfully added the application to a portal page, you will add a few blog entries to it.

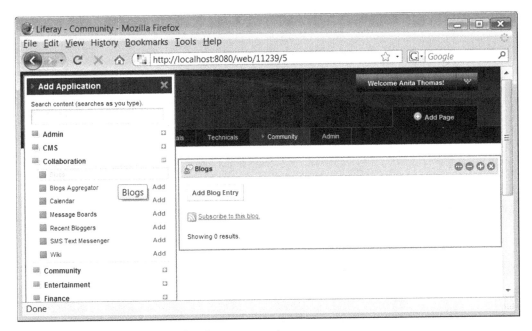

Figure 6-1. *Adding the Blogs application to a portal page*

Adding a Blog Entry

To add a blog entry, follow the steps listed here:

1. Select the *Community* page where you added the *Blogs* application.

2. Click the *Add Blog Entry* button. You will see the screen shown in Figure 6-2.

3. In the *Title* edit box, type **Have Markets bottomed out?**

4. In the *Display Date* fields, select the desired date for your blog entry. By default, this is the current date and time. You can leave these fields to their default values.

5. In the *Content* field, type the body of your entry, expressing your views (and evidence) on whether the markets are currently bottomed out.

6. Format your contents using the WYSIWYG (What You See Is What You Get) editor.

7. Leave the check mark in the *Allow Incoming Trackbacks* check box.

8. Leave the *Trackbacks to Send* field blank.

9. Enter some text in the *Tags* edit box if you wish to tag the current blog entry with some index terms. (You learned about tags in Chapter 4.)

10. After you're done composing the blog entry, click the *Publish* button to publish it. You will now see your blog entry in the application's client area as shown in Figure 6-3.

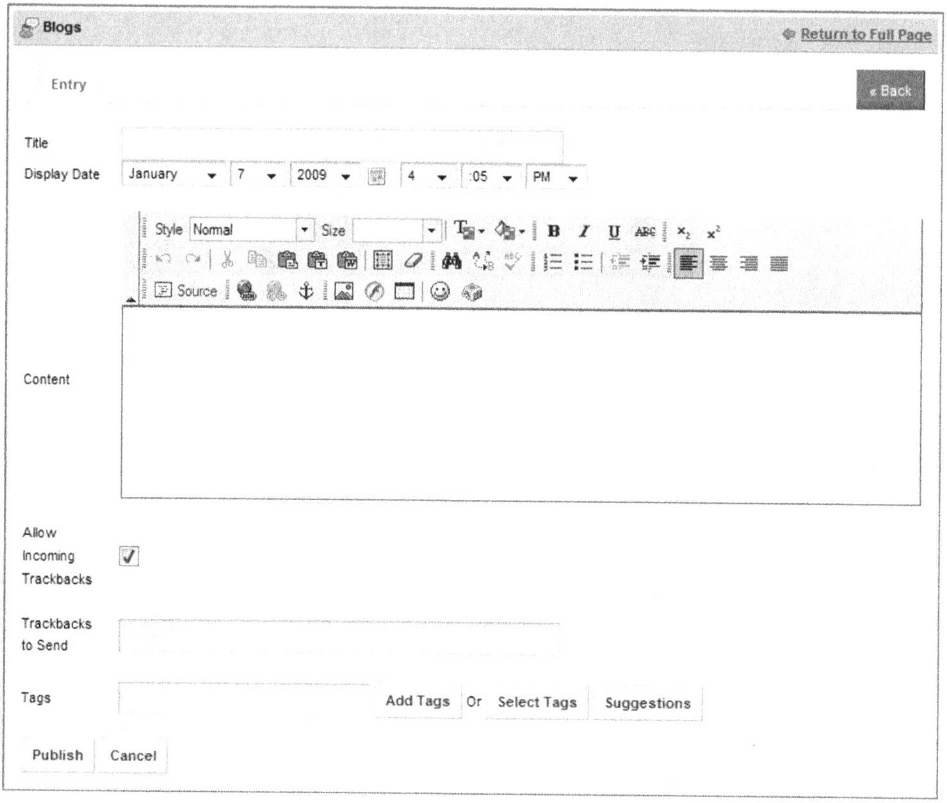

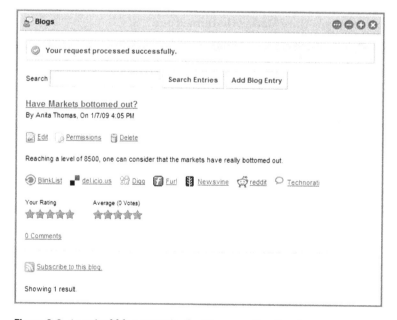

Figure 6-2. *Entering contents for a blog*

Figure 6-3. *A typical blog entry in the Blogs application browser*

Adding Multiple Entries

You can add as many entries to your blog as you wish. Each blog entry will generally have a new timestamp. When you have multiple blog entries on the application screen, they usually appear in reverse-chronological order (with latest blog entry at the top).

You will now add one more blog entry. Make a new blog entry with the following information:

- *Title*: Enter **Market sentiments are very high**.

- *Display Date*: Keep the current date and time values.

- *Content*: Enter **Investor sentiments are now very high considering the current market situation**.

- *Other fields*: Leave these to their default values.

Click the *Publish* button to publish the current blog entry.

Viewing Multiple Blog Entries

After you publish your second blog entry, you will see both your blog entries listed on the application screen as shown in Figure 6-4.

As you can see in Figure 6-4, the most recent entry appears at the top. Also, note the various options that allow you to perform the following actions on each entry:

- Edit

- Delete

- Share

- Rate

- Post comments

- Set user permissions

I will explain these actions in depth, but first I will discuss the *Search* facility that lets you locate a desired blog.

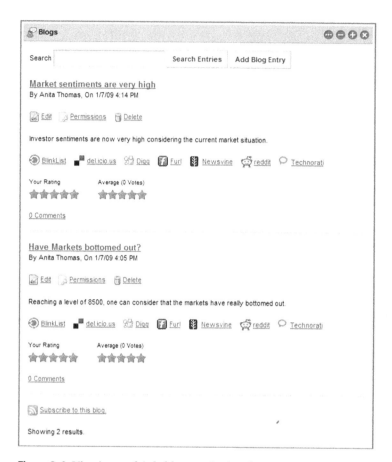

Figure 6-4. *Viewing multiple blog entries in a browser*

Searching for an Entry

As the number of blog entries grows, the *Search* facility comes in handy when you want to locate entries containing certain keywords. For example, you can search all blog entries for the word "market" by entering the keyword **market** in the *Search* edit box and clicking the *Search Entries* button. You'll now see all blog entries that contain your keyword (see Figure 6-5), and you can click an entry's title link to view its contents.

Figure 6-5. *Result of the "market" keyword search*

Editing an Entry

To edit an entry, perform the following steps:

1. Scroll to the desired entry.

2. Click the *Edit* link shown below the entry title.

3. Look at the selected entry in the WYSIWYG editor. This is the same editor you used while creating the entry.

4. Make any desired changes to the entry, such as formatting its contents, changing its title, changing the timestamp, or adding tags.

5. Click the *Save* button to save your changes, which should be reflected in the *Blogs* browser display.

Deleting an Entry

To delete an entry, perform the following actions:

1. Scroll to the desired entry.

2. Click the *Delete* link below the entry title.

3. Confirm whether you want to delete the entry. When you return to the browser display, note that the entry has disappeared.

Note When you delete an entry, all comments made on the entry will be deleted as well. (You'll read more about comments in the section "Posting Comments.")

Sharing an Entry

If you find a blog entry useful and you want to share it, you can choose from several sites that let you do that. Links to many such sites appear below each blog entry in the browser display:

- BlinkList
- del.icio.us
- Digg
- Furl
- Newsvine
- reddit
- Technorati

You need to register on these sites in order to share your discoveries with other users of the site. Once you share a blog entry on Technorati, for example, other Technorati members will be able to view your recommendation. Such sharing is a good way to popularize a blog entry.

These sites also crawl the Internet and create an index of various blog entries so that the sites' members can search the entire web for the indexed terms. This indexing, sometimes used by the press, proves useful for collecting public opinion on a particular topic.

Rating an Entry

No doubt you'll like some blog entries better than others. The *Blogs* application allows you to give each entry a rating between one and five stars. Rating an entry is easy. Under the entry, you will find five stars below the *Your Rating* label (see Figure 6-6).

Figure 6-6. *Rating an entry*

If you want to give a three-star rating to the current blog entry, click the third star. The first three stars become red in color, and the *Average* stars change to reflect the average rating of all the votes made on this article. Because this entry has only one vote, the average rating is the same as your personal rating (three stars).

Tip Log on to the portal as some other user and locate the entry that you want to rate. Cast your vote, assuming that you have the permission to do so. The *Average* rating displays the number of votes cast, and the number of stars shown in red changes to reflect the new average of all the votes cast so far.

Posting Comments

In addition to rating blog entries, you will also be able to post comments on them. To comment on an entry, follow these steps:

1. Locate the entry on which you wish to comment.

2. Click the *Comments* link at the bottom of the entry.

3. Click the *Post Reply* link to open an edit box for your comment text (see Figure 6-7).

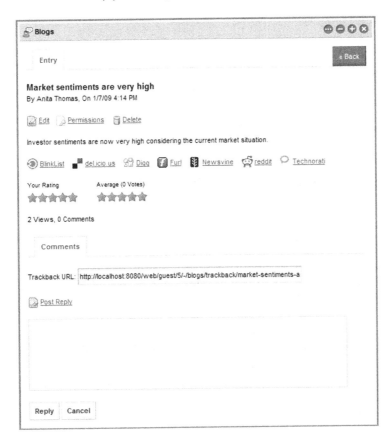

Figure 6-7. *Posting a reply to a blog entry*

4. Enter your reply message and click the *Reply* button.

You should see your reply below the original message in the browser (see Figure 6-8).

Blogs
Entry
« Back
Market sentiments are very high
By Anita Thomas, On 1/7/09 4:14 PM
Edit
Permissions
Delete
Investor sentiments are now very high considering the current market situation.
BlinkList
del.icio.us
Digg
Furl
Newsvine
reddit
Technorati
Your Rating
Average (0 Votes)
9 Views, 1 Comments
Comments
Trackback URL:
http://localhost:8080/web/guest/5/-/blogs/trackback/market-sentiments-a
Post Reply
Threaded Replies
Author
Date
The market will be volatile in these days.
Robert Prill
1/7/09 4:33 PM
The market will be volatile in these days.
Posted on 1/7/09 4:33 PM.
Robert Prill
Post Reply
Top
Edit
Delete

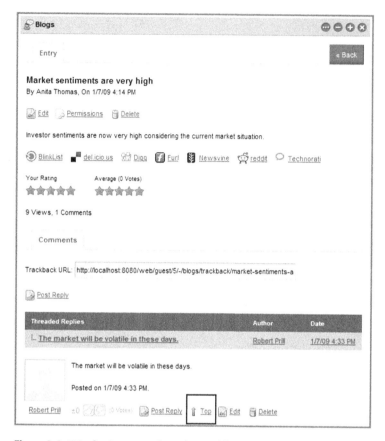

Figure 6-8. *Displaying a user's reply to a blog entry*

Navigating Comments

If you examine Figure 6-8, you will notice that a navigation tree appears immediately under the blog entry. Here you will find the hierarchy of all the replies on the original entry, with a link to each reply. A sample navigation hierarchy is shown in Figure 6-9.

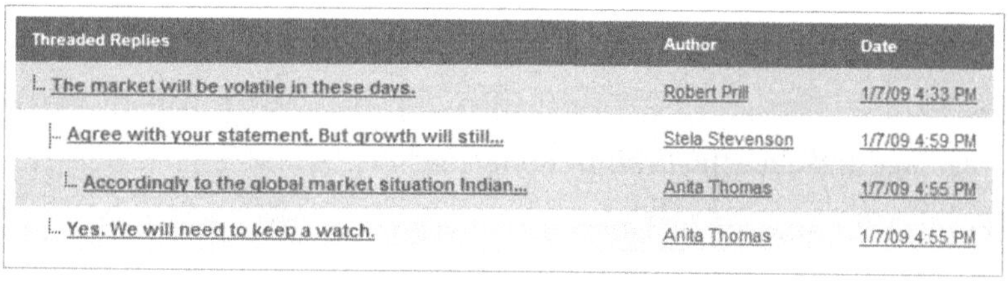

Threaded Replies
Author
Date
The market will be volatile in these days.
Robert Prill
1/7/09 4:33 PM
Agree with your statement. But growth will still...
Stela Stevenson
1/7/09 4:59 PM
Accordingly to the global market situation Indian...
Anita Thomas
1/7/09 4:55 PM
Yes. We will need to keep a watch.
Anita Thomas
1/7/09 4:55 PM

Figure 6-9. *Displaying the navigation hierarchy of replies*

Clicking any of the links will open the corresponding reply in your *Blogs* application browser.

■**Tip** If you are too deep in the reply hierarchy, you can jump straight to the top entry by clicking the *Top* button at the bottom (see Figure 6-8).

Replying to a Comment

When you are looking at somebody else's comment on a blog entry, you might want to add your own comment to the existing comment, assuming you have been assigned permission to do so. To post a reply to a comment, perform these steps:

1. Click the *Post Reply* button at the bottom of the selected comment to pull up a text box (see Figure 6-10).

Figure 6-10. *Posting a reply to a comment*

2. Enter your comment and click the *Reply* button.

3. Verify that your message has posted under the selected comment by examining the navigation tree.

Editing a Comment

If you wish to edit the comment that you posted (once again, assuming you have the required permissions), follow the steps listed here:

1. Click the *Edit* link at the bottom of the comment to open the comment in the edit box.

2. Make the desired changes to the contents.

3. Click the *Update* button and view your changes in the browser window.

Deleting a Comment

To delete a comment, click the *Delete* link at the bottom of the comment display. The current comment will be deleted after your confirmation.

Note When you delete a comment, all its subcomments are not deleted. The *Blogs* application retains them and moves them up in the hierarchy.

Setting User Permissions

When you add a blog entry, you will definitely want to set permissions to limit what other users can do with it. To set user permissions on a blog entry, click the *Permissions* link underneath it. You will see the usual permissions screen with the list of current roles and permissions assigned to each role.

By default, the guest user has only the *View* permission and the owner has all the permissions. You'll now assign permissions to the portal's power-user role by following these steps:

1. In the permissions display screen, select the *Power User* check box.

2. Click the *Update Permissions* button to get the screen shown in Figure 6-11.

Figure 6-11. *Setting permissions on a blog entry*

3. On this screen, you will be able to assign permissions for adding, deleting, and updating discussions. You can also allow the user to see the *Permissions* option itself.

4. Using the two arrows, assign or revoke the desired permissions.

5. Click the *Finished* button to save your changes and display them in the *Power User* tab.

I will now discuss the meanings of the various permissions.

Add Discussion

Assigning the *Add Discussion* permission allows the user to add a reply to the current message or its replies. If you grant this permission, the user will see the *Post Reply* link at the bottom of the blog entry and its replies. This link is highlighted in Figure 6-12.

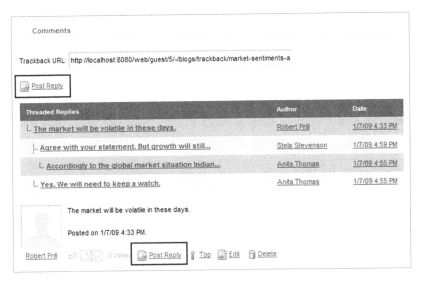

Figure 6-12. *The display seen by a user after the Add Discussion permission is granted*

Delete Discussion

The *Delete Discussion* permission allows a user to delete any of the replies to the current blog entry. Such a user will have access to the *Delete* link at the bottom of the entry.

Update Discussion

The *Update Discussion* option lets a user modify the contents of any reply to the current blog entry. Such a user will see the *Edit* link at the bottom of the entry.

Delete

Granting the *Delete* permission allows the user to delete the original blog entry. Whenever a blog entry is deleted, all its replies will also be deleted. A user with this permission will see the *Delete* link at the bottom of the original blog entry.

Update

Granting the *Update* permission allows the user to edit the original blog entry. An *Edit* link appears at the bottom of the original blog entry whenever this permission is granted.

View

By default, the *View* permission is granted to all users. However, if you explicitly deny this permission for a certain blog post, users will not be able to see the entry. You should always enable the *View* permission to encourage readership on your portal's blog.

Permissions

If you deny a user the *Permissions* permission, the *Permissions* link that you see at the bottom of the blog entry will be removed from the display. This user cannot change permissions on the current blog entry.

Note Setting the permissions on a selected blog entry affects only the currently selected entry and does not affect the remaining entries in the blog. If you want to grant or deny permissions on multiple blog entries, you must do so for each entry individually. Generally, the blog-entry author sets these permissions when she creates the entry.

Tip You can set some general permissions at the application level. These will apply to all blog entries. You can read more about this in the section "Setting General Permissions" under "Configuring the Blogs Portlet."

Configuring the Blogs Portlet

So far, you've seen how to use the *Blogs* portlet for setting up blogs, viewing blog entries, responding to blog messages, and so on. You'll now look at how to customize the *Blogs* portlet itself. Primarily, you will learn to

- Set what is displayed on the application browser while users view the blog entries
- Set permissions for the entire user base

Controlling Output

To configure how blogs are displayed, click the *Configuration* icon in the *Blogs* application. You will see the screen shown in Figure 6-13.

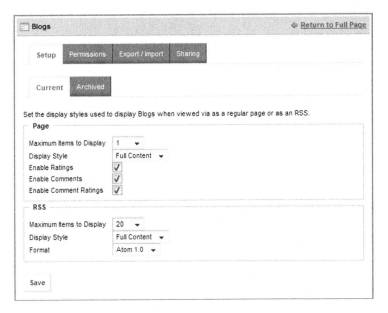

Figure 6-13. *Configuring the Blogs application*

Here you will see two options for controlling the output display: *Page* and *RSS*. Let's look at the various settings under each heading.

Page Output Options

The *Page* output option allows the following settings:

- *Maximum Items to Display*: This option lets you control the number of blog entries you display per page. This number can range from 1 to 100, as indicated in the drop-down list. The default value is 1.

- *Display Style*: This option gives you three choices:

  - *Full Content*: Displays the full contents of the blog; this includes both the abstract and the title.

  - *Abstract*: Displays only the abstract, which consists of the blog entry's first few lines. This view provides a *Read More* link at the bottom of each abstracted entry so that the user can view the full blog contents when desired.

  - *Title*: Displays only the entry's title. This option is useful if you want to save the real estate on your screen. This view also provides a link to the full content.

- *Enable Ratings*: This option is checked by default. Unchecking it will remove the star-rating display from the blog-entry view. The screenshot in Figure 6-14 shows the result of disabling this option.

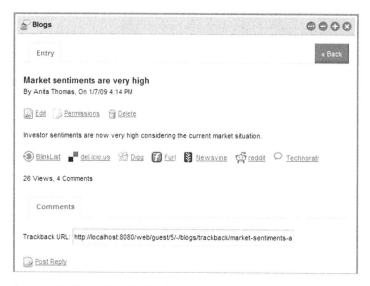

Figure 6-14. *Disabling the Enable Ratings option*

- *Enable Comments*: This option is also checked by default. Unchecking it removes the *Comments* link from the display screen so that the user will not be able to add comments to the posted blog entries.

- *Enable Comment Ratings*: Leaving this option checked allows users to rate the comments made by other users.

Note If you disable ratings at some point, the previous ratings on a blog entry or its comments do not get destroyed. The system retains them and redisplays them whenever you enable the ratings again.

RSS Output

Users can view the blog entries in RSS format. A typical view of a blog output in RSS format is shown in Figure 6-15.

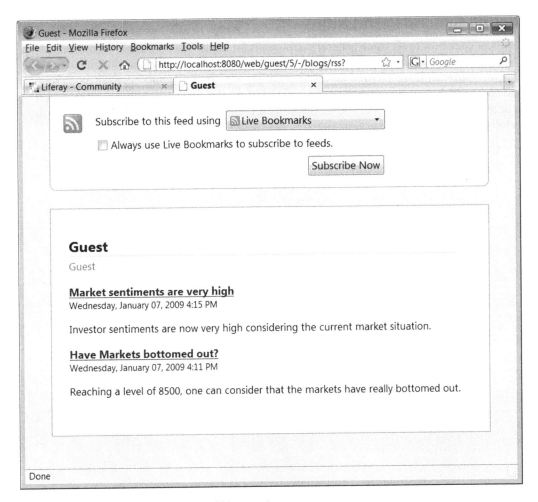

Figure 6-15. *Displaying an RSS view of blog entries*

In the *RSS* area of the *Blogs* application's configuration screen, you can control the following:

- *Maximum Items to Display*: This drop-down list resembles the one in the *Page* area of the configuration screen. The default value is 20.

- *Display Style*: Like the option of the same name in the *Page* area, it offers full-content display, abstract display, or title-only display.

- *Format*: This option lets you select the output format: RSS 1.0, RSS 2.0, or Atom 1.0. The default is Atom 1.0.

Setting General Permissions

Now you'll see how to set some general permissions for the users of our *Blogs* application. Click the *Permissions* tab to get the regular screen for setting application permissions. It displays the currently assigned roles for the application user. The *Available* tab displays all roles that are available for assignment. Use this tab to look up the permissions that you can assign to or revoke from a power user. You'll now assign permissions to the portal's power-user role by following these steps:

1. Check the *Power User* role in the displayed list.

2. Click the *Update Permissions* button to see the screen shown in Figure 6-16.

Figure 6-16. *Setting general permissions for a power user*

3. Set the desired permissions using the two arrows. You can choose from three types of permissions:

   a. *Add Entry*: Allows the user to add a new blog entry.

   b. *Configuration*: Allows the user to configure the blog.

   c. *View*: Allows the user to view the blog; this is assigned by default.

4. Click the *Finished* button to save your changes and put the newly assigned permissions into effect.

Using the Recent Bloggers Application

With luck, you'll encounter many active bloggers after opening up the community page to your portal users. Knowing who your most recent posters are can help you quickly identify new entries made by your favorite bloggers. Liferay provides an application called *Recent Bloggers* that helps you get this information. In fact, the Liferay site itself, which runs on the Liferay Portal engine, has this application installed on its *Community* page. Open the URL http://www.liferay.com/web/guest/community/home in your browser and you will see the screen similar to the one shown in Figure 6-17.

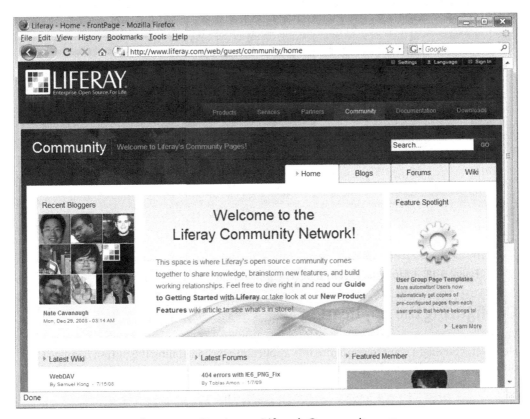

Figure 6-17. *The Recent Bloggers application on Liferay's Community page*

In the screen's top-left corner, you will see the *Recent Bloggers* application running. It displays the photos of recent bloggers; hovering the mouse over a photo displays the blogger's name underneath.

I will now show you how to set up this facility on your ISI portal.

Installing the Application

To install the *Recent Bloggers* application, follow these steps:

1. Select the *Community* page created in the previous section. (You can select any other page where you wish to add the new application.)

2. Select the *Add Application* menu.

3. Select *Recent Bloggers* under the *Collaboration* category.

4. Add the application to the page. You should get a screen like the one shown in Figure 6-18, and the application view should show the list of recent bloggers.

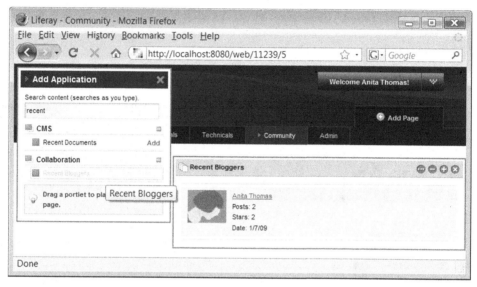

Figure 6-18. *Adding the Recent Bloggers application*

Configuring the Application

You've just seen the *Recent Bloggers* application display the list of recent bloggers onscreen. However, you might want to configure this application by controlling the output display. Click the *Configuration* button in the application window to get the screen shown in Figure 6-19.

Figure 6-19. *Configuring the Recent Bloggers application*

Here, you will find three options that you can configure to customize the output of the *Recent Bloggers* application: *Organization*, *Display Style*, and *Maximum Bloggers to Display*. I will discuss each of these.

Organization

You can choose the organization by clicking the *Select* button and selecting the desired organization from the displayed list. Several organizations defined in your portal might use your blog, especially in the case of multinational corporations with offices in different parts of the world. Each office works as an independent organization, so you might have organizational units in the United States, the United Kingdom, Denmark, China, and so on. While defining the portal, you will need to create organizations for each such unit.

Note You learned how to create organizations in Chapter 3.

By selecting an organization, you are choosing to display only the recent bloggers from that organization. We have only one organizational unit in our ISI portal, so all the portal's recent bloggers will be displayed in the list.

Note Unfortunately, Liferay does not allow you to select a community instead of an organization. Our ISI portal has two communities, both defined within the same organization. Thus, you will not be able to differentiate between the postings made by the two user communities.

Display Style

The *Display Style* option offers two choices: *User Name and Image*, and *User Name*. The first choice displays the user name along with an image, which the user provided when he created an account. Generally, bloggers provide photos of themselves to use in the image display. If no photo is provided, a default image is used. (Instead of a photo, a user might provide a cartoon image or other picture.)

The second choice displays only the user name. You might opt for this choice if you want to display a large number of users, most of whom have not set up images on their profiles.

Maximum Bloggers

This option controls the number of bloggers to display on screen. This, once again, is a discrete value in the range of 1 to 100. The default value is 10.

Using the Blogs Aggregator Application

Instead of viewing the full blog contents, you might find it more convenient to look at the aggregated view of the blogs and then retrieve the full blog entries only for the posts you find interesting. Liferay provides an application called *Blogs Aggregator* for this purpose. In this section, you will learn to install and use this application.

Installing the Application

To install an instance of the *Blogs Aggregator* application on your portal page, follow these steps:

1. Select the *Community* page you created earlier, or any other page where you want to add the application.

2. Select the *Install Application* menu.

3. Select the *Blogs Aggregator* application under the *Collaboration* category.

4. Add the application to the portal page. You should get a screen like the one shown in Figure 6-20, where you'll see an aggregated view of blog entries.

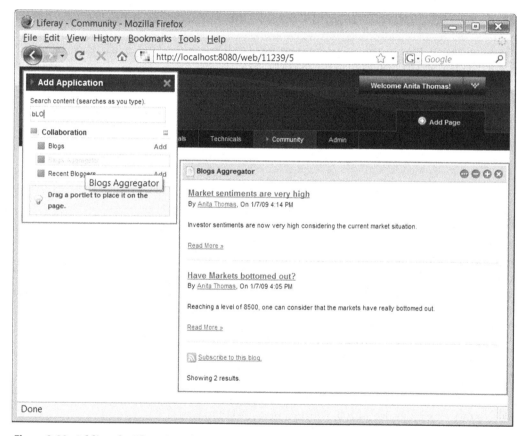

Figure 6-20. *Adding the Blogs Aggregator application*

Configuring the Application

Like all the applications discussed so far, *Blogs Aggregator* provides customization. To customize the application, click the *Configuration* icon in the application window. You will see the screen shown in Figure 6-21.

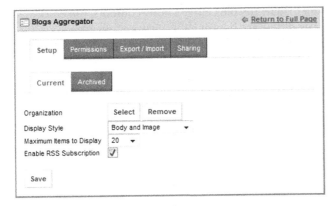

Figure 6-21. *Customizing the Blogs Aggregator application*

Here you will find four customization options:

- *Organization*
- *Display Style*
- *Maximum Items to Display*
- *Enable RSS Subscription*

I will now discuss each of these options.

Organization

The *Organization* option allows you to filter blog entries for a desired organization. As you did with the *Recent Bloggers* application, you can select the organization filter by clicking the *Select* button and selecting the desired organization from the displayed list. Our ISI portal defines only one organization, so this filter will not be useful in this case.

Display Style

The *Display Style* option provides several choices:

- *Body and Image*
- *Body*
- *Abstract*
- *Abstract without Title*
- *Quote*
- *Quote without Title*
- *Title*

The *Body and Image* option lets you display the blog entry's body contents, the entry's title, and the blogger's profile image. The difference between this view and the view provided in the *Blogs* application discussed earlier in this chapter is that the options for rating, commenting, editing, and so on are not displayed on the screen of the *Blogs Aggregator* application. So you can read the entries quickly rather than get distracted with several links and buttons on each blog entry. The screen output when this option is selected is shown in Figure 6-22.

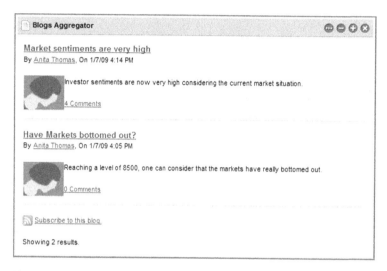

Figure 6-22. *The Body and Image view of the Blogs Aggregator application*

Choosing the *Body* option displays the title and body of each blog entry without the blogger's image. This saves some real estate on the screen and makes it easier to focus on the contents.

The *Abstract* view provides the title and the first few words of the body contents. A link called *Read More* lets a user retrieve the full body contents. The *Abstract without Title* option provides the same view as *Abstract*, except that the blog title is not displayed.

The *Quote* option displays the contents of the blog entry in double quotes. As the name suggests, the *Quote without Title* option provides the same view as *Quote*, but without the title. Finally, the *Title* option displays only the title of each entry.

Maximum Items to Display

The *Maximum Items to Display* option lets you set the maximum number of posts to display onscreen. As in the case of the *Recent Bloggers* application, this is a discrete number in the range of 1 to 100. The default value is 20.

Enable RSS Subscription

The *Enable RSS Subscription* option, which is enabled by default, displays a *Subscribe to this blog* link at the bottom of the application window. A user can click the link to subscribe to this blog and receive updates regularly in RSS-feed format. (See Chapter 4 for instructions on customizing the RSS feed and its format.)

Summary

In this chapter, you set up blogging, which is a very important feature of any portal. Liferay provides three applications to help you implement blogging on your portal: *Blogs*, *Recent Bloggers*, and *Blogs Aggregator*. The *Blogs* application allows users to create their own blog entries, post replies to existing entries, navigate posts, view and edit entries, and so on. It also provides a WYSIWYG editor for formatting blog entries.

The *Recent Bloggers* application displays the list of users who have recently posted blog entries, so you can identify your regular bloggers when you visit the portal's blog page. The *Blogs Aggregator* application provides a consolidated view of the blogs, where you can see many blog entries on one screen. You can then read a full entry by clicking the link provided on each.

CHAPTER 7

■ ■ ■

Establishing a Wiki

If you're reading this book, you're almost certainly familiar with Wikipedia. Wikipedia is an online encyclopedia created and maintained entirely by Internet users. If you have expertise in a certain field and want to share that knowledge with other users worldwide, you can post that information on Wikipedia. Anyone can contribute to the site.

The ISI portal that we are creating for stock-market investors can certainly benefit from the types of features that Wikipedia offers. Luckily, Liferay comes with an application to provide wiki functionality on its portals. In this chapter, you'll augment the ISI portal with a wiki that lets users post definitions and other information about investing and markets. This wiki will benefit the entire user community, from novices to seasoned investors, from short-term investors to long-term investors, from fundamental analysts to technical analysts.

This chapter will start with an overview about wikis, then show you how to

- Install and use Liferay's *Wiki* application
- Create nodes
- Add pages and subpages
- Configure pages' display settings and permissions
- Move and delete pages
- Manage wikis
- Track page changes
- List and manage recently changed pages
- List and manage orphan pages

What Is a Wiki?

Wikis have some similarities to the applications you've seen in earlier chapters, but they have some differences too. Like discussion forums and blogs, wikis facilitate collaboration among users. But whereas forums and blogs are controlled by individuals, wikis are controlled by a large number of users. And because the number of contributors to a wiki is potentially endless, wikis are vulnerable to abuse. Thus, the effective use of a wiki lies in its users' honest use and adherence to certain guidelines.

Wikipedia defines "wiki" as follows:

A wiki is a page or collection of Web pages designed to enable anyone who accesses it to contribute or modify content, using a simplified markup language. Wikis are often used to create collaborative websites and to power community websites.

As stated in the definition, a wiki is a web page or a collection of pages. Any user with appropriate permissions, which are generally granted by default, can create a new page and add it to a wiki. Ideally, this page should contain useful information that's helpful to other users, but the accuracy of the information cannot be guaranteed in most cases. If the information is incorrect, though, other users can fix it. The wiki tracks the changes that different users make to each entry, so one can revert back to the original entry if the modified information is technically incorrect. A classic example of a wiki is Wikipedia, which is entirely authored and edited by a large number of worldwide users with expertise in different areas.

Wikis also prove useful in business. A large multinational corporation can set up wikis on their intranets to publish company policies. The regional changes made to such policies can be directly entered and edited by employees belonging to those individual regions. Such wikis can also be useful for sharing knowledge and experience among colleagues, especially since the wiki retains that information long after employees leave the organization.

The first wiki software program was developed by Ward Cunningham. The application was called *WikiWikiWeb* and was described as "the simplest online database that could possibly work."[1] According to Wikipedia, "wiki" stands for "What I Know Is," but this is apparently a "backronym" (an acronym constructed for the word after the word had already been in existence). "Wiki," incidentally, is a Hawaiian word for "fast" or "quick."

Installing the Wiki Application

The Liferay installation comes with an application called *Wiki* to provide wiki functionality on Liferay portals. You will now learn to use it. First, install the *Wiki* application on the ISI portal by following these steps:

1. Open the *Community* page that you created in the last chapter.

2. Add a child page called *Wiki* to the *Community* page.

3. Alternatively, you can create a public page called *Wiki* under the *Fundamental Analysts* community.

4. Select the *Add Application* menu.

5. Select the *Wiki* application under the *Collaboration* category.

6. Add the application to the page. Your screen with the *Wiki* application should look like the one shown in Figure 7-1.

---

1 Wiki.org, "What Is Wiki," http://wiki.org/wiki.cgi?WhatIsWiki, 2002.

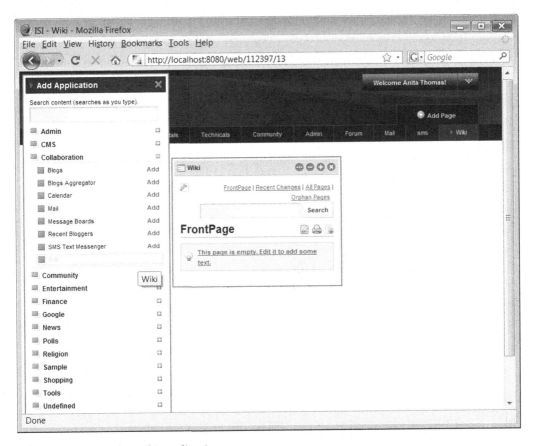

Figure 7-1. *Adding the Wiki application*

As you can see in Figure 7-1, the *Wiki* application has created a default node for you and has added a page called *FrontPage*. The page is empty, so you will need to edit it to add some content.

Note You can change the default name assigned to the page, which I'll describe in the "Advanced Actions" section under "Adjusting Page Properties."

Working with Nodes

A wiki consists of several nodes. You'll now add a few nodes of your own.

Creating Nodes

You'll add two nodes based on the classifications of our community users: *Fundamental* and *Technical*. The *Fundamental* node will carry information useful to fundamental analysts, while the *Technical* node will carry information for those who are interested in technical analysis. To add these nodes, follow the steps listed here:

1. Locate the small toolbox icon above the *FrontPage* heading (see Figure 7-2). You'll see a tool tip titled *Manage Wikis* when you hover the mouse over this icon.

Figure 7-2. *Icon for managing wikis*

2. Click this toolbox icon to pull up the screen shown in Figure 7-3. The screen shows the list of currently defined nodes and displays a button to let you add new nodes.

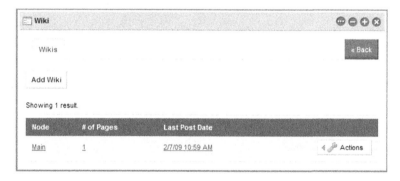

Figure 7-3. *Adding nodes to a wiki*

3. Click the *Add Wiki* button to create a new node. You will see the screen shown in Figure 7-4.

4. Enter **Fundamental** as the node name.

5. Enter a description for the node.

6. With the *Configure* link, you would be able to set the user permissions for the node you're adding. Leave the default settings for these. Note that the screenshot in Figure 7-4 shows the configuration options expanded, so the *Configure* link itself is not visible in the screenshot.

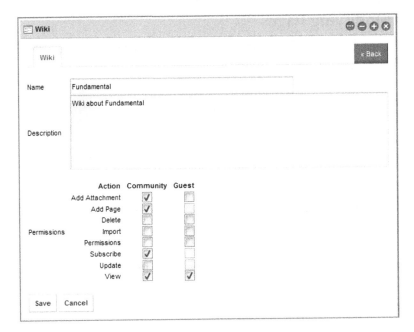

Figure 7-4. *Creating a new node*

7. Click the *Save* button. You will return to the screen shown in Figure 7-3, where you'll see the new node added to the displayed list.

8. Go back to step 3 and add one more node called **Technical**. After you have added the two nodes, the screen will look like the one shown in Figure 7-5.

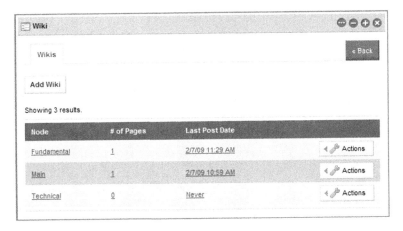

Figure 7-5. *List of created wikis*

Now that you've added the desired nodes, you can customize each one by editing its pages. You'll learn to modify the default pages created at the time of node creation, and you'll also learn to add child pages and configure them.

Adding and Modifying Pages

When you create a node, a default *Main* page is created for you. You'll now learn to edit the contents of this page.

Editing Contents

You'll start by customizing the *Fundamental* node you created in the previous section. To customize the node, follow the steps listed here:

1. Click the *Edit* icon shown in the top-right corner of the node (see Figure 7-6).

Figure 7-6. *Icon for editing a page*

2. The *FrontPage* page of the *Fundamental* node opens up for editing, as shown in Figure 7-7.

3. Select one of these options from the *Format* drop-down list:

   a. *Creole*: This is a markup language created by the WikiCreole community, which is headed by wiki inventor Ward Cunningham. This language is easy to learn, easy to teach, and fast to type. It uses readable markup that's nondestructive.

   b. *HTML*: In this mode, you will see the FCKeditor, which is a WYSIWYG editor for creating HTML text. It offers functionality similar to Microsoft Word or OpenOffice, although with limitations.

4. Select *HTML* format for the time being. Using this HTML editor, you can add text, images, and links to the page.

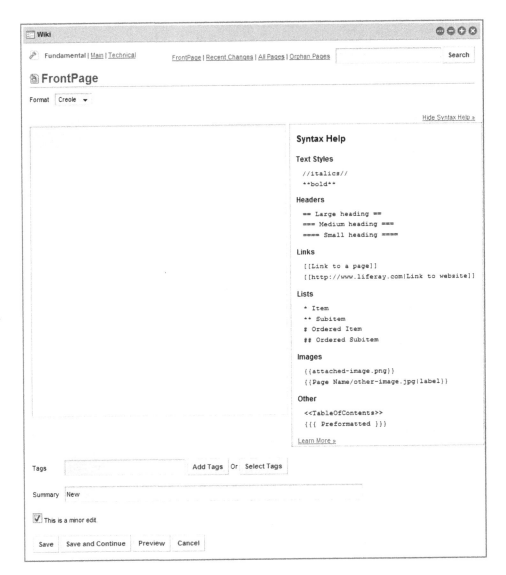

Figure 7-7. *Editing a wiki page*

5. Enter a description as shown in Figure 7-8.

6. Add tags to the page if you wish.

7. You can add a short abstract using the *Summary* edit box.

8. You can preview the edits before saving the page by clicking the *Preview* button. If you're satisfied with the edits, click the *Save* button to save your changes to the page. You should now see the screen shown in Figure 7-8.

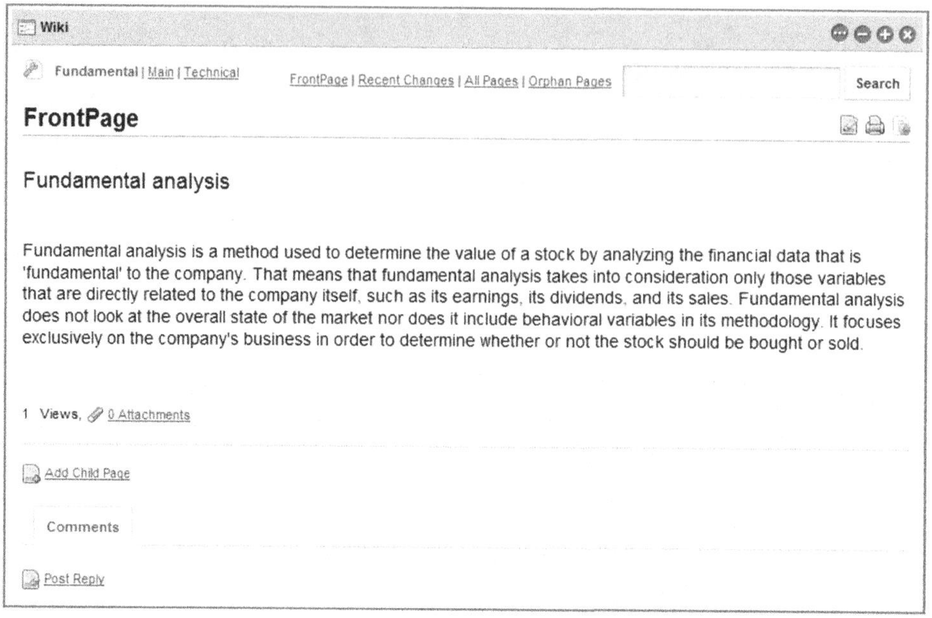

Figure 7-8. *A completed wiki page*

Once a page has been edited to include a title and description, you can add attachments, add child pages, or post replies to it. We will now look at all of these options.

Adding Attachments

When you define a wiki page and provide some description on it, you might want to support your contribution with external documents. You can do this by attaching the supporting files to the wiki page. To attach an external document to a page, follow these steps:

1. Click the *Attachments* link at the bottom of the page. If the page has any existing attachments, the *Wiki* application will display them onscreen. If this is the first time you are adding an attachment, the list will be empty.

2. Click the *Add Attachment* button. The resulting screen is shown in Figure 7-9.

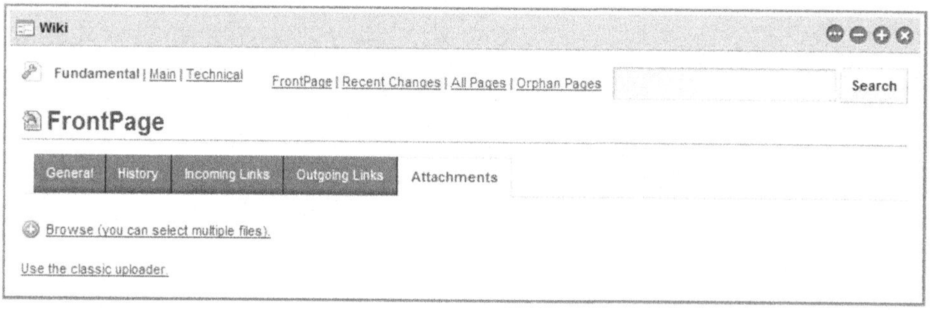

Figure 7-9. *Adding attachments to a page*

3. Click the *Browse* button to pull up the file-selection dialog.

4. Browse the folder structure and select one or more files that you'd like to upload. After selecting multiple files, you'll get a screen similar to the one shown in Figure 7-10.

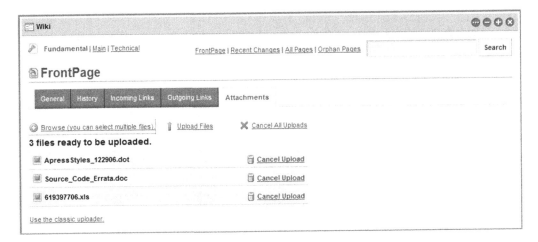

Figure 7-10. *Selecting multiple files for upload*

5. You can cancel the upload of any of the selected files by clicking the *Cancel Upload* link to the right of the file name.

6. Click the *Upload Files* link to upload the selected files to the server.

7. Click the *Use the classic uploader* link to use the classic uploader, which lets you upload three files at a time. Alternatively, you can use the new uploader by clicking the *Browse (you can select multiple files)* link, which allows you to upload any number of files at a time.

   The application checks the file extension before uploading the file and shows the message shown in Figure 7-11 if it doesn't recognize the extension.

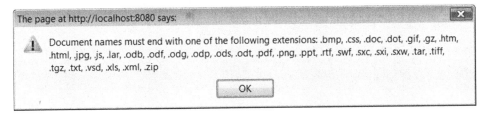

Figure 7-11. *Valid extensions for the file to be uploaded*

8. Return to the page view, where you'll see the number of attachments associated with the page (see Figure 7-12).

Figure 7-12. *The link showing the number of attachments*

The community users will now be able to view these attachments along with the main text of your page.

Adding Child Pages

You've created the main page for your wiki node and attached a few justifying documents. Now you can add child pages to the main page. Generally, as an owner of a wiki node, you would allow your community users to add child pages to your node so that they can provide additional information on your topic or fill any gaps. Don't worry about the permissions for now; just continue adding child pages with the owner rights that you have.

To add a child page, follow these steps:

1. Click the *Add Child Page* link at the bottom of the wiki entry (see Figure 7-13). Doing this pops up the page editor that you used earlier.

Figure 7-13. *Adding a child page*

2. Enter the title, body text, tags, and summary in the editor.

3. Click the *Save* button to save your changes. You will return to the previous screen, which lists the newly added child page.

4. Add multiple child pages as desired. When you return to the wiki entry, you'll see a list of all child pages displayed at the bottom (see Figure 7-14).

Figure 7-14. *List of all added child pages*

5. Click the link of a child page to view it. The page will show up in full-screen view.

■**Tip** Child pages are equivalent to your main page. You can add further child pages to each individual child page, you can add attachments to a child page, and your users can post replies to a child page. You can edit and configure a child page, as well as set permissions on it—just as you can for your main page. In short, whatever you can do on a main page, you can do on a child page.

Posting a Reply

When you post a wiki page, your users might want to post replies to it. Such replies might consist of supporting content or even dissenting views. To post a reply to a wiki entry, follow the steps listed here:

1. Log in as a different user. For example, you can log in as another user that you created earlier. Make sure that the selected user account has permissions to post a reply.

2. Select the wiki page on which you want to comment.

3. Hit the *Post Reply* link at the bottom of the body text. This opens an edit box underneath the link on the same screen (see Figure 7-15).

Figure 7-15. *Posting a reply to a wiki page*

4. Type your comment in the edit box and click the *Reply* button. The application returns you to the previous screen, where you can see your reply at the bottom of the wiki page (see Figure 7-16).

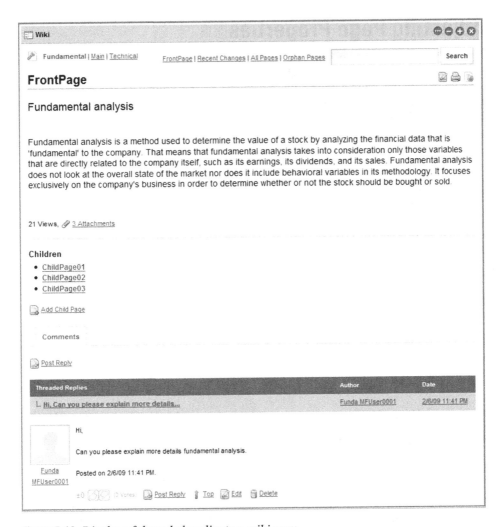

Figure 7-16. *Display of threaded replies to a wiki page*

5. When different users post their replies, all such replies will be shown in a tree hier-archy under the *Threaded Replies* heading. Click any of the displayed links to jump directly to that reply. You can always quickly return to the top of the reply list by clicking the *Top* link.

6. You can edit or delete a reply by using the corresponding links shown at the bottom of it.

Note The *Edit* and *Delete* links will be visible to you only if you have permissions to perform these actions.

Adjusting Page Properties

So far, you've learned to add new pages to a wiki node and create child pages for it. Now, you will learn to set the various page properties. The properties are maintained for each page individually, so you first need to select the page you want to modify. To look up the page's current properties and set new values for them, use the *Properties* icon shown in the top-right corner of the page (see Figure 7-17).

Figure 7-17. *The Properties icon*

When you click the *Properties* icon of the selected page, you will bring up the following tabbed options:

- *General*
- *History*
- *Incoming Links*
- *Outgoing Links*
- *Attachments*

We will now look at each of these options in detail.

General Properties

The *General* properties tab of a typical wiki page is shown in Figure 7-18.

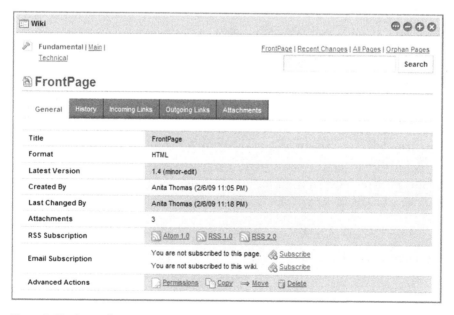

Figure 7-18. *General properties of a wiki page*

The *General* properties screen shows several generally useful properties and also allows you to perform certain actions on the selected page. We'll now look at the interpretations of the various properties and actions:

- *Title*: This displays the page title.
- *Format*: This shows the page format, which can be either *HTML* or *Creole*.
- *Latest Version*: This shows the version number for the last edit to the page.

Note The *Wiki* application maintains the versions for your edits on the page. Whenever you edit the page and save it, the app assigns a new version number to the page. The original page is retained and the edited page is saved under the new version number.

- *Created By*: This shows the page creator, plus the date and time of creation.
- *Last Changed By*: This shows the user who edited the page last, plus the date and time of the last edit.

Tip Any user can edit a wiki, assuming she has been granted permission to do so. (Wikis differ from blogs in this manner.) In fact, this is the intention behind wikis: allowing users to edit entries so they can incorporate accurate content and fill in any gaps.

- *Attachments*: This shows the number of files attached to the current page. As I mentioned earlier, the page creator or anybody having requisite permissions can attach supporting documents to a page.
- *RSS Subscription*: This property lets you choose whether to view the page in Atom 1.0, RSS 1.0, or RSS 2.0. When you view the page in RSS, you will see all of a page's versions displayed in a browser window (see Figure 7-19).
- *Email Subscription*: This shows your subscriptions to the page and the wiki. If you are not currently subscribed, you can subscribe by clicking the *Subscribe* link to the right of the desired option. After you subscribe, the link changes to *Unsubscribe* so you can unsubscribe to the feed at any time. (This property is accessible only to users who have the permission to subscribe.)
- *Advanced Actions*: This provides you four important actions:
  - *Permissions*
  - *Copy*
  - *Move*
  - *Delete*

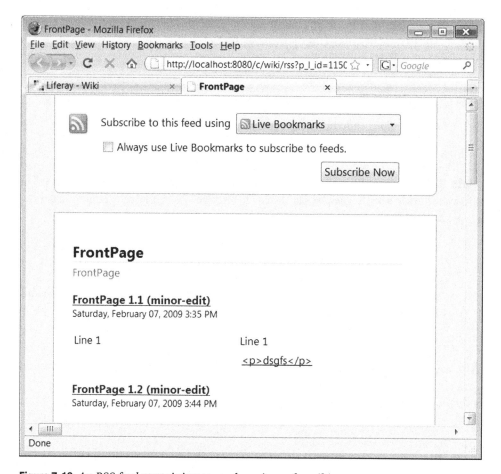

Figure 7-19. *An RSS feed containing several versions of a wiki page*

I'll discuss each of these options in the next section.

Advanced Actions

The *Advanced Actions* property lets you set user permissions on a page, copy a page under a new name, move a page to another location, or simply delete a page. Let's look at each action in detail.

Permissions

You saw in earlier chapters how to set permissions for users with different roles; the process for setting permissions on a wiki page is similar. To set the permissions, follow the steps listed here:

1. Click the *Permissions* link under the *Advanced Actions* option. You will see the list of roles and permissions assigned to each role.

2. Look up the *Available* roles under *Regular Roles* and *Community Roles* and select the desired role for which you want to set permissions.

3. Click the *Update Permissions* button to look up the available permissions for assignment:

   a. *Add Discussion*

   b. *Delete*

   c. *Permissions*

   d. *Subscribe*

   e. *Update*

   f. *View*

The permissions in the preceding list have the same meanings as the ones associated with the other Liferay applications that you studied in earlier chapters. The *Add Discussion* permission allows you to post replies. The *Delete* permission lets you delete an entry. The *Permissions* option enables the user to assign rights to other users. The *Subscribe* option enables the user to subscribe to a feed. The *Update* option allows the user to modify the entry. The *View* option, which by default is a required feature, allows the user to view the entry.

Copy

Selecting this option under *Advanced Actions* in the *General* properties tab allows you to copy the page under the new name. When you click the *Copy* link, a new page opens in the page editor with no name assigned to it. All the contents of the selected page are copied into the new page, except for the page name. You just need to enter the desired name for the page and click the *Save* button. The new page now appears in the list of pages available on the wiki. These newly added pages are not linked to any other page, so they're essentially "orphan" pages at this point.

Move

Selecting the *Move* action facilitates the following:

- Renaming the page
- Changing the page's parent

When you select the *Move* action, the page opens with tabs called *Rename* and *Change Parent* (see Figure 7-20).

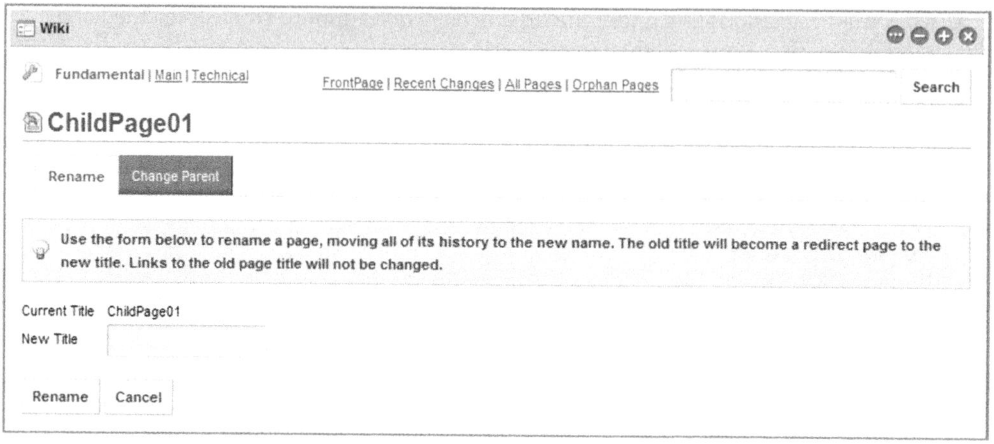

Figure 7-20. *Assigning a new name to a page*

To rename the page, simply enter the new name in the *New Title* edit box and click the *Rename* button. The page will now be saved under its new name.

Tip This is also the way you can change the default *FrontPage* name that's assigned to a page when you create a new node.

To move the page under a different parent, follow the steps listed here:

1. Select the *Change Parent* tab to pull up the screen shown in Figure 7-21.

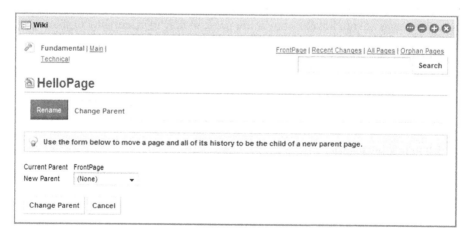

Figure 7-21. *Changing the parent association for the current page*

2. Select the desired parent from the *New Parent* drop-down list.

3. Click the *Change Parent* button. This moves the current page under the new parent.

Delete

Clicking the *Delete* option under *Advanced Actions* deletes the current page after the application asks for your confirmation to do so.

Now that you've seen the various general properties and actions, take a look at the next option tab: *History*.

History

The *History* page-properties option displays the history of all your edits to the current page. Each time you edit a page and save it, the *Wiki* application assigns a new version number to the page. Both the original and revised pages are saved under their respective version numbers. Rather than saving the full page, the *Wiki* application saves only the changes made to the page. You can always request to see the changes made between each version (see the "Comparing Versions" section following the "Viewing" section). First, let's look at how to display the different versions of a selected page.

Viewing

When you select the *History* tab, you see the screen shown in Figure 7-22.

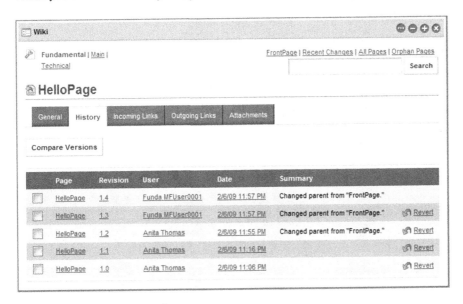

Figure 7-22. *A page-revision history*

As you can see in Figure 7-22, the screen displays a list of all different versions of the page. For each entry, you'll see the following information:

- *Page*: This displays the page name.
- *Revision*: This shows the revision number.

- *User*: This shows the person who revised the page.

- *Date*: This shows the date and time of revision.

- *Summary*: This shows the summary of changes made with respect to the previous version.

Also note the *Revert* button to the right of each entry. It allows you to revert your wiki page back to the selected version.

■ **Note** A page edit might involve changing the page name itself. This, however, would not be reflected in the revision history. When you look up the revision history under the new page name, you would see the entire history of the earlier edits to the page.

Comparing Versions

As you saw in the preceding "Viewing" section, the *Summary* column summarizes the changes you have made to a page. You can get more information about the changes by asking for a detailed comparison between versions. To do so, perform the following steps:

1. Select the two versions that you want to compare by marking the corresponding check boxes on the *History* page.

2. Click the *Compare Versions* button to display the detailed list of changes in the window. A typical comparison is shown in Figure 7-23.

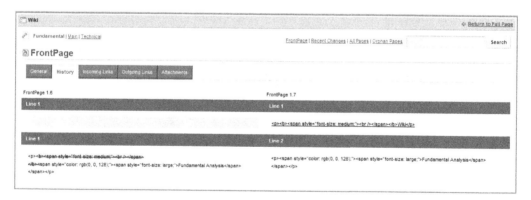

Figure 7-23. *Comparing revisions to a page*

Creating Page Links

Now you will examine the links to and from a wiki page by using the *Incoming Links* and *Outgoing Links* tabs. A page can have both incoming and outgoing links. But before you look at the display of these links, you need to create a few first. Follow these steps to add a few pages and to create interconnecting links:

1. Open the *FrontPage* page for editing.

2. You must use *Creole* syntax for editing, so confirm that you are in *Creole* mode.

3. Add a link by typing [[**Fundamental Analysis Research**]] in the editor's body-text window. This would create a link to the page called *Fundamental Analysis Research* after you save your edits—if that page were to exist. But you do not have a page with this name, so the application creates the link and shows it in red. Clicking this link opens the new document in which you can add your contents. Save your edits.

4. Now, you will add one more link from this page (*Fundamental Analysis Research*) to another new page.

5. Follow the procedure in step 3 to add a new page called *Fundamental Analysis Report* with an interconnecting link between the two pages.

You have now set up the required pages and the interconnected links. You will examine the display of these links in the next section.

Incoming Links

Open the *Fundamental Analysis Research* page. Click the *Properties* icon and select the *Incoming Links* tab. You will see a screen similar to the one shown in Figure 7-24.

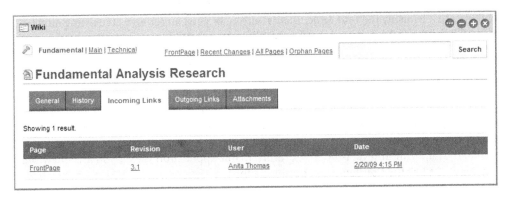

Figure 7-24. *Display of incoming links to a page*

Outgoing Links

The *Outgoing Links* option is similar to the *Incoming Links* option, except that it shows the outgoing links instead. To view the outgoing links, open the *FrontPage* page. Click the *Properties* icon and select the *Outgoing Links* tab. You will see an outgoing link to the *Fundamental Analysis Research* page.

Attachments

When you click the *Attachments* properties tab, you will see a screen similar to the one shown in Figure 7-25.

Figure 7-25. *Displaying attachments on a page*

The screen in Figure 7-25 shows all current attachments on the page. You can add new attachments to it by using the *Add Attachments* button, or you can remove an existing attachment by clicking the *Delete* button associated with the unwanted file.

Setting Application Properties

So now you've seen how to set up wikis, add pages, add child pages, customize pages, and so on. Next, you'll learn what properties are available at the application level, how they're important, and how to set them.

To set the application-level properties, return to full-application view if you are still within the application. Click the *Configuration* button on the top-right corner of the screen. You will see the following tabbed options:

- *Setup*
- *Permissions*
- *Export/Import*
- *Sharing*

I'll explain each of these configuration options in detail.

Setup

When you select the configuration option in the application menu, the first tab that you see is the *Setup* tab (see Figure 7-26).

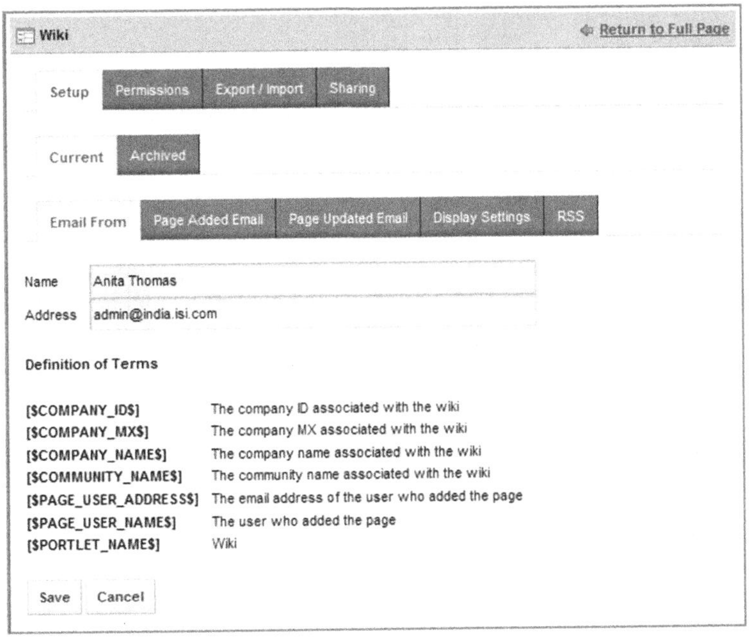

Figure 7-26. *The page-setup options*

Here, you will see the five tabbed options for setup:

- *Email From*
- *Page Added Email*
- *Page Updated Email*
- *Display Settings*
- *RSS*

Email From

The *Email From* option allows you to set the sender information for messages that the application sends to an outsider. Usually, the application will send automatic mail notifications to its e-mail subscribers whenever a new page is added or updated on the wiki. As Figure 7-26 shows, this screen accepts the *Name* and *Address* of the sender. After entering this information, you can save your changes by clicking the *Save* button. The mail notifications will now carry this sender information in each message.

Page Added Email

The *Page Added Email* option asks you to enter the subject, body, and signature for the message format. Whenever a new page is added to the wiki, the application will generate a mail message using the format defined on this page.

Note Defining e-mail formats for notifications was discussed in Chapter 3.

Page Updated Email

The *Page Updated Email* option allows you to set the subject, body, and signature information as you did in the *Page Added Email* case. The application will use the defined format for composing notification messages that alert users to page updates.

Display Settings

The *Display Settings* option shows a screen like the one in Figure 7-27.

Figure 7-27. *The wiki display settings*

You can adjust the following settings on this screen:

- *Enable Comments*: By marking this check box, you allow the users to post their comments on wiki pages. Of course, a user must have the *Add Discussion* permission to do this.

- *Enable Comment Ratings*: Selecting this option allows the users to rate the comments entered by other users.

- *Visible Wikis*: The two list boxes under this heading display which wikis are visible and which are hidden from view. You can move the entries from one list box to another with the help of the right and left arrows.

RSS

Using the *RSS* option, you can customize the RSS output. You can set these two parameters for the RSS output:

- *Maximum Items to Display*: From the drop-down list, you can select a discrete value ranging from 1 to 100.

- *Display Style*: You can choose whether to display a page's full content, its abstract, or its title only.

Permissions

The *Permissions* tab lets you set the user permissions at the application level. As with Liferay's other applications, you can set the permissions for both *Regular* and *Community* roles. For each type of role, you can view the currently assigned and available permissions. The following three permissions are available at the application level for all types of roles:

- *Add Node*
- *Configuration*
- *View*

The *Add Node* permission, as the name suggests, allows the user to add a new node to the wiki. The *Configuration* permission assigns the user rights to configure the *Wiki* application itself. The *View* permission allows the user to view the wiki pages; this is the bare-minimum permission required by any user to use the application effectively.

Export/Import

Whereas some of the tabbed options in the *Wiki* application also appear elsewhere in Liferay, you haven't yet encountered the *Export/Import* tab because it is either unavailable or insignificant in the other applications you've seen so far. When you select this option, you will see two secondary tabs:

- *Export*: Allows you to export your configuration settings and data
- *Import*: Allows you to import previously saved configuration settings and data

The *Export* settings screen is shown in Figure 7-28.

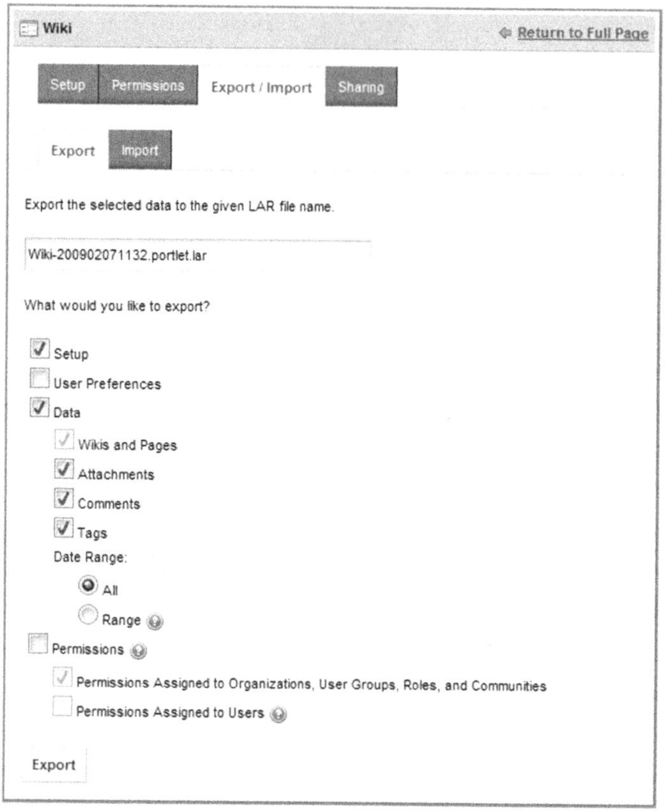

Figure 7-28. *Exporting wiki data and configuration settings*

As you can see in Figure 7-28, the *Export* option allows you to save not only the configuration, but also the data. While exporting the data, you can select the date range for the selection of data. You can also export the permissions assigned to users.

The *Import* tab displays a list of items that you can import into the wiki (see Figure 7-29).

After you have set the desired import parameters, you will need to locate and select the file for import using the *Browse* button. After you are satisfied with the settings, click the *Import* button to import data and settings from the selected archive file into the wiki.

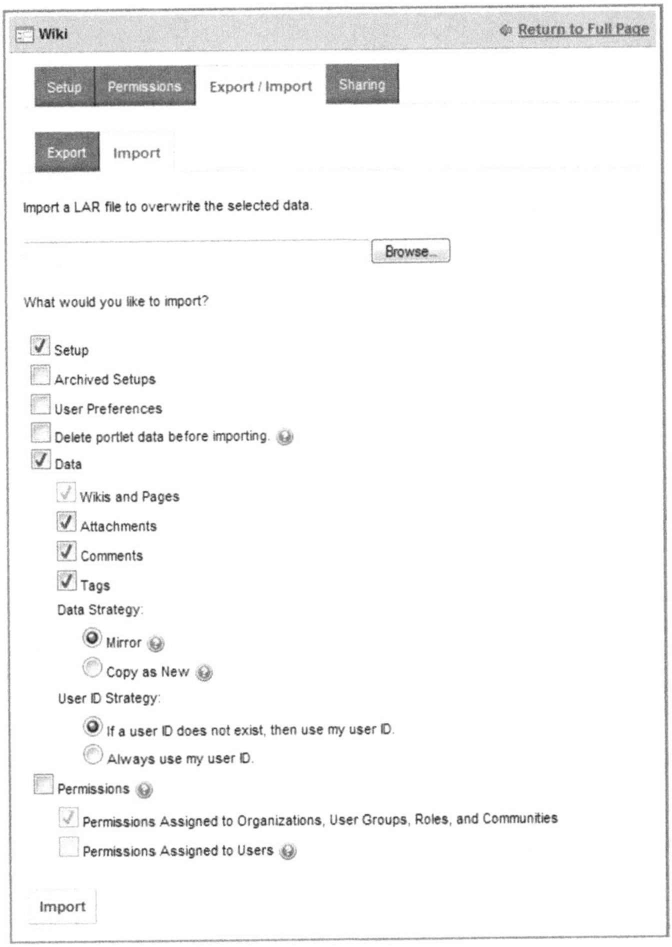

Figure 7-29. *Importing data and configuration settings to a new wiki*

Note The *Export/Import* option is a required feature for a wiki application. Wikis are created over long periods of time, so they often host valuable information that will need to be archived and transferred to another wiki application in the future. Compare this with the community-forum and blog applications that you studied in previous chapters: although an archive of data for such applications is desirable, you never *need* to make this data available in other applications.

Sharing

The *Sharing* option allows you to share the current application with any other web site or on Facebook.

Other Features

The *Wiki* application offers some other useful functionality for the effective use of wikis. Specifically, it lets you view a list of the following:

- *Recent Changes*
- *All Pages*
- *Orphan Pages*

You will notice the presence of these three links (beside the link to FrontPage) at the top-right corner of the application screen (see Figure 7-30).

Figure 7-30. *Viewing lists of pages*

Recent Changes

When you click the *Recent Changes* link, you will see all the pages that have undergone recent changes. A typical list of such pages appears in Figure 7-31. (Note that the screen resembles the page-revision history shown in Figure 7-22.)

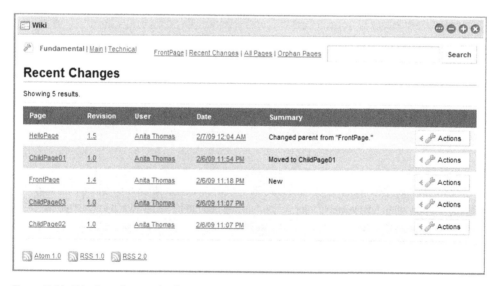

Figure 7-31. *Display of recently changed pages*

For each entry in the list, the following details are listed:

- *Page*: Page name; it might change between revisions if a user has edited the name
- *Revision*: Revision number

- *User*: User who made the change
- *Date*: Date and time on which the changes were made
- *Summary*: Summary of changes made with respect to the previous version

Also note the *Actions* button that appears with each item listed. If you click it, you will see a list of typical operations:

- *Edit*: Allows you to edit the current page
- *Permissions*: Allows you to set permissions on the current page
- *Copy*: Allows you to copy the page and rename it
- *Move*: Allows you to move the page to a new location under a new parent
- *Subscribe*: Allows you to subscribe to the page so that you'll be alerted to page changes via e-mail or RSS (this option changes to *Unsubscribe* when you are subscribed)
- *Delete*: Allows you to delete the currently selected page after you confirm

All Pages

Selecting the *All Pages* option displays a list of all pages in the wiki. The list displays similar information to what's shown in the *Recent Changes* list. On each entry, you can perform any or all of the actions described in the previous section. Additionally, you can add a new wiki page by clicking the *Add Page* button.

Orphan Pages

The *Orphan Pages* option displays the list of orphan pages, which are pages with no parent connections. Because a wiki is community-run, it's likely that users will move pages from one location to another. Doing this can result in pages that are no longer associated with a parent page. So even though these pages exist in the system, users cannot navigate to them. Thus, in a way, orphan pages are useless to us. You must either move them back to their original locations or simply remove them from the system. You will be able to do so using the *Actions* button against each orphan page.

Summary

In this chapter, you studied yet another Liferay application called *Wiki*. The *Wiki* application, which comes with the Liferay installation, enables you to set up wikis on your Liferay portals. A wiki is a collaborative means of sharing information. Users can contribute to the wiki by adding pages and external documents containing valuable information related to their areas of expertise.

Users can also post replies to entries made by others, rate those entries and replies, move pages around according to their significance, and remove pages permanently. The user-managed nature of a wiki can result in smaller issues such as orphan pages and larger issues such as site misuse. But generally, the benefits offered by a wiki's vast amount of information outweighs these risks. Along with discussion forums and blogs, wikis can provide your portal with much-needed collaboration features.

CHAPTER 8

■ ■ ■

Implementing a Shared Calendar

Most communities host organized events such as meetings, gatherings, or parties. People usually find some occasion or pretext to get together. Members of online communities can benefit from such meetings because they can use the opportunities to share their ideas with others. To schedule such meetings and events for an online community, you need a sharable calendar where an event organizer can schedule a meeting and post its details. Members who subscribe to the shared calendar receive notification about the event, after which they can visit the calendar to learn the event details. In this chapter, you will learn how to set up and use a shared calendar on your Liferay portal. In particular, you will learn how to

- Add the *Calendar* application to your portal page
- Define events
- Set event characteristics and periodicity
- View events in different formats
- Set permissions on events
- Export and import event data and configurations
- Configure the *Calendar* application

Shared calendars are very popular these days—you will find them on portals such as Google, MSN, and Yahoo!. As you can imagine, the use of shared calendars greatly enhances the usability of portals with large communities. Our ISI portal, where technical and fundamental specialists rub shoulders with general investors, would benefit from a shared-calendar application. The application would help members organize events of general interest to the community such as regional meetings, seminars, tech events, and the like. The Liferay installation comes with an application called *Calendar* that allows you to implement shared-calendar functionality on your portal.

Installing the Calendar Application

To install the *Calendar* application on your portal, follow these steps:

1. Log in to the portal using your administrator account.

2. Create a new public page called *Shared Calendar* under either the *Fundamental* or *Technical* community. Or you could create a general page that's accessible to both groups.

3. Select the *Add Application* menu item.

4. Open the *Collaboration* category and click the *Add* link associated with the *Calendar* application (see Figure 8-1).

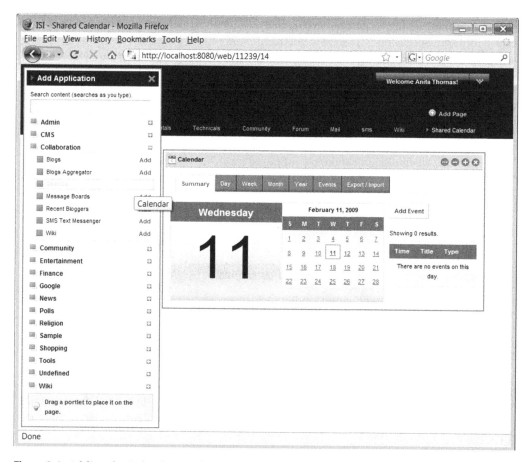

Figure 8-1. *Adding the Calendar application*

After you add the application to the page, you can add events to it immediately. You will now learn to add an event to the shared calendar.

Setting Up Events

You'll probably be dealing with events of different types. For example, suppose you want to call upon all regional members to discuss a new investment strategy or to discuss the current market outlook. You might want to announce and demonstrate a new analysis tool that you have developed. You might want to hold a training session for the newbies or an advanced seminar for the seasoned technical analysts. The reasons for holding such meetings could be numerous, but we classify them all as "events" in the shared calendar. You can now easily announce and organize such events by defining them in the *Calendar* application.

Adding an Event

To set up an event, follow these steps:

1. View the *Calendar* application, which initially shows the calendar for the current system date (see Figure 8-2).

Figure 8-2. *Initial view of the Calendar application*

2. Select the date on which you want to set the event.

Tip Notice that the default *Summary* view of the *Calendar* application allows you to select a date only in the current month. There are no navigation buttons to select a future date. To select a future date, you will either have to change to another view such as *Day*, *Week*, *Month*, or *Year* (which I'll discuss in the "Viewing Events" section), or do the date selection in the event-addition screen that's accessible through the *Add Event* button.

---

3. Click the *Add Event* button. You will see the screen shown in Figure 8-3.

4. Select the date and time for the event.

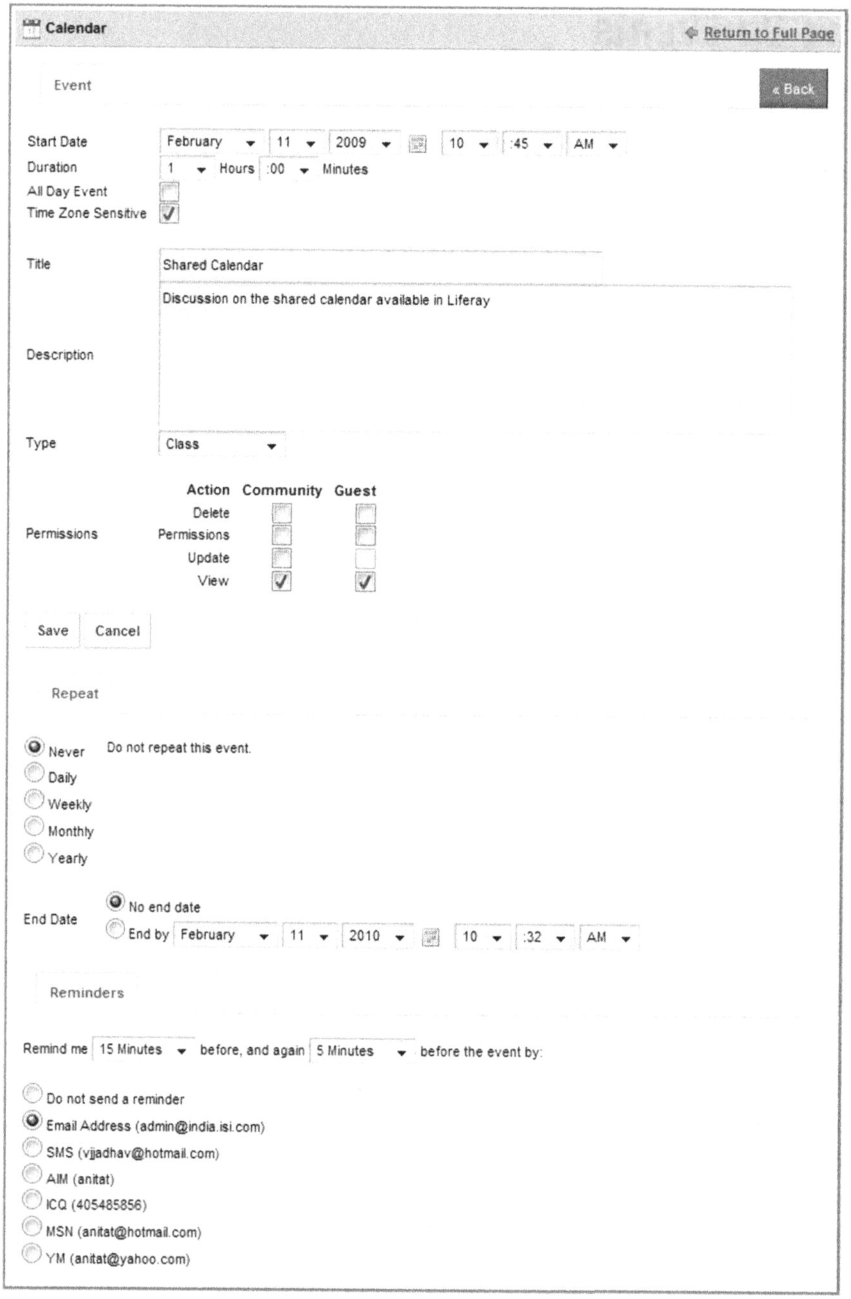

Figure 8-3. *Defining a new event*

■**Note** As I mentioned earlier, you can select any future or past date here by clicking the small calendar icon that appears between the drop-down boxes for date and time selection.

---

5. Select the event duration by selecting hours and minutes from the two displayed drop-down boxes. If it is an all-day event, check the corresponding check box.

6. If your event is conducted at a location that abides by Daylight Saving Time, check the *Time Zone Sensitive* check box.

7. Enter the event title in the *Title* edit box.

8. Enter the event description in the *Description* edit box.

9. Select the type of event from the *Type* drop-down list.

Note The *Calendar* application provides several predefined categories for event types, such as Anniversary, Birthday, Appointment, Sports, Training, TV Show, Vacation, and so on. The list is exhaustive and covers almost every type of event that you could ever imagine. Having such a large number of choices, the community users can effectively use the *Calendar* application for everything from personal needs to corporate requirements.

---

10. Next, you will set the permissions on this event. When you click the *Permissions* link, you will see the menu for setting permissions for *Community* users and *Guest* users (see Figure 8-4). You will be able to set *Delete*, *Update*, and *View* permissions for each type of user. You can also enable the user to assign or deny permissions to others by using the *Permissions* check boxes.

Figure 8-4. *Possible permissions assignments*

11. After you have entered the desired information, click the *Save* button.

You have now succeeded in adding the event to the calendar. The application will return you to the event-view screen.

Adding Multiple Events

Because many users share the calendar, it's likely that you'll have multiple events scheduled on the same day. To add more events, follow the procedure you used to add the first event:

1. Click the *Add Event* button in the *Summary* view.

2. Fill in the event details on the displayed form.

3. Click the *Save* button.

You will now return to the *Summary* screen that shows the list of events for the selected day. You will find the newly listed event displayed with the previously defined events (see Figure 8-5).

Figure 8-5. *View of multiple events scheduled on the same day*

Repeating an Event

Some events that you define in a calendar have a repetitive nature. For example, an introductory one-day course on technical analysis might be offered on the first Monday of every month. Rather than defining 12 individual events for this training course, you can define the event only once. Let's look at the steps to do this:

1. Select the start date of the event and enter all of the event's required details.

2. Under the *Save* button on the event-entry screen, locate the *Repeat* tab (see Figure 8-6).

Figure 8-6. *Defining the periodicity for an event*

3. Choose whether to repeat the event on a *Daily*, *Weekly*, *Monthly*, or *Yearly* basis. If you select the *Weekly* option, for example, the event would be shown every week on the same day of the week in the shared calendar.

   Alternatively, you can choose not to repeat the event. In this case, the event would be offered only once on its start date.

4. When you repeat an event, you also need to set up the end date beyond which the event will not be offered. You specify the end date by selecting the desired date in the *End Date* portion of the screen (see Figure 8-7).

Figure 8-7. *Defining an event-ending date*

5. If you don't want to specify an end date, mark the *No end date* radio button. This means that the event will recur indefinitely.

Establishing Reminders

Typically, an event is announced in the shared calendar a few months before its scheduled start date. To prevent users from signing up for an event and forgetting about it later, you can send reminders to the registered users. You can set up reminders on an event in the *Reminders* tab at the bottom of the event-entry screen (see Figure 8-8).

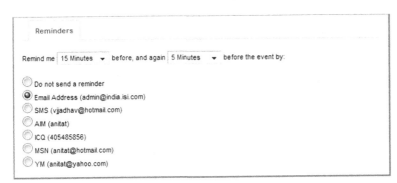

Figure 8-8. *Creating event reminders*

You can implement up to two reminders for each event:

1. Set up the first reminder by selecting the time frame in the *Remind me* drop-down list. You can choose a discrete time-frame value ranging from five minutes to two weeks.

2. Set up the second reminder in the next drop-down list.

3. Select the communication mode for the reminder. You get the following choices for communication:

   a. *By e-mail*: An e-mail notification will be sent to the registered user. You will be able to configure the reminder e-mail, as I'll discuss in the "Setup" section under "Configuring the Application."

   b. *SMS*: Note that SMS here does not send a traditional SMS message to a mobile phone; rather, it sends a message to the recipient's e-mail ID.

   c. *AIM*: The user is notified on AOL Instant Messenger (AIM).

   d. *ICQ*: The user is notified on her ICQ messaging service.

   e. *MSN*: The user is notified on her Windows Live Messenger account.

   f. *YM*: The user is informed on her Yahoo! Messenger service.

4. You also have a choice of not sending a reminder at all. Do this by selecting the *Do not send a reminder* radio button.

Now that you've learned to define events and repeat them over a period of time, you'll see how to view the available events in the shared calendar.

Viewing Events

The *Calendar* application allows you to view the available events in six different modes:

- Summary
- Daily
- Weekly
- Monthly
- Yearly
- All

The Summary View

You saw the *Summary* view while defining your first event (see Figure 8-9).

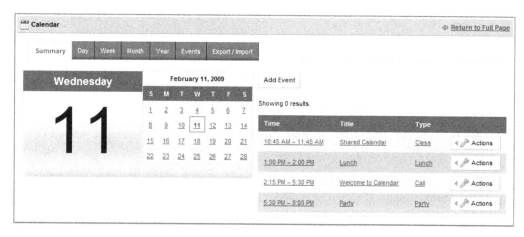

Figure 8-9. *Summary view of today's events*

The *Summary* view displays the following:

- The event date, which is the selected date in the calendar

- The calendar for the month in which the event is taking place

- A list of events scheduled on the selected day

The Daily View

The daily view, accessible through the *Day* tab, displays all the events scheduled on a selected date (see Figure 8-10).

Figure 8-10. *A day view of scheduled events*

The selected date appears at the top of the screen with two arrow buttons on either side. Clicking these buttons allows you to navigate to the next and previous days. When you navigate to a new date, the list of scheduled events at the bottom of the screen updates accordingly.

By default, events of all types appear in the list. You can filter the list by event type by selecting the appropriate type in the *All Events* drop-down box.

The daily view also allows you to add a new event for the currently selected day. You do this by clicking the *Add Event* button. You can also perform a few actions on each event displayed in the list; I'll discuss them in the section "Performing Actions on Events."

The Weekly View

The weekly view, accessible through the *Week* tab, displays the calendar for the selected week. For each day of the week, the table lists all the events for that day (see Figure 8-11).

Figure 8-11. *Weekly view of scheduled events*

As with the daily view, you can navigate to the next and previous week by clicking the two arrow buttons on either side of the current week (see Figure 8-12).

Figure 8-12. *Week navigation buttons*

You can also filter the list by event type using the same *All Events* drop-down list that you used in the daily view.

If you wish to add a new event on a particular day in the displayed week, you can do so by clicking the + icon next to the date in the first column of the table. This is shown highlighted in Figure 8-13.

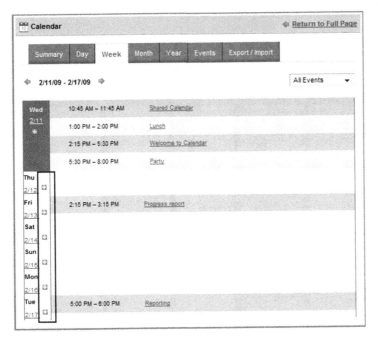

Figure 8-13. *The + icons for event addition*

The Monthly View

In the monthly view, accessible through the *Month* tab, you can see all the scheduled events in a selected month (see Figure 8-14).

As in the other views we've discussed, you can navigate to a different month using the two arrow buttons on either side of the current month. You can also filter the output by event type and add a new event by clicking the + icon associated with the desired date.

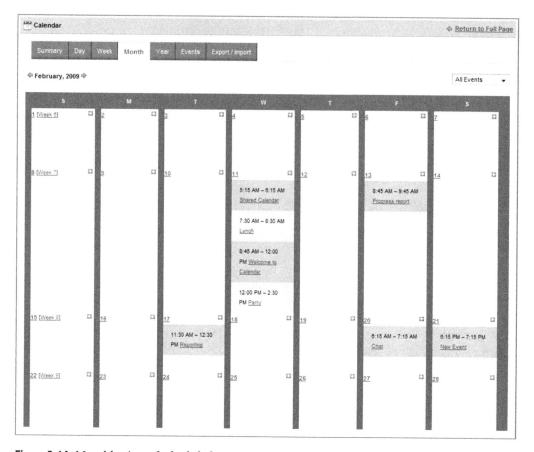

Figure 8-14. *Monthly view of scheduled events*

The Yearly View

The yearly view, accessible through the *Year* tab, displays the entire year's calendar (see Figure 8-15).

As you might have noticed, no events are displayed onscreen in the yearly view. So how do you know what events are taking place throughout the year? In this view, the current date is highlighted with a square around it and each date is underscored. The dates on which the events are scheduled carry a dot underneath this underscore (except for the current date). The display for the month of February is shown in Figure 8-16.

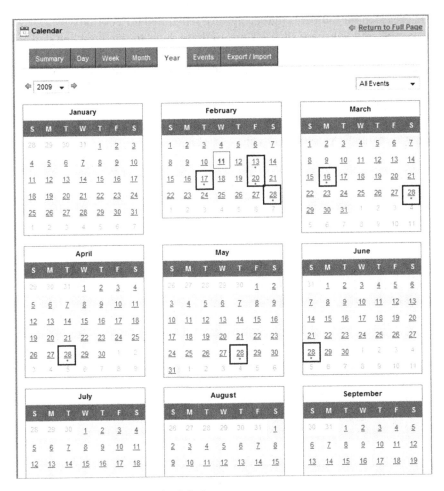

Figure 8-15. *Yearly view of scheduled events*

Figure 8-16. *Dates marked with scheduled events*

In Figure 8-16, the calendar indicates that events are scheduled for February 13, February 17, February 20, and February 28. Click any of these dates to see the scheduled events for that date.

As in the other calendar views, you can navigate to any year by using the two navigation arrows, and you can filter the display by event type.

Tip The yearly display is very useful for setting up your full-year planner.

The All View

Selecting the *Events* tab displays all the events defined in the shared calendar (see Figure 8-17).

Figure 8-17. *Listing all scheduled events*

In this mode, the application displays the date, time, title, and type for each registered event. The *Actions* button to the right of each entry allows you to perform several prelisted actions on it, as I'll discuss in the section "Performing Actions on Events."

Displaying Event Details

You've now seen several different ways to view the events defined in the shared calendar. Most of these views either display the title of the event or give you an indication that some event is scheduled on a particular day. When you click the link provided, you can retrieve the full details of the concerned event. For example, Figure 8-18 shows all the details of a typical event.

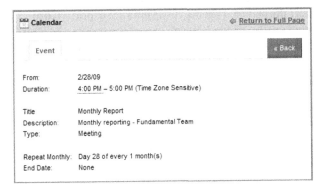

Figure 8-18. *A detailed view of an event*

Here you will see the date and time of the event, its duration, its title, its description, and its type. This view also displays the end date if the event continues over multiple days.

Performing Actions on Events

When you list the events onscreen, you can perform certain actions on each one:

- *Edit*
- *Export*
- *Permissions*
- *Delete*

The action-selection menu appears when you click the *Actions* button (see Figure 8-19).

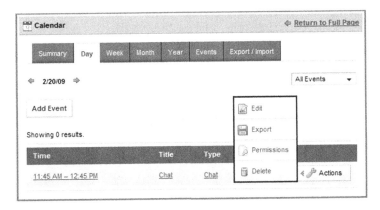

Figure 8-19. *The predefined actions on an event*

The *Edit* action opens the event in the event editor, which you used while creating a new event. You can use this editor to make any desired changes to the event. When you save the edits, the changes will be immediately reflected in the subsequent display of the event.

The *Export* option allows you to export the selected event. The events are exported to a file of type *iCalendar*, which carries a file extension of .ics. You can export the events and later import them into some other instance of the calendar. You can also import the events into apps that can read .ics files, such as the Mac's iCal program. I'll discuss how to import and export events in the next section.

The *Permissions* action opens the screen that lets you set up user permissions. You're quite familiar with this option by now, as you have studied it in the context of Liferay's other applications. You can set permissions for users with *Regular* and *Community* roles. The typical permissions available for the *Guest* role are *View*, *Delete*, and *Permissions*. The typical permissions available for the *Community* role include *View*, *Delete*, *Permissions*, and *Update*.

The *Delete* action allows you to delete the currently selected event—after you confirm your intention to do so, of course.

Exporting and Importing Events

Over time, your users might create a large number of events, and you might want to import these events into another instance of the calendar. To accomplish this, you first need to export the events to a file. The *Calendar* application allows you to export and import event data easily. Start by selecting the *Export/Import* tab on the main application screen (see Figure 8-20).

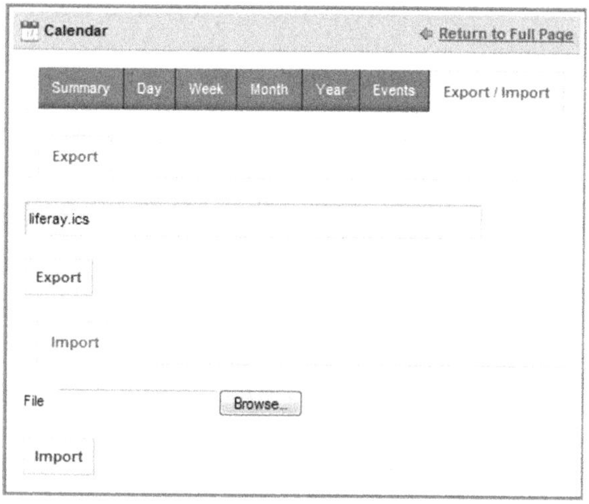

Figure 8-20. *Exporting and importing event data*

You'll notice that the default file name appearing in the edit box at the top of the screen is liferay.ics. If you stick with this file name and click the *Export* button, Liferay exports the data into a file called liferay*xxxxx*.ics, where *xxxxx* is a counter. The application maintains this counter internally. It also includes this counter in file names that you create yourself. For example, if you rename the export file to MyEvents.ics in the edit box, Liferay saves the file as MyEvents*xxxxx*.ics, where *xxxxx* is the counter. In any case, the application exports all the calendar data and stores it in a new file.

You can later import all the calendar data by browsing to the file name in the *Import* portion of the screen and clicking the *Import* button.

Tip You can configure the fields for export or import in the application's *Configuration* screen.

Now that you've looked at the various options in setting up a shared calendar, you'll see how to configure the application itself.

Configuring the Application

To configure the *Calendar* application, click the *Configuration* icon in the main application window. You'll see the typical tabbed options listed here:

- *Setup*
- *Permissions*
- *Export/Import*
- *Sharing*

Setup

The *Setup* tabbed option allows you to configure the formats for your mail-notification messages and control the settings of the output display. You will be able to adjust the following settings in this tabbed option:

- *Email From*: In this option, you can set the sender information for the mail notifications. You will need to enter the sender's name and e-mail ID on this screen (see Figure 8-21).

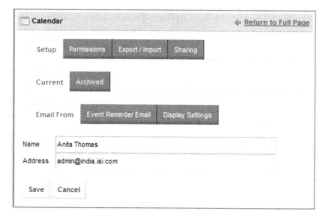

Figure 8-21. *Defining the sender ID for e-mail notifications*

- *Event Reminder Email*: You can configure the message format for the reminder e-mail in this option. On this screen, you can set the subject and the body of the e-mail message. The format uses several predefined tags, which are listed below the *Body* field (see Figure 8-22).

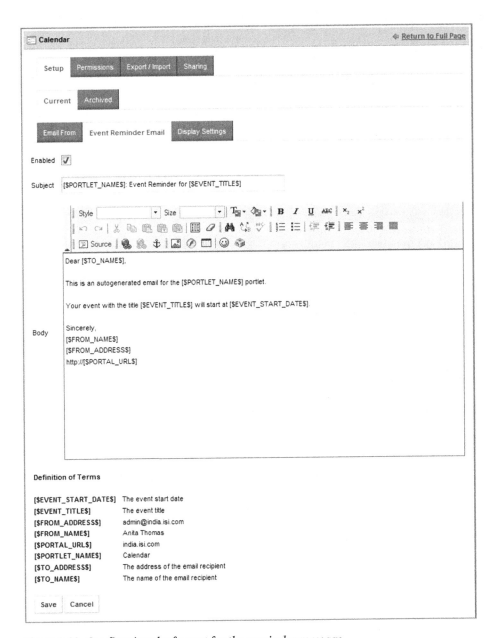

Figure 8-22. *Configuring the format for the reminder message*

- *Display Settings*: You can control the display output using the various settings provided on this screen (see Figure 8-23).

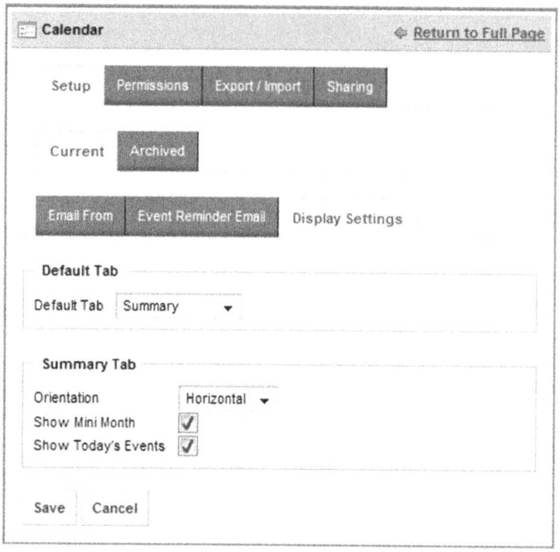

Figure 8-23. *Configuring display settings*

You must have noticed so far that the *Calendar* application screen opens with the *Summary* tab selected by default. You can change this default by selecting the appropriate tab name from the drop-down list of *Default Tab* settings in the *Display Settings* screen.

To customize the look of the *Summary* page itself, you can adjust three settings in the *Summary Tab* area of the *Display Settings* screen:

- *Orientation*: This can be either *Horizontal* or *Vertical*. The default is *Horizontal*, whereby the calendar and event list appear side by side on the *Summary* screen (see Figures 8-5 and 8-9). Selecting the *Vertical* orientation arranges the calendar and event list vertically, with one on top of the other (see Figure 8-24).

- *Show Mini Month*: Enabling this option results in the display of the monthly calendar on the *Summary* screen.

- *Show Today's Events*: Enabling this option results in the display of today's events. If this is disabled, no events are displayed on the *Summary* screen.

Figure 8-24. *Vertical orientation of the Summary screen*

Permissions

The *Permissions* option allows you to set up application-level permissions for its users. As usual, you can set permissions for *Regular* and *Community* roles. Under *Regular* roles, you can grant or deny the following three permissions:

- *View*: Granting this permission enables the user to view the shared-calendar portlet.

- *Configuration*: Granting this permission allows the user to adjust the configuration settings on the shared-calendar portlet.

- *Export All Events*: Granting this permission allows the user to export all the shared-calendar data to a file. You can later import this file back into the shared calendar, into another instance of the shared calendar, or into any other application that supports the iCalendar data format.

Under *Community* roles, you can grant or deny the three preceding permissions, plus the *Add Event* permission. The *Add Event* permission allows the user to define a new event and add it to the calendar.

Export/Import

Selecting the *Export/Import* tabbed option on the *Configuration* screen lets you configure the settings that come into play when you export event data using the *Export/Import* tab of the *main* application screen. On this screen, you can decide what fields to export.

Selecting Fields for Export

The fields that you can export to a file are as follows:

- *Setup*: The configuration settings of your shared calendar
- *User Preferences*: The user-preference settings in your calendar
- *Data*: Either all the data, or data in a specific date range
- *Permissions*: The permissions, classified into two categories:
  - *Permissions Assigned to Organizations, User Groups, Roles, and Communities*: This option is the default. All these permissions would be saved to the exported file along with the event data.
  - *Permissions Assigned to Users*: By marking this check box, you can save user-permission data to the exported file as well.

After you have selected the desired fields for export, set a desired name for the file under which you wish to save the data. You can use the default file name, which includes the current date for easy identification (see Figure 8-25).

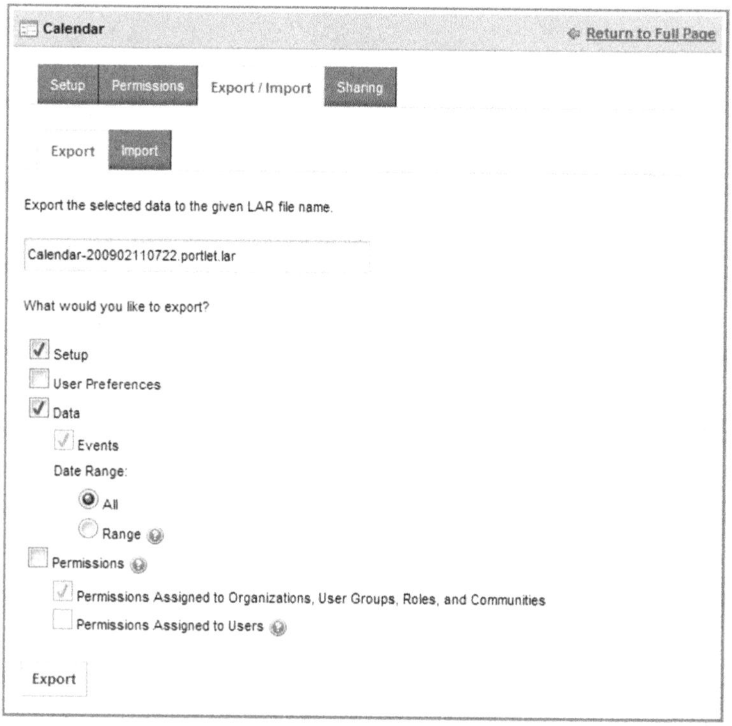

Figure 8-25. *Selecting fields to export*

Selecting Fields for Import

The data that you exported to a physical file in the previous section can be imported into the same instance or a new instance of the shared calendar. You can accomplish this using the *Import* tabbed option. To import the data, you first need to enter the name of the data file in the file-name field. Then you need to select the fields for import. These are as follows:

- *Setup*: This field contains configuration settings of the previous calendar stored in the backup data file.

- *Archived Setups*: Calendar data that is exported to a file consists of the current settings plus all previous settings that are archived every time you save the data. Selecting this option allows you to import all such archived setups along with the current settings.

- *User Preferences*: This field contains the user-preference settings of the previous calendar.

- *Delete portlet data before importing*: Selecting this option starts the calendar with a clean slate; that is, all the existing data would be deleted from the calendar and the new data from the archived file would replace it.

Caution The data in the current instance might be referenced by other applications. Deleting all the data and cleaning up the application instance might give rise to broken links in other applications when they try to look up this data.

- *Data*: Here, by default all the event data is imported. You have to decide on two types of strategies while importing data; I'll discuss these shortly.

- *Permissions*: By default, all permissions related to organizations, user groups, roles, and communities would be imported. You can optionally select to import the permissions assigned to users.

Tip The amount of user-permission data might be very large, so you should export and import such data only after careful thought. Of course, if the data is important, you do not have a choice here—you must export it regardless of its size.

Now let's return to the two types of data-import strategies I just mentioned: the *data strategy* and the *user ID strategy*. With the data strategy, you have two options: you can either copy the data as new data, or mirror the data instead.

If you choose the *Copy as New* option, the data is imported as a new item. So the first time the data is imported, a new event entry will be created for every archived entry. The next time the data is imported from the same file, an additional entry would be created for the same event. So you'd have multiple copies of the same event when you import the file multiple times.

Now suppose you mirror the data instead. The first time you import the data, a new entry is added for each imported event and a link to the original event is created. The next time you import data from a file, the newly added entry is *updated* and no additional entries for the same event are created.

You also need to choose a *user ID strategy* for importing data. Because the user who originally created an event may or may not exist in the new instance of the portal, you need to choose one of these options:

- If a user ID does not exist in the new calendar instance, then use your ID in place of the missing ID.

- Regardless of whether the user ID exists in the new system, always use your ID while importing data.

After selecting the desired fields and strategies, click the *Import* button to import the data to your calendar.

Sharing

The *Sharing* option produces the code that you can embed in other web sites to make the application available elsewhere. It also allows you to share the application on Facebook.

Summary

This chapter covered yet another important application for community collaboration. The *Calendar* application that comes with the Liferay installation facilitates the creation of a shared calendar.

A shared calendar allows users to create and list events throughout the year. Any user with appropriate permissions can schedule an event in the shared calendar. The item can be a one-time event or a recurring event. You can specify the event's name, duration, description, and event type. The *Calendar* application provides several predefined classifications for this event type, and you can use these types to filter your event list.

You can view the events in several ways: daily, weekly, monthly, or yearly. Plus, you can get a quick summary of today's events, and even list all of the events in the entire calendar. You can set reminders on these events so registered users don't forget about them.

You can also export and import the event data. All of your calendar data can be exported to a physical file for backup purposes or for later import into another installation or another instance of the *Calendar* application. You have several choices in terms of what fields you want to export, and what strategies you want to use for data import. With all this functionality, it's easy to see why shared calendars are becoming so popular in the online world.

CHAPTER 9

■ ■ ■

Managing Content

In the last few chapters, you studied several means of providing community collaboration on your portal. In this chapter, you will learn one more important aspect of community sharing: managing documents and images. Our ISI portal caters to investment analysts who collect data from corporations, stock exchanges, and so on. They analyze the data, make charts, and offer recommendations, and then publish these findings and analyses in various formats such as PDFs, image files, Word documents, and spreadsheets. These analysts should be able to upload their files to our portal easily, and other users should be able to browse and search the files.

Over time, the portal will accumulate many such documents, so they must be well-organized. We thus need a good application for content management. Fortunately, Liferay provides several good applications to address this need, some of which we will examine in this chapter. In particular, you will learn to

- Understand document management
- Install the *Document Library* application
- Create a folder hierarchy for document storage
- Add documents to various folders
- Upload documents to a server
- Create shortcuts to documents and folders
- Set user permissions on documents and folders
- Search and locate documents
- List your documents and recently added documents
- Export and import the document database
- Use the *Document Library Display* and *Image Gallery* applications

Implementing Document Management

First, we will consider text-based documents in various formats, such as PDFs, Word documents, spreadsheets, and so on. For managing such documents, Liferay provides two important applications:

- *Document Library*
- *Document Library Display*

You will now study the use of these applications, starting with *Document Library*. The *Document Library* application allows you to organize and manage your documents. You use it to create a tree-structured hierarchy where the documents are published and stored. Thus, you can organize the document storage logically so that users can easily locate the files.

Adding the Application

To add the *Document Library* application on our ISI portal page, follow the steps listed here:

1. Log in as *Administrator* on the ISI portal.

2. Create a new page called *Document Library* under our predefined communities, or at any other location you'd like.

3. Select the *Add Application* menu.

4. Select and add the *Document Library* application from the *CMS* category (see Figure 9-1).

Now you're ready to create a folder structure for document storage. You'll create a hierarchy of folders for storing documents created by our analysts and categorize the documents into two types:

- Fundamental Analysis Documents
- Technical Analysis Documents

These classification names derive from the type of analysis that the documents contain. For each category of documents, you'll further classify the documents based on who the author is. For simplicity, call these authors Analyst1, Analyst2, and so on. So you'll create a folder for each analyst and store the analysts' documents in their respective folders. Begin by creating the folder hierarchy.

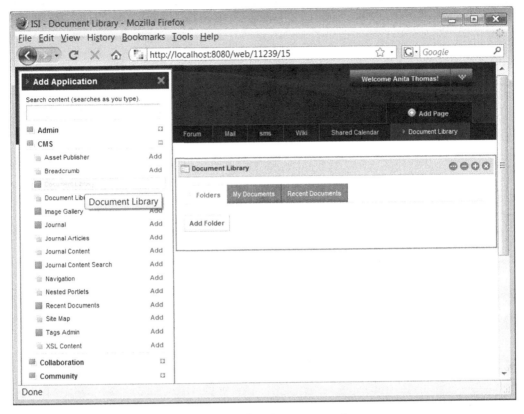

Figure 9-1. *Adding the Document Library application to a portal page*

Creating a Folder

To create a folder in the *Document Library* application, follow these steps:

1. Navigate to the *Document Library* page that you created in the previous section.

2. Click the *Add Folder* button in the *Document Library* application.

3. Take action on the following fields in the displayed dialog (see Figure 9-2):

   a. *Name*: Enter **Fundamental**.

   b. *Description*: Enter **This folder contains analysis reports created by prominent fundamental analysts**.

   c. *Permissions*: Leave these settings at their default values.

4. Click the *Save* button to save your changes. You will automatically return to the main application screen after your changes have been saved.

5. You will now add another folder called *Technical* to organize the technical analysis documents produced by the portal's leading technical analysts. Follow steps 2, 3, and 4 to create the *Technical* folder.

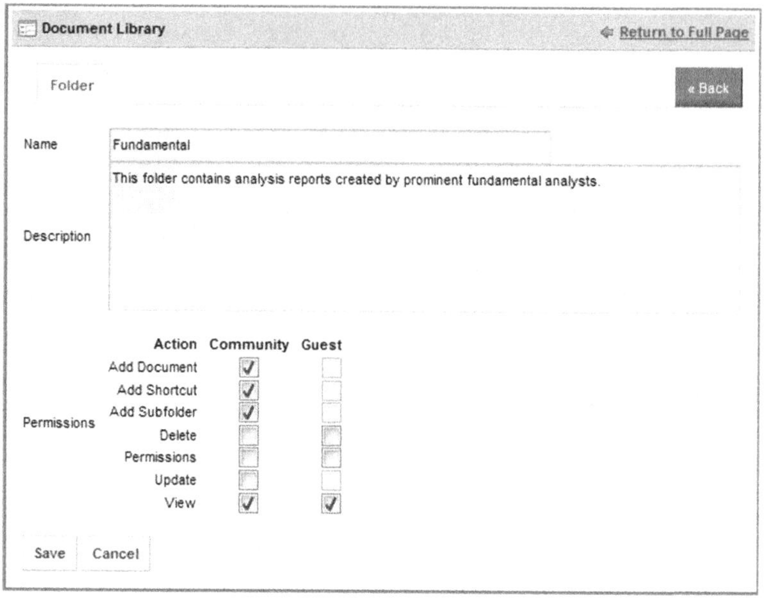

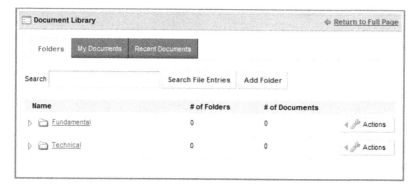

Figure 9-2. *Creating a new folder*

When you return to the main application screen, you will notice that the newly added *Fundamental* and *Technical* folders are listed on the main page (see Figure 9-3).

Figure 9-3. *The folders list*

You'll now add subfolders in the folder hierarchy.

Adding a Subfolder

First, you'll add subfolders under the *Fundamental* folder. Follow these steps to do so:

1. Click the *Fundamental* link in the folders list displayed on the main application screen.

2. Click the *Add Subfolder* button on the displayed screen.

3. Take action on the following fields in the displayed dialog:

   a. *Name*: Enter **Analyst1**.

   b. *Description*: Enter **The documents in this subfolder are provided by Analyst1**.

   c. *Permissions*: Leave these settings at their default values.

4. Click the *Save* button to save your changes.

5. Add two more subfolders under the *Fundamental* folder by following steps 2 through 4 again, but call these subfolders **Analyst2** and **Analyst3** and update the description text accordingly.

6. Save your edits. When you return to the *Fundamental* folder screen, it should look like the one shown in Figure 9-4.

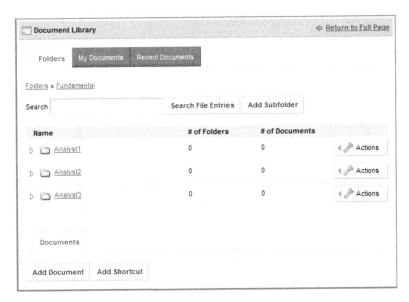

Figure 9-4. *List of subfolders*

Note that the three subfolders you created appear under the *Fundamental* folder. Also, notice the folder-navigation links that appear above the *Search* edit box. Looking at these links, you can easily see the current folder's position in the hierarchy. You can jump to any folder by clicking its name in the series of navigation links.

Now follow the preceding steps to create subfolders called **Analyst1**, **Analyst2**, and **Analyst3** under the *Technical* main folder. Next, you'll learn to store documents in the folder hierarchy that you have created so far.

Adding Documents

To add documents to our document library on the portal, follow the steps listed here:

1. Navigate to the *Fundamental/Analyst1* subfolder.

2. Click the *Add Document* button.

3. Click the *Browse* link to select the documents.

4. Select the desired analysis reports for uploading (you can select multiple documents if desired). At this stage, your screen would look like the one shown in Figure 9-5.

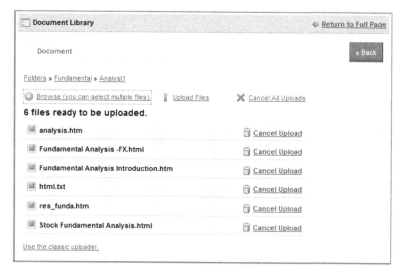

Figure 9-5. *List of files displayed in the new uploader*

5. Click the *Upload Files* link to upload the files to the server.

Using the Classic Uploader

You can use either the new uploader or the classic uploader to upload files to the server. In the previous section, you used the new uploader by clicking the *Browse (you can select multiple files)* link. In this section, you'll use the classic uploader by clicking the *Use the classic uploader* link on the upload page (see Figure 9-6).

Perform the following actions to complete the classic uploader entry screen:

1. Type the name of the file to be uploaded in the *File* edit box. If you are not sure of the file's full path, use the *Browse* button to locate the file and add its name to the edit box.

2. Enter the desired title for the file in the *Title* edit box.

3. Enter the desired description for the file in the *Description* edit box.

4. Enter the tags in the corresponding edit box. You can create new tags here by typing the index word and clicking the *Add Tags* button. Alternatively, you can tag the current file by selecting from the predefined tags that pop up when you click the *Select Tags* button.

5. Set the user permissions by clicking the *Configure* link.

6. Finally, after you complete all your inputs, click the *Save* button to upload the file to the server.

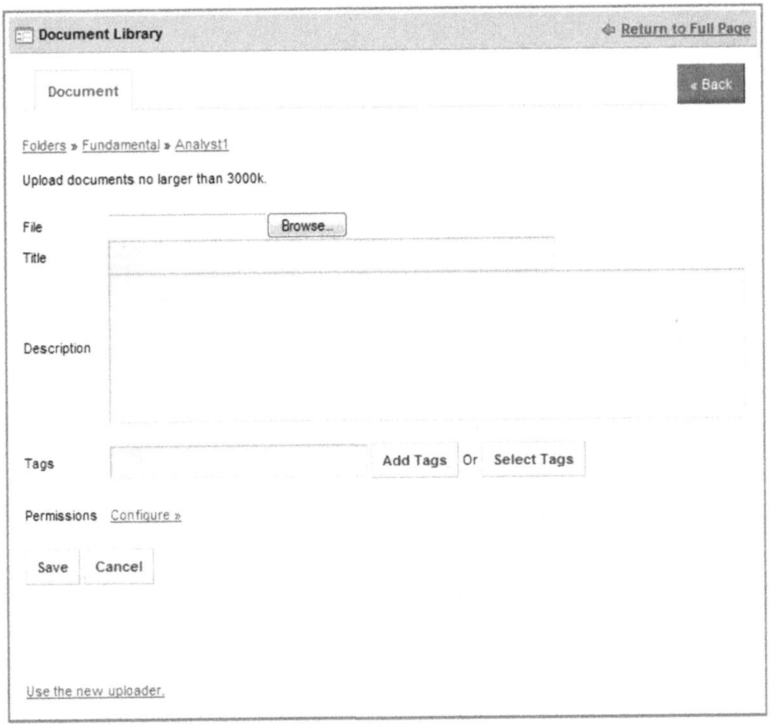

Figure 9-6. *The classic uploader*

Note The classic uploader allows you to select only one file at a time for uploading, but the upside is that you can tag the file. The new uploader allows multiple file selections, but does not facilitate tagging.

Caution You cannot upload a file with the same title to the server multiple times. If you try to upload a file with the same title as a file that already exists in the target folder on the server, the uploader will reject your request to upload the file.

Creating a Shortcut

If you find a document useful, you might want to create a shortcut to it so you can locate it more easily the next time. You obviously must have at least a read permission on the document to create a shortcut to it. Once you create the shortcut, you can grant permissions on it to other users so that they can also locate the document easily.

Note Before you create a shortcut, you first need to add a few documents by logging in as another user or selecting another community. See the preceding "Adding Documents" section for details.

To create a shortcut to a document, follow the steps listed here:

1. On the screen that lists the documents, locate and click the *Add Shortcut* button.

2. On the displayed screen, click the *Select* button to the right of the *Community* label. You will see the list of communities as shown in Figure 9-7.

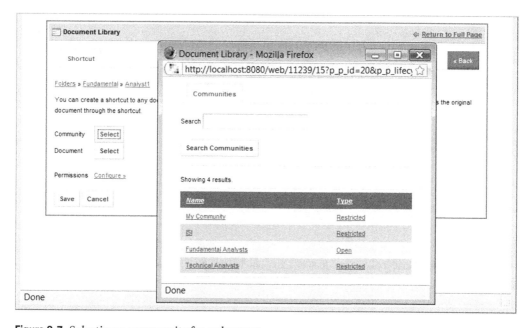

Figure 9-7. *Selecting a community for a shortcut*

3. Select the desired community from the list. After you do this, the pop-up window closes automatically.

4. Click the *Select* button to the right of the *Document* label.

5. Navigate to the desired document and select it. Again, the pop-up window closes automatically.

6. Assign the desired permissions for the shortcut (you can use the defaults, in this case).

7. Click the *Save* button. The newly created shortcut will appear in the list of documents.

Tip The current Liferay application creates the shortcut to a document in the same folder as the document itself. This obviously is a bug in the application, making the shortcut useless to the user. Hopefully, the Liferay team will have fixed this bug by the time you read this.

Performing Actions on Documents

Now that you've added a few documents and created a few shortcuts to these documents, we will look at what actions you can perform on them. You can perform these actions on each document displayed in the document list:

- *View*
- *Edit*
- *Permissions*
- *Delete*

You see the actions menu when you click the *Actions* button in the document list (see Figure 9-8). Now I'll explain how each of these actions operates.

Figure 9-8. *The actions menu for documents*

The View Action for Documents

Selecting the *View* action displays important information about the document or its shortcut; the nature of the information varies depending on which you choose. If you select a document in the list and perform a *View* action on it, you'll see a screen similar to the one shown in Figure 9-9.

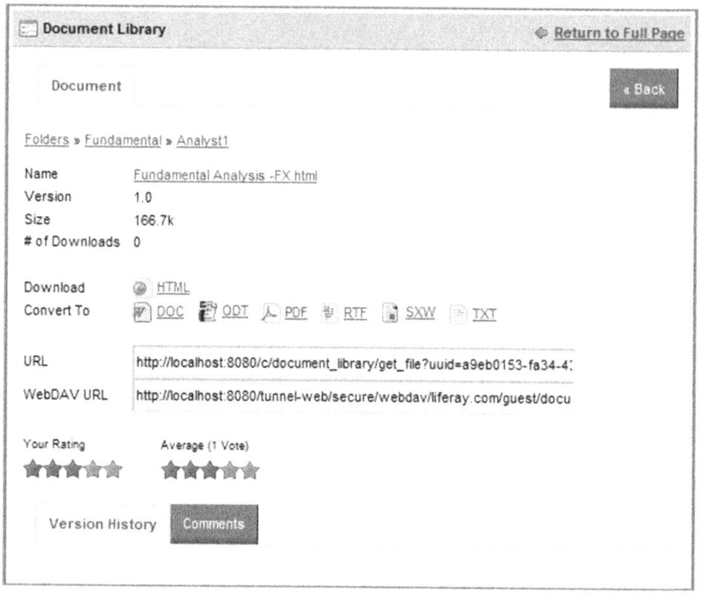

Figure 9-9. *Performing the View action on a document*

The *Document* tab at the top of Figure 9-9 shows that the currently selected item is a document rather than a shortcut. (You'll see a *Shortcut* label in the tab if you choose a shortcut instead.) The screen displays the document's name, version, size, and number of downloads. The latter statistic helps you judge the document's popularity. The screen also provides a *Download* link for downloading the document to your desktop. When you download the document, you can convert it to any of the formats displayed in the *Convert To* list.

■ Tip To enable the document conversion, you will need to start the OpenOffice services at port 8100 by running the following command on the command prompt from your OpenOffice installation folder:

```
c:\..\<open office installation folder\program>
       soffice -headless -accept="socket,host=127.0.0.1,port=8100;urp;"
```

The document-conversion feature is available only if the OpenOffice conversion option is enabled in the *Admin* portlet. You will learn more about this in Chapter 12.

You can also rate the current document by using the same five-star system you've seen in Liferay's other applications. By clicking the desired number of stars at the bottom of the screen, you can give the document a rating between 1 and 5 (see Figure 9-10). Your rating immediately affects the adjacent average rating, which is shown with the number of votes cast so far.

Figure 9-10. *Rating the document*

In addition to rating the document, you can add your comments to it. Click the *Comments* tab at the bottom of the screen to see the *Post Reply* link (see Figure 9-11). Click this link to open an edit box for the comment text. Enter your comment in this edit box and click the *Reply* button. Your comment will post immediately and appear in the *Threaded Replies* section of the document-view screen. When different users post their replies on a document, the application arranges all such replies hierarchically under *Threaded Replies* (see Figure 9-11).

Figure 9-11. *Threaded replies on a document*

Finally, the *Version History* tab at the bottom of the document-view screen allows you to view the various versions of the current document available on the server.

The Edit Action for Documents

The *Edit* action allows you to edit certain information about the document (see Figure 9-12). It's not an action for editing the document itself.

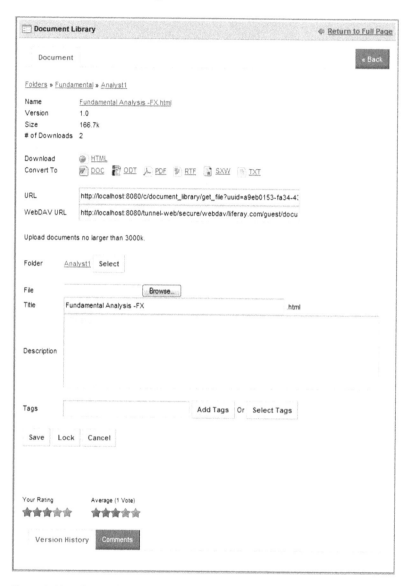

Figure 9-12. *Editing document information*

On this edit screen, you can set the folder where the document is stored, set the document's title and description, tag the document with your own index words, rate the document, and add comments to the document. In the case of shortcuts, the *Edit* action allows you to change the currently assigned community to whom access is granted.

Most important, if you modify the document's contents, you can upload the document again through this screen. When you do so, the version number displayed under the document's name increments to indicate that the document has been updated.

The Permissions Action for Documents

This option allows you to set permissions on the current document or shortcut for various user and community roles. The permissions that you can grant or deny under *Regular* or *Community* roles are:

- *View*: Allows the user to view the document or shortcut
- *Delete*: Allows the user to delete the document or shortcut
- *Permissions*: Allows the user to set permissions for other users
- *Update*: Allows the user to update the properties of the document or shortcut
- *Add Discussion*: Allows the user to post replies to the document

For a *Guest* user, you can assign only the *View*, *Delete*, and *Permissions* permissions—not *Update* or *Add Discussion*.

The Delete Action for Documents

This action, as the name suggests, allows you to delete the selected document or shortcut after you confirm to do so.

Performing Actions on Folders

Just as you can perform various actions on a document or its shortcut, you can perform certain actions on the folders in which you have arranged your documents. To perform an action on a folder, go to the folder-display view and click the *Actions* button to the right of the folder's name. You will see three action menus: *Edit*, *Permissions*, and *Delete* (see Figure 9-13).

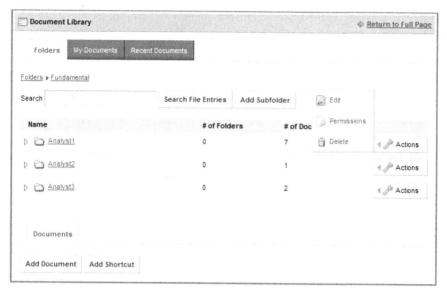

Figure 9-13. *The actions menu for folders*

The Edit Action for Folders

When you perform the *Edit* action on a folder, you can set a new parent folder or remove an existing one. You can also set the folder's name and description (see Figure 9-14).

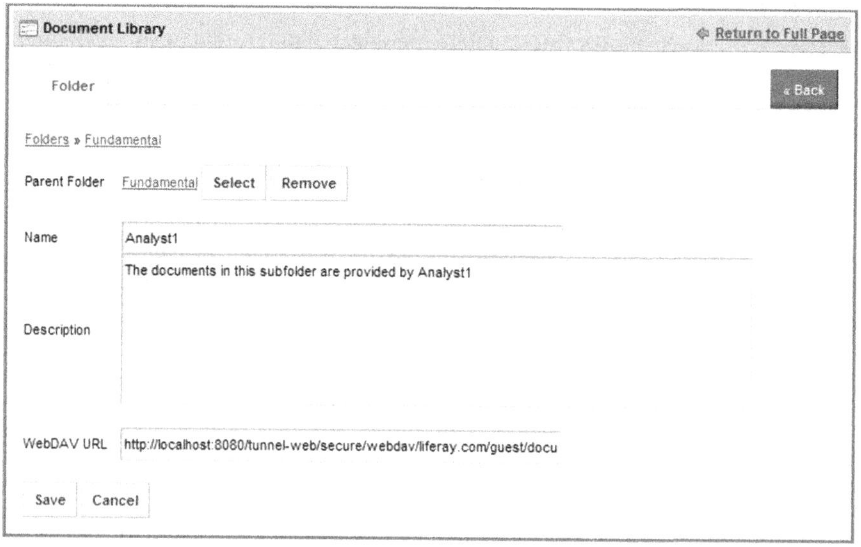

Figure 9-14. *Editing folder information*

The Permissions Action for Folders

As in the earlier cases, you can use the *Permissions* action to grant or deny permissions to users having *Regular* or *Community* roles. Under *Regular* or *Community* roles, you can grant or deny the following permissions:

- *View*: Allows the user to view the folder
- *Delete*: Allows the user to delete the folder
- *Permissions*: Allows the user to set permissions for other users
- *Update*: Allows the user to update the folder's properties
- *Add Shortcut*: Allows the user to create a shortcut in the current folder
- *Add Subfolder*: Allows the user to create a subfolder under the current folder
- *Add Document*: Allows the user to add a document in the current folder

For a *Guest* user, you can assign only *View*, *Delete*, and *Permissions*.

The Delete Action for Folders

The *Delete* action, as the name suggests, allows you to delete the selected folder after you confirm you want to do so.

Searching Documents

Over time, your document-library database will accumulate a large amount of files, so you'll want the ability to search for a certain file. The *Document Library* application provides a built-in facility for searching the database.

On the application's main screen, you will find a *Search* edit box. To search for a document, enter the desired search text in this edit box and click the *Search File Entries* button next to it. The application will search the entire database and display the list of file names that match the specified criterion. The application performs the search on the document's file name, description, and contents.

Note Liferay uses Apache Lucene as its default search engine. It can also use Apache Solr, which is—among other things—a clusterable wrapper around Lucene. Both create indexes with the text to be searched. The indexing mechanism can also make use of document-content extraction, which allows the content of a PDF document, for example, to be indexed and thus searched. A number of common document types can be indexed and searched using this feature.

A typical search result is shown in Figure 9-15.

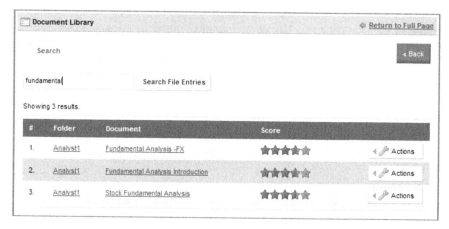

Figure 9-15. *List of searched items*

The search results display the folder name where the document is stored. Clicking any document name opens the document for viewing or allows you to download the document to your machine if an appropriate viewer is not registered for that document type.

Listing Documents

So far, you've seen how to create a folder hierarchy and add documents to it, as well as search the document-library database for files matching a specific search term. But the *Document Library* application's search feature doesn't locate files based on the users who uploaded the files. What if you want to locate only files that you yourself have uploaded? Locating your own documents in the database could prove to be a nontrivial effort. To address this, the *Document Library* application provides a feature that lets you easily list your documents and recently added documents.

Displaying My Documents

On the application's main screen, you will find the tab called *My Documents*. If you click this tab, you'll see a list of all documents that you've added to the document library (see Figure 9-16).

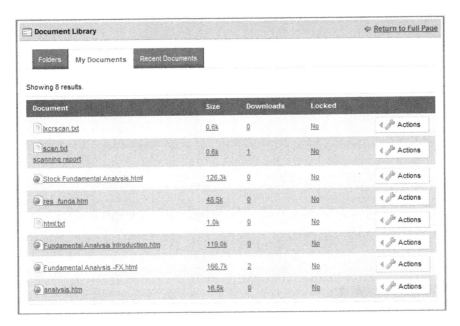

Figure 9-16. *List of My Documents*

From this screen, you can open any document for viewing or downloading. You can also perform various actions on any document, as discussed in the preceding "Performing Actions on Documents" section.

Displaying Recent Documents

Just as you can display your own documents, you can view recently added documents by selecting the *Recent Documents* tab on the main application screen.

Configuring the Application

Now we will look at the configuration options that you can set at the application level. When you click the *Configuration* button on the application's main screen, you will see the typical four tabbed options:

- *Setup*
- *Permissions*
- *Export/Import*
- *Sharing*

We will now discuss each of these options in detail.

Setup

Under the *Setup* tab, you will find several configuration options. There are four second-tier tabs:

- *Display Style*
- *Folders Listing*
- *Documents Listing*
- *Ratings*

Display Style

Under the *Display Style* option, you can select one of two views: the Classic view (see Figure 9-17) or the Tree view (see Figure 9-18).

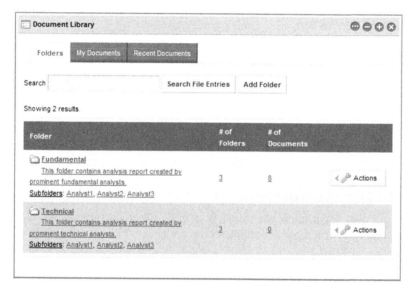

Figure 9-17. *Classic view of folder hierarchy*

Figure 9-18. *Tree view of folder hierarchy*

Folders Listing

The *Folders Listing* tab provides several configuration options for folder display (see Figure 9-19):

- *Show Breadcrumbs*: Selecting this option displays the list of folder-navigation links.

- *Show Search*: This option enables users to search folders in the database.

- *Show Subfolders*: This option enables the display of subfolders. When this check box is marked, the application will display subfolders in a tree hierarchy (see Figure 9-18). To view a subfolder, you click the small arrow to the left of the folder name.

- *Folders per Page*: This option allows you to select the number of folders to display in the folder list. The default value is 20.

- *Show Columns*: This option allows you to select the columns to display in the list. The *Folder* option displays a column containing the name of the folder. The *# of Folders* option displays a column containing the number of subfolders within the specified folder. The *# of Documents* option displays a column containing the number of documents within the specified folder. The *Action* option displays the *Actions* button in each row of the folder list.

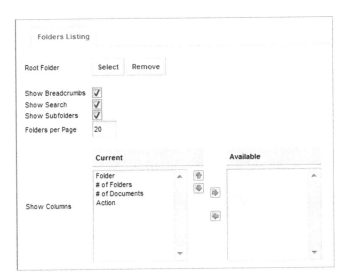

Figure 9-19. *Display options for the folder list*

Documents Listing

The *Documents Listing* tab lets you set various options to determine how documents will be listed onscreen (see Figure 9-20):

- *Show Search*: This option allows you to enable or disable the display of the search option on the document-list screen.

- *Documents per Page*: This sets the number of documents to be displayed per page. The default value is 20.

- *Show Columns*: This option allows you to select from five columns for display. The *Document* column displays the document name, the *Size* column displays the document's size, the *Downloads* column displays the number of downloads so far, the *Locked* column indicates if the document is currently locked for editing, and the *Action* column displays the *Actions* button in the row.

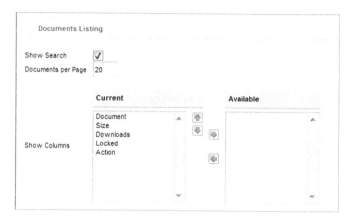

Figure 9-20. *Options to set for listing documents*

Ratings

The *Ratings* tab allows or prevents the user from rating the document (see Figure 9-21).

Figure 9-21. *The Ratings screen*

Permissions

The *Permissions* option allows you to set application-level permissions for your users. As usual, you can set permissions for *Regular* and *Community* roles. The following permissions can be granted or denied:

- *View*: Denying this permission makes the application itself inaccessible to the user.
- *Configuration*: Granting this permission allows the user to adjust the configuration settings on the application.
- *Add Folder*: Granting this permission allows the user to add a new folder to the database.

For the *Guest* role, you can grant or deny only the *View* and *Configuration* permissions.

Export/Import

As your document database grows, you need to archive it to a safe place periodically. The *Export* option on the application's configuration screen allows you to do so. When you export, the application archives the data related to the current community served by the current application instance. If the portal administrator were to use this export option for backing up the data, she would need to do so for each community. Alternatively, a system administrator can be made responsible for the entire data backup. Obviously, the administrator would need to know the underlying storage used by the current Liferay installation for maintaining the document repository. The data that you export to backup storage can be restored via the *Import* facility.

Export Tab

When you select the *Export* tab, you will see the screen shown in Figure 9-22.

As the screen in Figure 9-22 shows, you can select various fields for backup. By default, all folders and its documents are backed up. Along with this, you can save shortcuts, ranks, comments, ratings, tags, and so on. Simply mark the check box in front of each field that you wish to back up. Clicking the *Export* button exports the selected fields to the file specified in the filename edit box at the top of the screen.

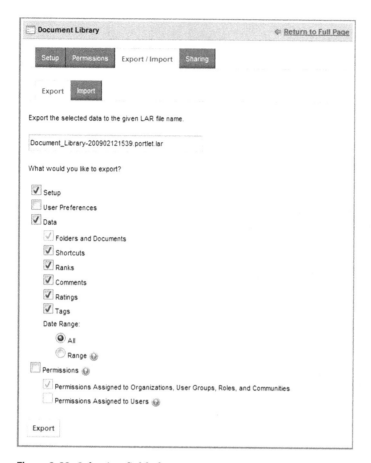

Figure 9-22. *Selecting fields for export*

Import Tab

When you select the *Import* tab, you will see the screen shown in Figure 9-23.

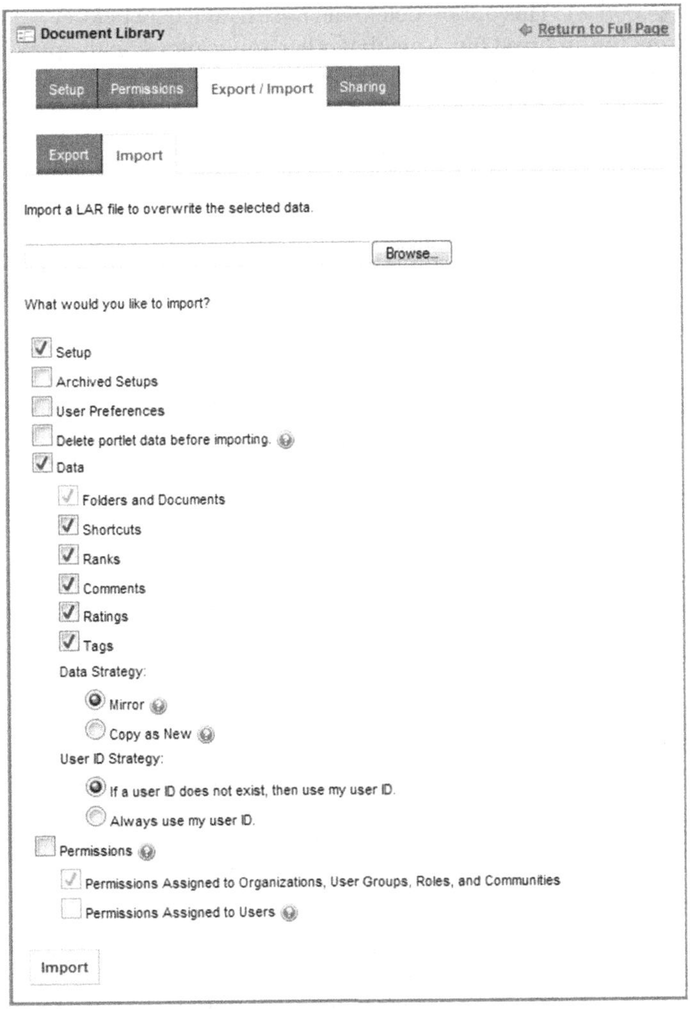

Figure 9-23. *Selecting fields for import*

On this screen, you first need to select the file from which you wish to import data. Do this by clicking the *Browse* button and navigating to the desired file name. After selecting the data file, select the various fields for import:

- *Setup*: This option imports the previously configured setup options.

- *Archived Setups*: This option results in the import of archived setups, if the backup database contains any.

- *User Preferences*: This option imports the user preferences.

- *Delete portlet data before importing*: This option deletes all the existing data before importing the new data from the archived file. Note that other applications on the portal might reference some of the documents in your database, so deleting all the data might result in orphan links in those applications.

- *Data*: You have to decide on two types of strategies while importing data; I'll discuss these shortly.

- *Permissions*: By default, all permissions related to organizations, user groups, roles, and communities would be imported. You can optionally choose to import the permissions assigned to users.

Tip The amount of user-permission data might be very large, so you should export and import such data only after careful thought. Of course, if the data is important, you do not have a choice here—you must export it regardless of its size.

Now let's return to the two types of data-import strategies I just mentioned. You must decide on the *data strategy* and the *user ID strategy*. With the data strategy, you have two options: you can either copy the data as new data, or mirror the data instead.

If you choose the *Copy as New* option, the data is imported as a new item. So the first time the data is imported, a new entry will be created for every archived entry. The next time the data is imported from the same file, an additional entry would be created for the same document. So you'd have multiple copies of the same document when you import the file multiple times.

Now suppose you mirror the data instead. The first time you import the data, a new entry is added for each imported document and a link to the original document is created. The next time you import data from a file, the newly added entry is *updated* and no additional entries for the same document are created.

You also need to choose a user ID strategy for importing data. Because the user who originally created a document may or may not exist in the new instance of the portal, you need to choose one of these options:

- If a user ID does not exist in the new instance, then use your ID in place of the missing ID.

- Regardless of whether the user ID exists in the new system, always use your ID while importing data.

After selecting the desired fields and strategies, click the *Import* button to import the data to your database.

Sharing

The *Sharing* option produces the code that you can embed in other web sites to make this application available elsewhere. It also allows you to share the application on Facebook.

Displaying the Library Contents

All of this chapter's preceding content involved creating a document library using Liferay's *Document Library* application. Liferay also provides an application that allows you to display the contents of this library. This application is known as *Document Library Display*.

Installing the Application

To install the *Document Library Display* application, follow the steps listed here:

1. Log on to the portal with *Administrator* rights.

2. Navigate to the *Document Library* page you created in the "Adding the Application" section toward the beginning of the chapter.

3. Select the *Add Application* menu option.

4. Select the *Document Library Display* application under the *CMS* category.

5. Add the application to the page by clicking the *Add* button. The resultant screen is shown in Figure 9-24.

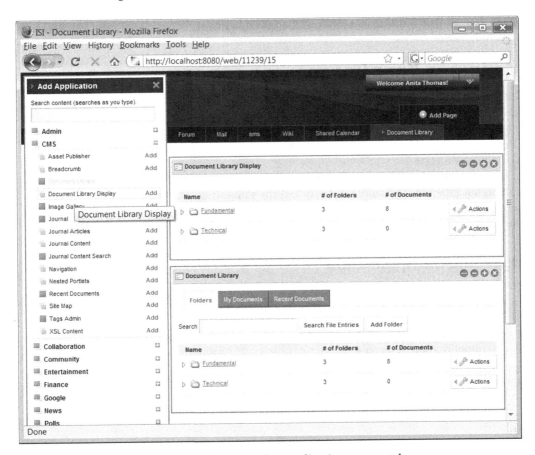

Figure 9-24. *Adding the Document Library Display application to a portal page*

Using the Application

Using the *Document Library Display* application is easy. The application opens with a screen displaying the first level of folders in the document library (see Figure 9-25).

Name	# of Folders	# of Documents	
▷ 📁 Fundamental	3	8	◁ 🔧 Actions
▷ 📁 Technical	3	0	◁ 🔧 Actions

Figure 9-25. *Main screen of the Document Library Display application*

The folder list displays the folder name, the number of subfolders within it, and the number of documents within the selected folder and associated subfolders. You can navigate to the subfolders by clicking the expansion arrows associated with the top-level folders. When you reach the lowest-level node, you'll see the list of documents inside the selected node. You can click any document name to view or download the document.

Managing Your Images

The *Document Library* application works well for managing documents such as PDFs, text files, and so on. But images generally require special attention and special programs to render them. You cannot simply store the images alongside your text-based files. For this reason, Liferay has provided another application called *Image Gallery* that allows you to manage a database of images.

The *Image Gallery* application shares many features with the *Document Library* application because their functionality is more or less the same. They differ only in the type of data storage and in the way their contents are rendered to the user. Thus, we will focus mainly on the features that set *Image Gallery* apart from *Document Library*.

Installing the Application

To install the *Image Gallery* application on our ISI portal, follow the steps listed here:

1. Log in as *Administrator* on the ISI portal.

2. Create a new page called *Image Library* under our predefined communities, or at any other location that you'd like.

3. Select the *Add Application* menu.

4. Select and add the *Image Gallery* application from the *CMS* category (see Figure 9-26).

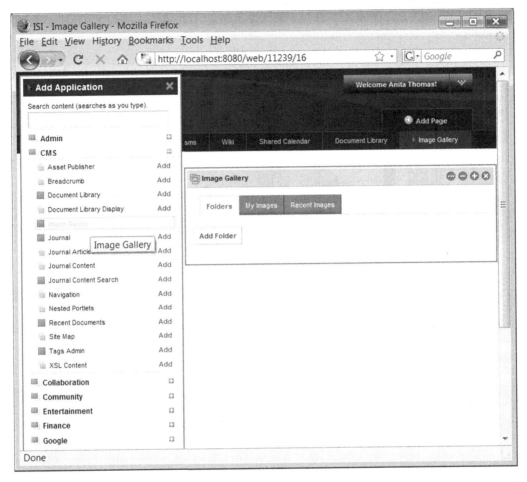

Figure 9-26. *Adding the Image Gallery application*

Using the Application

If you look at the main screen of the *Image Gallery* application, you'll see many similarities to the *Document Library* application. Just the way you organize your documents in a folder hierarchy, you will need to organize your images under logical folders on your site. The application shows three main tabs:

- *Folders*
- *My Images*
- *Recent Images*

The *Folders* tab, as in the *Document Library* application, allows you to create folders and subfolders. It allows you to add images to a folder and upload them to the server. The default file extensions for recognized images are .bmp, .gif, .jpeg, .jpg, .png, .tif, and .tiff. Most of the industry's popular image viewers recognize these formats.

A typical image-view screen is shown in Figure 9-27.

Figure 9-27. *Listing images in the Image Gallery application*

On this screen, you can also search images against the text in the images' description fields. Additionally, you might have noticed another button called *View Slide Show*. Clicking this button opens a new window and starts a slide show of all the images in the current folder (see Figure 9-28).

The slide-show viewer allows you to pause the show any time by clicking the *Pause* button. You can then navigate to the next or previous image by clicking the respective buttons. You can resume the slide show by clicking the *Play* button. Finally, you can set the speed of the slide show by selecting the duration value for each image (in seconds) from the drop-down list box.

Note The rest of the functionality of the *Image Gallery* application is similar to that of the *Document Library* application, and is thus not discussed further.

Figure 9-28. *Slide-show window*

Configuring the Application

The *Image Gallery* application's configuration does vary from the configuration of the *Document Library* application. When you click the *Configuration* icon in the main application window, you will see the following three tabbed options:

- *Permissions*
- *Export/Import*
- *Sharing*

Notice the absence of the *Setup* option. The *Image Gallery* application does not provide any setup options. I won't address the *Sharing* option here because it closely resembles its counterpart in the *Document Library* application. But we'll review *Permissions* and *Export/Import*.

Permissions

As in the case of the *Document Library* application, the *Permissions* tab allows you to set user-level permissions for both *Regular* and *Community* roles. You can assign the following permissions:

- *View*: Allows the user to view the application
- *Configuration*: Allows the user to perform various configuration tasks
- *Add Folder*: Allows the user to add folders

The *Add Folder* permission cannot be granted to a *Guest* user.

Export/Import

The *Export/Import* tab allows you to export and import your image database. When you click this tab and select the *Export* second-tier tab, you will see the screen shown in Figure 9-29.

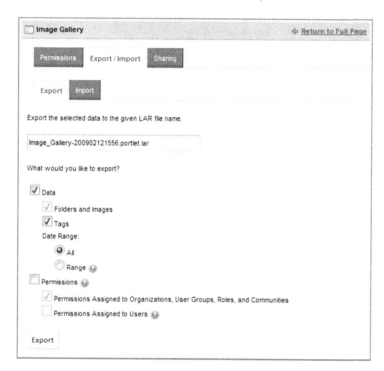

Figure 9-29. *Selecting fields for export*

Note that this screen has fewer fields for selection compared to the *Document Library* application. While selecting the images to be archived, you can specify a date range or select all the images. When you set a date range, only the images added to the database in the specified range would be added to the archive.

The second-tier *Import* tab, which resembles its counterpart in the *Document Library* application, allows you to select the fields to be imported.

Summary

In this chapter, you learned to create and manage a database of text-based documents and a database of images for your portal. You used Liferay's *Document Library* application to manage text documents and its *Image Gallery* application to manage images. To view the documents in the existing document library, you used yet another application called *Document Library Display*.

A document library generally consists of a large number of documents created by community members and domain experts. These documents must be neatly organized so the portal's users can locate them with ease. The *Document Library* application allows you to organize the documents in various folders and subfolders. It also facilitates easy searching.

To add documents to these folders, you can use one of two uploaders provided by the application: the classic uploader or the new uploader. The classic uploader allows you to select and upload only one document at a time, but it allows you to tag each document. The new uploader allows you to select and upload multiple documents at a time, but it doesn't let you do any tagging.

The *Document Library* application allows you to archive the entire database using its export facility. The import facility allows you to rebuild your lost database.

The *Image Gallery* application resembles the *Document Library* application in many ways, but it manages images rather than documents. The *Image Gallery* application also provides a slide viewer that facilitates slide shows.

CHAPTER 10

■ ■ ■

Publishing Dynamic Content

In the last chapter, you used Liferay to manage static content that your portal can retain and use over a long period of time. But you might also find it useful to manage dynamic content and publish it on your portal. News and announcements are examples of such dynamic content.

By "dynamic content," I do not mean content that's generated on the fly as in the case of dynamic web pages. Instead, I'm referring to material that changes periodically and often. Liferay offers several content-management applications that let you manage dynamic content and make it available to your users. In this chapter, you will

- Learn to use the *Journal* application to create both free-form and template-based articles

- Create structures for journal articles

- Define templates for journal articles

- Manage an article database

- Learn to use the *Journal Articles* application, which facilitates the display of an article list based on a certain article category

- Learn to use the *Journal Content* application, which lets you display individual articles

- Learn to use the *Journal Content Search* application, which lets you search for an article within the journal database

Installing the Journal Application

The application that we are going to use for creating regularly changing content is called the *Journal* portlet. First, you need to install this application on the ISI portal. Follow these steps to perform the installation:

1. Log on to the ISI portal using your *Administrator* account.

2. Create a public page called *Dynamic* under one of our communities, or at any other location of your choice.

3. Select the *Add Application* menu.

4. Locate the *Journal* application under the *CMS* category.

5. Add the application to the page. Your screen should now look like the one shown in Figure 10-1.

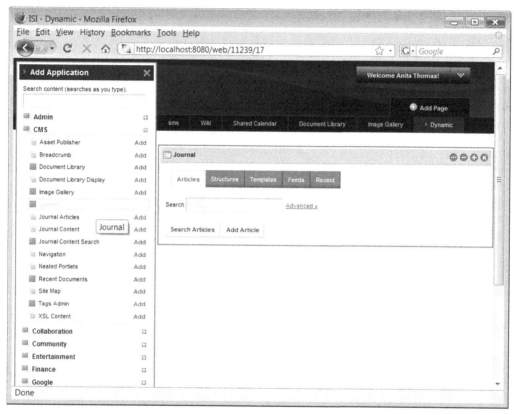

Figure 10-1. *Adding the Journal application*

At this point, you are ready to create journal articles. When you create a journal article, it can be a free-form article like the one you created in Chapter 2 using the *Journal Content* application. (You'll also read more about *Journal Content* in this chapter's "Using the Journal Content Application" section.) In a free-form article, the writer can include any content and format it as desired. But it is a better programming practice to define a document structure on which authors can base their article content. Also, you might want to define the way the document is rendered to the user. You achieve these two tasks in the *Journal* application by creating *structures* and *templates*. The structure defines what needs to be included in the document, and the template defines how the contents are rendered in the user's browser. You will now learn to create structures and templates, plus an article based on them.

Creating Article Structures

To create a new journal-article structure, follow these steps:

1. Click the *Structures* tab in the main application window of the *Journal* portlet. You will see the screen shown in Figure 10-2.

Figure 10-2. *The Structures screen*

The screen shows a list of available structures. As no structures are currently defined, this list is blank.

2. Click the *Add Structure* button to create a new structure. At this stage, your screen should look like the one shown in Figure 10-3.

3. Take these actions on this screen:

   a. *Autogenerate ID*: Each structure has its own unique ID. If you do not wish to track your own IDs, allow the application to autogenerate the IDs by marking this check box.

   b. *Name*: Enter **Announcement Structure**.

   c. *Description*: Enter **This defines the structure for the announcement type of article.**

   d. *Permissions*: This section allows you to set various permissions at *Community* and *Guest* levels. Leave these at their default values.

4. Before you click the *Save* button, you need to define the XML schema for the structure. The schema defines the various fields to be included in the document. I will discuss this next.

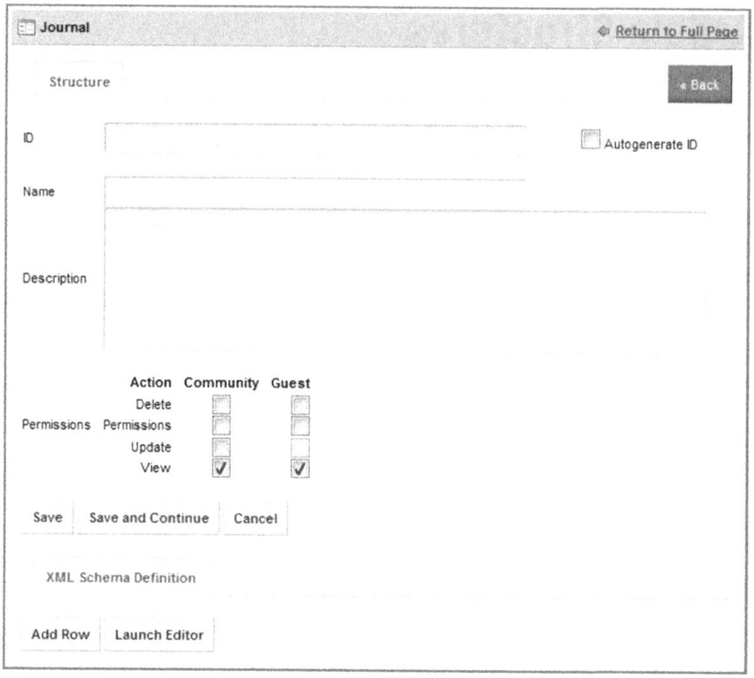

Figure 10-3. *Creating a new structure*

Defining Your XML Schema

You can use one of two ways to create the XML schema that will contain the fields for our structure:

- Using the provided graphical interface
- Directly coding the schema definition in the provided XML editor

Using the Graphical Interface

To use the graphical interface to create the XML schema, follow these steps:

1. On the screen for creating a new structure, click the *Add Row* button under the second-tier *XML Schema Definition* tab. A new row with a drop-down list appears (see Figure 10-4).

Figure 10-4. *Creating a schema definition*

2. Enter **Title** in the edit box. This sets the title field for the content.

3. In the drop-down list next to the edit box, select *Text* as the content type. You have several choices for the content type; you will be using the other types soon.

4. Add one more field to the structure by clicking the *Add Row* button.

5. Name this field **Description** and set its type to *Text*.

6. Add another field called Image and set its type to *Image*. At this stage, your screen should look like the one shown in Figure 10-5.

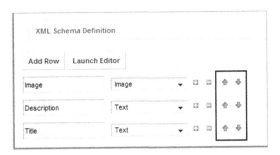

Figure 10-5. *Schema definition with three fields*

Rearranging Schema Fields

You can easily change the order of the schema fields by using the two arrows shown next to each field. The down arrow moves the field down by one position and the up arrow moves it up by one position. These arrows are highlighted in Figure 10-5.

Adding Subfields

Each field can contain an inner field. To add a subfield, use the + icon to the right of the field name. You'll now add two subfields to the *Description* field:

1. Click the + icon next to the *Description* field to add a subfield under it.

2. Enter **Abstract** in the edit box and select *Text* as the content type.

3. Click the *Description* field's + icon one more time.

4. Enter **Details** in the edit box and select the *Text* content type. The *Details* subfield appears as the first one under the *Description* field.

5. Rearrange the two subfields using the associated arrows so that the *Details* field follows the *Abstract* field. Your screen should now look like the one in Figure 10-6.

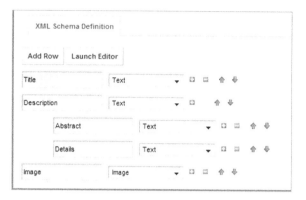

Figure 10-6. *Schema definition with subfields*

Removing Fields

If you wish to remove a previously added field or subfield, you can do so easily by clicking the – (minus) icon to the right of it. The corresponding field disappears from the structure.

Caution When you remove a field or subfield, the application does not ask for your confirmation first.

So you can see how easy it is to define an article structure using the graphical interface. However, if you still insist on coding the structure, you can use the second method of creating it: using the XML editor.

Using the XML Editor

To use the XML editor to create an article structure, click the *Launch Editor* button under the *XML Schema Definition* tab. An editor window pops up on the screen. If you already created some of the structure using the graphical-interface method, the corresponding XML code for the structure appears in the editor (see Figure 10-7).

The editor provides two views for the code: *Plain* and *Rich*. You can add more fields and subfields to the structure by directly editing the displayed code in either of the two views. To do this, you must understand XML coding.

Once you're satisfied with the changes, click the *Update* button to update the structure. Your changes will be reflected in the structure's graphical view.

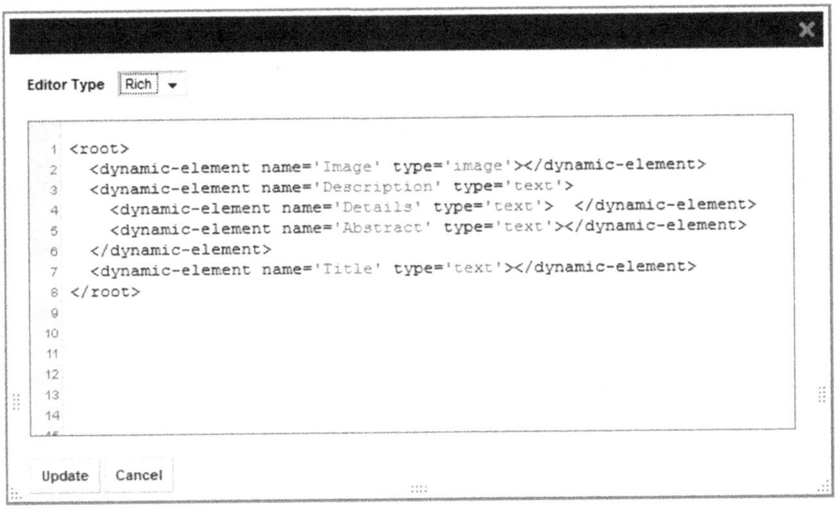

Figure 10-7. *XML schema definition in the XML editor*

Viewing and Searching Structures

After you have created a structure and saved it, it will appear in the list of structures on the *Structures* screen in the main application view (see Figure 10-8).

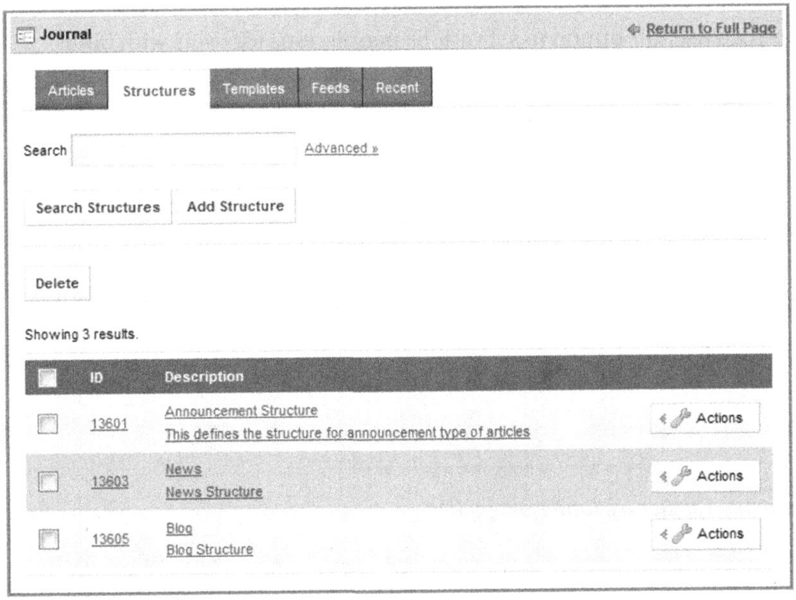

Figure 10-8. *Structures list*

If your structures list grows large, you might find it tedious to locate a desired structure. In that case, use the *Search Structures* button to narrow down your search and get a list of structures matching a given search criterion.

Using the Actions Menu

You will now be able to perform certain actions on these structures. To do so, click the *Actions* button to the right of the desired structure name. An *Actions* menu will appear (see Figure 10-9).

Figure 10-9. *List of actions you can perform on a structure*

You can perform these actions on a structure:

- *Edit*: Clicking this menu option opens the current structure in the graphical editor. You can now modify the structure and update its definition by saving the changes.

- *Permissions*: You can use this option to set various permissions for users with both *Regular* and *Community* roles.

- *Copy*: This option allows you to create a copy of the current structure under a new ID (see Figure 10-10).

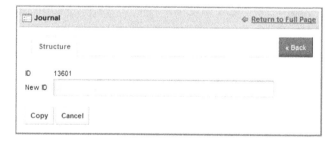

Figure 10-10. *Copying a structure under a new ID*

- *Add Article*: This option allows you to add a journal article to the database using the currently selected structure. (I will discuss the article-creation process in the sections "Creating Journal Articles" and "Creating Template-based Articles.")

- *View Articles*: This option shows all articles using the currently selected structure on the *Articles* screen.

- *Add Template*: This option allows you to create a new template based on the currently selected structure. I'll explain the template-creation process in the section "Defining Article Templates."

- *View Templates*: This option displays all templates that use this structure.

- *Delete*: This option removes the structure definition from the system.

Editing a Structure

In addition to using the *Edit* option in the *Actions* menu, you can also open a structure in the graphical editor by clicking its name in the structure list. You can now modify the structure's definition and save it under the same ID.

Deleting a Structure

In addition to using the *Delete* option in the *Actions* menu, you can delete a structure definition by marking the check box to the left of the desired structure name and clicking the *Delete* button (see Figure 10-8). This removes the structure definition from the system.

So far, you have learned to create journal-article structures by defining the fields that the document will contain. Now we will look at how to define templates that use these structures. A template uses a structure to capture the data from the article author and defines the overall formatting of the article. The application will format each field in the structure using the formatting instructions defined in the template.

Defining Article Templates

To create a new template or to view the existing templates, click the *Templates* tab in the main application window (see Figure 10-11).

Figure 10-11. *The Templates screen*

This screen displays a list of existing templates at the bottom. This list is currently blank because you haven't yet defined any templates. We'll remedy that now.

Adding a Template

To create a new template, follow the steps listed here:

1. Click the *Add Template* button. You will see the screen shown in Figure 10-12.

Figure 10-12. *Creating a new template*

2. Do the following things on the displayed screen:

   a. *Autogenerate ID*: Mark this check box. The application will now autogenerate the ID for the new template.

   b. *Name*: Enter **Announcement Template.**

   c. *Description*: Enter **This is a page template for the announcement type of journal article.**

    d. *Cacheable*: Leave this box checked (the default).

    e. *Structure*: Click the appropriate button to select or remove the earlier selected structures.

    f. *Language Type*: You get three choices here:

        i. *VM*: Velocity is a powerful Java-based template engine. It renders data from plain Java objects to various formats.

        ii. *XSL*: Extensible Stylesheet Language (XSL) is a language for expressing style sheets. Like CSS, it contains information on how to render an XML document.

        iii. *CSS*: Cascading Style Sheets (CSS) is a widely accepted standard for creating style sheets to define how web-page information will be rendered.

    g. *Script*: Specify the file that defines the template structure. Because you can create the template structure in VM, XSL, or CSS, you should select the appropriate file based on the language selection in the *Language Type* field. To locate the file on the system, use the *Browse* button. Alternatively, you can create a new file on the fly using the *Launch Editor* button.

Note As mentioned earlier, a template defines the formatting instructions for each field defined in the structure. When the user views the article, these formatting instructions will be applied to the various fields defined in the structure and the formatted output will be rendered in the user's browser. You can specify such formatting instructions in VM, XSL, or CSS, but describing the formatting instructions is beyond the scope of this book.

---

    h. *Format Script*: Mark this check box if you want to format your script. You must save the document by clicking the *Save and Continue* button or the *Save* button to see the effects of this action. The opportunity to format the script is especially useful if you created the script in an external editor and did not indent it properly.

    i. *Small Image URL*: Specify the URL of the image to be used for identifying the template.

    j. *Small Image*: Alternatively, you can specify an image from the local disk. To locate the image, use the *Browse* button.

    k. *Use Small Image*: If you have populated the *Small Image* field, check this box.

    l. *Permissions*: Use this section to set the various permissions for *Regular* and *Community* roles. For now, leave these at their default values.

3. Click the *Save* button to save your edits.

Viewing and Searching Templates

After you have created a template and saved it, it will appear in the list of templates on the *Templates* screen in the main application view (see Figure 10-13).

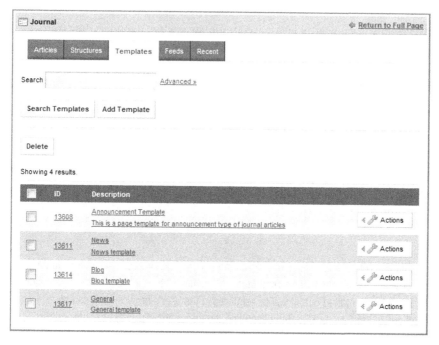

Figure 10-13. *View of predefined templates*

As in the case of structures, the view screen has a search facility that lets you narrow down the list of templates displayed. You can enter the search string in the *Search* edit box and click the *Search Templates* button to locate the templates matching the search criterion.

Performing Actions on Templates

The actions you can perform on templates are similar to the actions you can perform on structures:

- *Edit*: This allows you to edit the selected template. Selecting this action opens the template in the editor, giving you the opportunity to edit any of the fields.

- *Permissions*: This action allows you to set user permissions on the selected template for the *Regular* and *Community* roles.

- *Copy*: This option allows you to make a copy of the selected template under a new ID.

- *Add Article*: This action allows you to add a new article based on the current template. I'll discuss adding articles in the section "Creating Journal Articles."

- *View Articles*: This option displays all the existing articles based on the currently selected template.

- *Edit Structure*: A template uses a particular structure. With this menu action, you will be able to modify the structure that the current template is based on.

- *Delete*: This action deletes the currently selected template from the system.

Editing a Template

In addition to using the *Edit* option in the *Actions* menu, you can also open a template in the editor by clicking its name in the template list (see Figure 10-13). Then you can make modifications.

Deleting a Template

In addition to using the *Delete* option in the *Actions* menu, you can delete a template by marking the check box to the left of the template name and clicking the *Delete* button (see Figure 10-13).

Now that we've completed the groundwork for article creation by setting up structures and templates, we will delve into the process of creating a new article. In the "Creating Journal Articles" section, you will learn to create a free-form article; in the "Creating Template-based Articles" section, you'll learn to create an article based on a structure and template.

Creating Journal Articles

When you select the *Articles* tab in the main application view, you will see the screen shown in Figure 10-14.

Figure 10-14. *The Articles screen*

The *Articles* screen shows the list of currently available articles. This list is empty because you haven't yet created any articles.

Adding an Article

To add a new article, click the *Add Article* button. Doing this pops up an editor that offers several options, each of which we'll discuss individually.

Editing Content

The main portion of the screen is the editor for entering article data (see Figure 10-15).

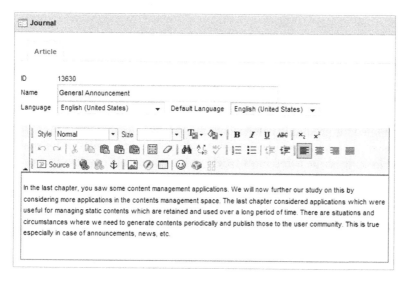

Figure 10-15. *Creating a new article*

On this screen, you would enter the following information:

- *Name*: Enter the article name here. This name will appear in the article list; it will also prove useful when users search for an article.

- *Body*: Enter the body of the journal article in the rich-edit control. You can format the text using the icons in the toolbar.

- *Permissions*: Use this section to set user permissions on the article for *Regular* and *Community* roles. You'll find it under the rich-edit control on the article-addition screen.

Abstract

The *Abstract* option, under the *Permissions* section, allows you to add an abstract to your journal article. The abstract subscreen is shown in Figure 10-16.

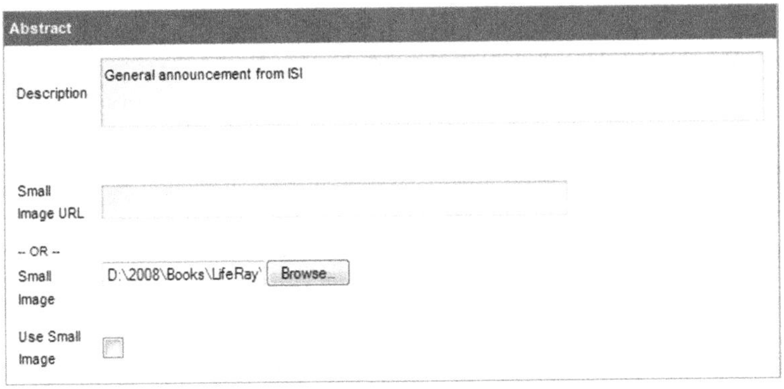

Figure 10-16. *Adding an abstract and image to a new article*

Perform the following tasks on this subscreen:

- *Description*: Enter **General announcement from ISI**.

- *Small Image URL*: Enter the URL of the image that will be used to identify the current article in the article list.

- *Small Image*: Alternatively, enter the name of the image file from your local drive. You can use the *Browse* button to locate the file.

- *Use Small Image*: Mark this check box if you have populated the *Small Image* field.

Workflow

The *Workflow* subscreen at the top-right corner of the article-addition screen simply displays the current status of the article (see Figure 10-17).

Figure 10-17. *Workflow status display*

Note that the status is *New* because we are currently creating a new article. When you open an existing article for editing at a later time, the status would be different.

Note The four possible workflow-status values are *New, Approved, Not Approved*, and *Expired*. After the administrator reviews and approves the article, it acquires the status *Approved*. If the article is rejected for publication, it gets the status *Not Approved*. Finally, if an article has been set to expire after a certain date and that date has passed, it acquires *Expired* status. The expiration date is generally set by the administrator at publication time, but it can be changed later. You can make an expired article "live" again by changing the expiration date to a future value.

Form and Presentation

The *Form and Presentation* subscreen, under the *Workflow* subscreen, allows you to select which structure and which template you'd like to use for the current article (see Figure 10-18).

Figure 10-18. *Selecting the structure and template for a new article*

Click the *Select* button to the right of the *Template* option. Doing this displays a list of existing templates on the screen. When you select the desired template, the corresponding structure used by the selected template would automatically display to the right of the *Structure* option.

■**Note** The editor on the left side of the screen automatically changes to display the fields defined in the selected structure.

Categorization

You can set the article category on the subscreen for categorization (see Figure 10-19).

Figure 10-19. *Selecting a category and tags for a new article*

An article can belong to one of the following categories:

- *Announcements*
- *Blogs*
- *General*
- *News*
- *Press Release*
- *Test*

Note The category type helps narrow down an article search. For example, the *Journal Articles* portlet discussed in the "Using the Journal Articles Application" section uses article categories to limit the amount of articles displayed in the list.

Tip You can add more categories by modifying the `portal.properties` file. However, this is beyond the scope of this book.

You will also be able to tag the article in this subscreen. You can tag the article with a pre-existing tag or a newly created tag.

Schedule

The schedule subscreen, near the bottom-right of the article-addition screen, is shown in Figure 10-20.

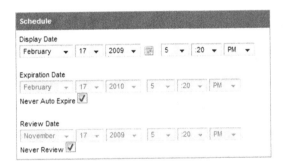

Figure 10-20. *Setting a publishing schedule for a new article*

In the *Display Date* field, you can set the date and time at which the current article will be made available to the portal members. The *Expiration Date* field allows you to set the date and time after which the article will no longer be available for viewing. If you mark the *Never Auto Expire* check box, the article will never expire and be available to members indefinitely. The *Review Date* sets the date for article review. Marking the *Never Review* check box indicates that an article review is not required for approval and publication.

Saving a New Article

After you've entered the desired information on the article-addition screen (see Figure 10-15), you get several options for saving the edits:

- *Save*: Clicking this button saves the edit, creates a new article with the given ID, and adds it to the database of the existing articles.

- *Save and Continue*: Clicking this button saves the current edits and keeps the editor open for you to make further changes.

- *Save and Approve*: Clicking this button saves the current edits and approves the current article for publishing.

Note The administrator must approve an article before it is published, even if she has chosen to skip the review process. An unapproved article does not appear in the articles list displayed to the user.

- *Preview*: This option gives you a preview of how the article will look to the user.
- *Download*: This option downloads the article from the server.

Note The *Preview* and *Download* buttons appear only if your article is based on a template and a structure. This is obvious: if you don't base the article on a template, you design it in the WYSIWYG editor and thus preview it along the way. In the "Creating Template-based Articles" section, you will create a full journal article based on a template. You will then appreciate the use of the *Preview* option.

- *Cancel*: This option cancels all the current edits and returns you to the main application screen.

Viewing an Article

After you create and save a new article, you will return to the main application screen, where a list of existing articles would be displayed (see Figure 10-21).

Figure 10-21. *Viewing a list of articles*

If you need to search for an article or articles matching a specific criterion, specify the search string in the *Search* edit box and perform the search by clicking the *Search Articles* button.

Performing Actions on an Article

You can perform the following actions on each of the articles displayed in the list:

- *Edit*: Selecting this menu option opens the article in the editor so you can make changes.

- *Permissions*: This option allows you to set various user permissions on the current article for *Regular* and *Community* roles.

- *Preview*: This option allows you to preview the article to see how it would be rendered on the user's screen.

- *Copy*: This option makes a copy of the current article under a new ID.

- *Delete*: This option deletes the article from the database.

Assigning an Expiration Date for an Article

Over time, articles might lose their importance. You can set expiration dates on such articles so they're no longer available for viewing. Do this by marking the check boxes to the left of the desired articles in the displayed list and clicking the *Expire* button (see Figure 10-21).

Deleting an Article

If you'd like to delete one or more articles, go the *Articles* screen and mark the check boxes to the left of the unwanted articles. Click the *Delete* button to remove them from the database permanently.

Viewing Recent Articles

After adding several articles over a period of time, you might want to obtain a list of only the recently added articles. When you click the *Recent* tab on the main application screen, you will see the list of recently added articles (see Figure 10-22).

You can also obtain the RSS feed of the articles by defining the feeds in the *Feeds* tab. (You can find details on RSS feeds in Chapter 6.) The *Feeds* tab allows you to define feeds that will expose the existing articles using a set of rules such as constraints and presentation settings.

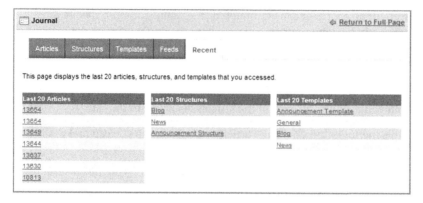

Figure 10-22. *Viewing recently added articles*

Configuring the Journal Application

Now we will study the configuration settings for the *Journal* portlet at the application level. When you click the application-configuration icon, you will see four tabbed options:

- *Setup*: Lets you set various e-mail formats
- *Permissions*: Lets you set permissions for different user roles
- *Export/Import*: Facilitates the export and import of data
- *Sharing*: Facilitates application sharing

We will now look at each of these options in detail.

Setup

Under the *Setup* option (see Figure 10-23), you can set up the formats for various e-mail messages, such as these:

- *Email From*
- *Article Denied Email*
- *Article Granted Email*
- *Article Requested Email*
- *Article Review Email*

Figure 10-23. *The Journal application setup screen*

Email From

In the *Email From* tabbed option, you can set the sender information for all the application-generated e-mail messages. In particular, you enter the sender's name and e-mail ID (see Figure 10-23).

Article Denied Email

The *Article Denied Email* tab allows you to set the format for the e-mail message that communicates an article rejection. If you decide to reject an article because its contents are unsuitable, the application sends an automated message to the author using the format specified on this screen (see Figure 10-24). The message format uses several predefined fields, which are listed at the bottom of the screen.

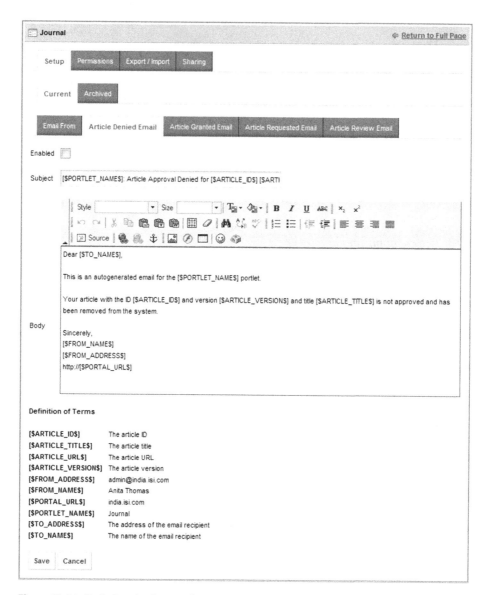

Figure 10-24. *Defining the format for an article-rejection message*

Article Granted Email

The *Article Granted Email* tab lets you define the format for the e-mail message that gets sent to a user whose article has been accepted for publication. Its settings resemble those for the *Article Denied Email* screen.

Article Requested Email

When a user submits an article for publication, the application generates a message for the portal administrator indicating that the user has requested an article approval. In the notification message, the author can mention the article's location (URL), ID, version, title, and any other relevant information. You can define the format for this notification message in the *Article Requested Email* tabbed option.

Article Review Email

You might want multiple reviewers to read and approve any submitted article. You use the *Article Review Email* screen to set up the e-mail message requesting a review.

Permissions

In the *Permissions* tabbed option, you can set several permissions for the *Regular* and *Community* roles.

Regular Roles

Under the *Regular* roles, you have four types of users:

- *Administrator*
- *Guest*
- *Owner*
- *Power User*
- *User*

A guest user has only two types of permissions: *View* and *Configuration*. The *View* permission is granted by default. Granting the *Configuration* permission allows the user to perform various configuration activities.

An administrator, owner, power user, and ordinary user can obtain several types of permissions:

- *Add Article*: Allows the user to add a new article
- *Add Feed*: Allows the user to add an article feed
- *Add Structure*: Allows the user to create a new structure
- *Add Template*: Allows the user to create a new template
- *Approve Article*: Allows the user to approve a submitted article
- *Configuration*: Allows the user to perform various configuration tasks
- *View*: Allows the user to view articles

Community Roles

Under *Community* roles, there are three types of users:

- *Administrator*
- *Member*
- *Owner*

All three types of users have access to all the permissions discussed in the "Regular Roles" section. These are *Add Article, Add Feed, Add Structure, Add Template, Approve Article, Configuration*, and *View*.

Export/Import

The *Export/Import* tabbed option facilitates the export and import of the journal-article database pertaining to the current community. When you click this tabbed option, you will see the screen shown in Figure 10-25.

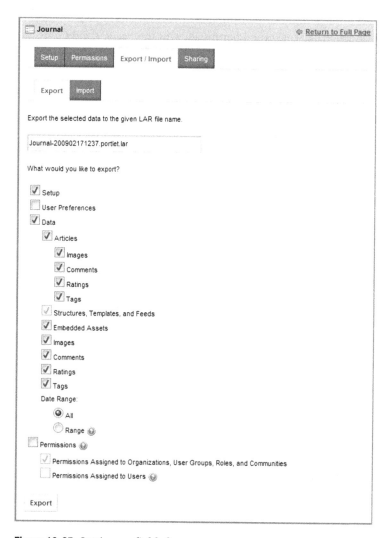

Figure 10-25. *Setting up fields for export*

On this screen, you can select the various fields you wish to export to the external database. The file name is specified in the LAR file-name edit box. By default, several fields are marked for export; you can uncheck any fields you don't want. You can also opt to export data only in a specified date range.

The *Import* tab allows you to select fields you wish to import into the new instance of the *Journal* application. While importing the data, you can choose to mirror the data or copy it as new data. Likewise, if a user is not defined in the new instance of the portal, you can choose to use your ID in place of the missing person's ID. Alternatively, you can decide to use your ID in all cases, irrespective of whether the user is defined in the new system.

Note The data strategy and user ID strategy for data import are explained in depth in Chapters 8 and 9.

Sharing

The *Sharing* option produces the code that you can embed in other web sites so you can make this application available elsewhere. It also allows Facebook sharing of the application.

Creating Template-based Articles

You fully explored the functionality of the *Journal* application in the previous two sections, and you explored the creation of structures and templates in the two sections before that. Now you'll put that new knowledge to use by going through an example of creating a template-based article. In the process, you'll see why and where to use the templates and structures.

Suppose that your portal users would like to share their recommendations on whether to buy or sell a particular security based on its market price for the day, its 52-week high, and its 52-week low. You'll create an article structure that will require the author to input the security's name, its high and low prices for the day, and its high and low prices over a 52-week period. The structure will also ask the author for his recommendations.

Creating the Structure

Use the following steps to create the new structure:

1. Open the *Journal* application.

2. Select the *Structures* tab and click the *Add Structure* button (see Figures 10-2 and 10-3).

3. Mark the *Autogenerate ID* check box.

4. Enter **52-week analysis data** in the *Name* field.

5. Enter **This defines the structure for the 52-week analysis report** in the *Description* field.

6. Leave the default settings in the *Permissions* section.

7. Using the *Add Row* button repeatedly, add several fields to the structure with the following names and content types (see Figure 10-4):

  a. Name: **Info**; Type: *Text*

  b. Name: **Symbol**; Type: *Text*

  c. Name: **High**; Type: *Text*

  d. Name: **Low**; Type: *Text*

  e. Name: **52WeekHigh**; Type: *Text*

  f. Name: **52WeekLow**; Type: *Text*

 8. You can rearrange the rows by using the up and down arrows, if desired (see Figure 10-5).

 9. Click the *Launch Editor* button to verify that the structure you created matches the one shown in Listing 10-1.

  Listing 10-1. *XML Document for the Created Structure*

```
<root>
  <dynamic-element name='Info' type='text'></dynamic-element>
  <dynamic-element name='Symbol' type='text'></dynamic-element>
  <dynamic-element name='High' type='text'></dynamic-element>
  <dynamic-element name='Low' type='text'></dynamic-element>
  <dynamic-element name='52WeekHigh' type='text'></dynamic-element>
  <dynamic-element name='52WeekLow' type='text'></dynamic-element>
</root>
```

 10. Click the *Save* button to save your edits.

Next, you will create the article template based on this structure.

Creating the Template

To create the new template, use the following steps:

 1. Return to the main screen of the *Journal* application, if you have not done so.

 2. Select the *Templates* tab and click the *Add Template* button (see Figures 10-11 and 10-12).

 3. Mark the *Autogenerate ID* check box.

 4. In the *Name* field, enter **52-week article template**.

 5. In the *Description* field, enter **This template defines the article structure for a 52-week analysis report**.

 6. Leave *Cacheable* checked (its default state).

 7. Click the *Select* button to the right of the *Structure* label and select the previously defined *52-week analysis data* structure from the displayed list of structures.

8. Select *XSL* from the *Language Type* drop-down list. You will use the XSL transformation to define the document formatting.

9. In the *Script* edit box, select the file called 52week.xsl by using the *Browse* button. Note that you do not have this file on your machine yet; you must enter the code from Listing 10-2 in any of your favorite text editors and store it in a file called 52week.xsl.

Listing 10-2. *The XSL Transformation Document*

```
<?xml version="1.0" encoding="UTF-8"?>

<xsl:stylesheet xmlns:xsl="http://www.w3.org/1999/XSL/Transform"
  version="1.0">
  <xsl:output method="html" omit-xml-declaration="yes"/>
  <xsl:template match="/">
    <xsl:value-of disable-output-escaping="yes"
         select="root/dynamic-element[@name='Info']/dynamic-content"/>
    <p/>
    <table width="50%">
      <tr>
        <td width="200">
          <font size="2" color="#0000FF">
            <b>Symbol</b>
          </font>
        </td>
        <td width="200">
          <font size="2" color="#0000FF">
            <b>High</b>
          </font>
        </td>
        <td width="200">
          <font size="2" color="#0000FF">
            <b>Low</b>
          </font>
        </td>
        <td width="350">
          <font size="2" color="#0000FF">
            <b>52 Week High</b>
          </font>
        </td>
        <td width="350">
          <font size="2" color="#0000FF">
            <b>52 Week Low</b>
          </font>
        </td>
      </tr>
```

```
        <tr>
          <td>
            <xsl:value-of disable-output-escaping="yes"
                    select="root/dynamic-element[@name='Symbol']/
                            dynamic-content"/>
          </td>
          <td>
            <xsl:value-of disable-output-escaping="yes"
                    select="root/dynamic-element[@name='High']/dynamic-content"/>
          </td>
          <td>
            <xsl:value-of disable-output-escaping="yes"
                    select="root/dynamic-element[@name='Low']/dynamic-content"/>
          </td>
          <td>
            <xsl:value-of disable-output-escaping="yes"
                    select="root/dynamic-element[@name='52WeekHigh']/
                            dynamic-content"/>
          </td>
          <td>
            <xsl:value-of disable-output-escaping="yes"
                    select="root/dynamic-element[@name='52WeekLow']/
                            dynamic-content"/>
          </td>
        </tr>
      </table>
      <p/>
      <xsl:value-of disable-output-escaping="yes"
              select="root/dynamic-element[@name='Detail']/dynamic-content"/>
      <p/>
    </xsl:template>
  </xsl:stylesheet>
```

10. Leave the rest of the fields at their default settings.

11. Click the *Save* button to save your edits.

12. Click the *Return to Full Page* link to return to the main screen of the *Journal* application.

Now, you and your community users can use this template to create journal articles.

Creating Articles

To create a new article based on a template, use the following steps:

1. Navigate to the *Journal* application main screen, if required.

2. Select the *Articles* tab and click the *Add Article* button (see Figures 10-14 and 10-15).

3. Enter **IBM Stocks** in the *Name* field.

4. Click the *Select* button to the right of the *Template* item in the *Form and Presentation* box on the right side of the screen.

5. Select *52-week article template* from the list of displayed templates. This is the template you just created.

6. Note the changes on the left side of the screen. The default editor changes to the list of fields you had defined in the *52-week analysis data* structure associated with the selected template.

7. Enter the following data in the displayed fields:

   a. Info: **My views on IBM stocks**

   b. Symbol: **IBM**

   c. High: **90.20**

   d. Low: **86.33**

   e. 52WeekHigh: **130.93**

   f. 52WeekLow: **69.50**

8. Leave all other fields on this screen at their default values.

9. Select the article's category type from the *Categorization* box on the right side of the screen.

10. Click the *Save and Approve* button to publish the article.

11. Note that the *Status* changes to *Approved* (see the *Status* column in the list of articles).

12. To preview the article, click its *Actions* button and select *Preview*. You will see the screen shown in Figure 10-26. This is what your users will see when they open the article in their portal window.

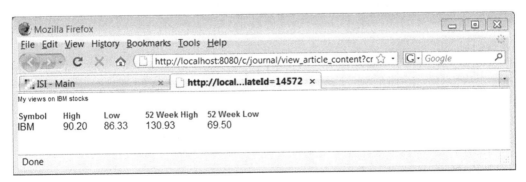

Figure 10-26. *Previewing the journal article*

In the next section, I will describe the *Journal Articles* application that you can use to view articles from the journal database based on their category assignments.

Using the Journal Articles Application

The *Journal Articles* portlet allows the user to view articles of a certain type from the repository, such as *Announcements* or *Blogs*. As an administrator, you will decide on what the user will see. To use this portlet on our ISI portal, follow the steps listed here:

1. Log on using your *Administrator* account.

2. Navigate to the *Dynamic* public page you created earlier in this chapter, or move to any other page where you wish to add this application.

3. Select the *Add Application* menu option.

4. Select the *Journal Articles* application under the *CMS* category.

5. Add the application to the portal page using the *Add* link. At this stage, your screen should like the one shown in Figure 10-27.

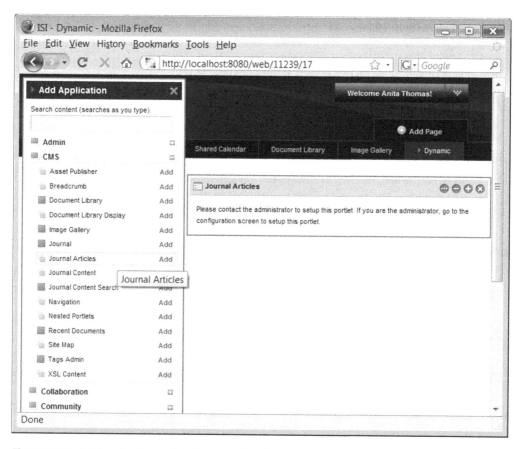

Figure 10-27. *Adding the Journal Articles application*

Before your users start using the *Journal Articles* application, an administrator needs to set it up. To set up the application, follow these steps:

1. Click the application-configuration icon. You will see the setup screen as shown in Figure 10-28.

Figure 10-28. *The application setup screen*

2. Choose the following options on the setup screen:

   a. *Community*: From this drop-down list, you need to select the community from all the available communities on your portal. The articles pertaining to the specified community will be displayed in the application portlet.

   b. *Article Type*: Select the article type. Note that a user can define his own type, after which it will appear in the selection list. Here are some examples of Liferay's pre-defined article types:

      i. *Announcements*

      ii. *Blogs*

      iii. *General*

      iv. *News*

      v. *Press Release*

      vi. *Test*

   c. *Display URL*: Leave this as the default value of *Maximized*.

   d. *Display per Page*: This option allows you to select the number of articles to be displayed in the list. The default value is 5.

   e. *Order By Column*: Here you can decide the sort order for the list of articles. You can sort the list by one of these parameters:

   i. *Display Date*

   ii. *Create Date*

   iii. *Modified Date*

   iv. *Article Title*

   v. *ID*

   f. *Order By Type*: This field determines whether the sort order is ascending or descending.

3. Save the edits by clicking the *Save* button.

4. Click the *Return to Full Page* link to go back to the main application screen.

You will now see the list of articles displayed in the application's main window (see Figure 10-29). You can view any article by clicking its link.

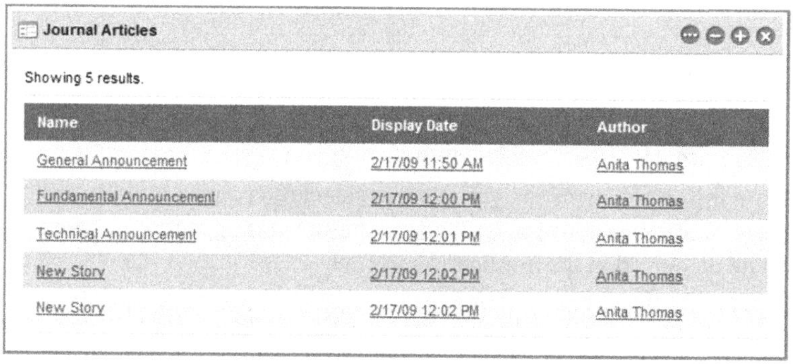

Name	Display Date	Author
General Announcement	2/17/09 11:50 AM	Anita Thomas
Fundamental Announcement	2/17/09 12:00 PM	Anita Thomas
Technical Announcement	2/17/09 12:01 PM	Anita Thomas
New Story	2/17/09 12:02 PM	Anita Thomas
New Story	2/17/09 12:02 PM	Anita Thomas

Journal Articles

Showing 5 results.

Figure 10-29. *List of articles in the Journal Articles application's main screen*

Using the Journal Content Application

Whereas the *Journal Articles* application facilitates the viewing of article lists according to category, the *Journal Content* application facilitates the viewing of individual journal articles. (You were introduced to the *Journal Content* portlet in Chapter 2.)

Note The primary function of the *Journal Content* portlet is to enable you to *view* an individual journal article, but you can also use it to *create* an individual article, as you saw in Chapter 2. When you click the *Add Article* icon within the *Journal Content* application, you're actually accessing a pared-down version of the *Journal* application. But if you want your portal to accommodate a lot of articles submitted by users, you should use *Journal* instead of *Journal Content* for article creation because it offers more functionality.

Neither *Journal Articles* nor *Journal Content Search* allows you to create articles. These applications facilitate viewing and searching only.

To use the *Journal Content* application on our ISI portal, follow the steps listed here:

1. Log on using your *Administrator* account.

2. Navigate to the *Dynamic* public page you created earlier in this chapter, or move to any other page where you wish to add this application.

3. Select the *Add Application* menu option.

4. Select the *Journal Content* application under the *CMS* category.

5. Add the application to the portal page using the *Add* link. At this stage, your screen should look like the one shown in Figure 10-30.

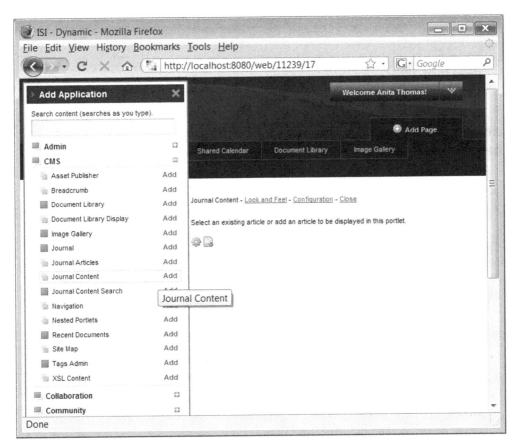

Figure 10-30. *Adding the Journal Content application*

6. At the bottom-left corner of the application screen, you will find two icons: one for selecting an article to view, and one for adding a new article.

7. If you do not have any existing articles, click the *Add Article* icon to open the article editor.

8. Create a new article, then click the *Save and Approve* button.

9. When you return to the main application screen, you can select the article for viewing (see Figure 10-31).

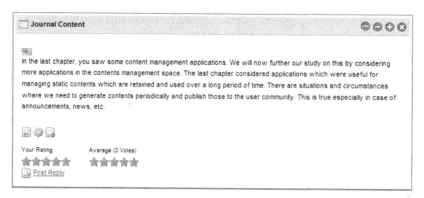

Figure 10-31. *Viewing an article*

10. You can edit the displayed article by clicking the *Edit* icon displayed at the bottom-left corner of the application screen.

Now you'll configure *Journal Content* at the application level. When you click the application-configuration icon, you will see the setup screen as shown in Figure 10-32.

You will see the list of articles displayed on the bottom of the setup screen. You will also see a list of setup options in the center of the screen:

- *Show Available Locales*: Checking this box results in the display of all locales in which the application is available.

- *Enable Ratings*: Selecting this option results in the display of ratings on the main application screen.

- *Enable Comments*: Selecting this option enables the user to comment on the current article.

- *Enable Comments Ratings*: This setting allows the user to rate the comments on the article.

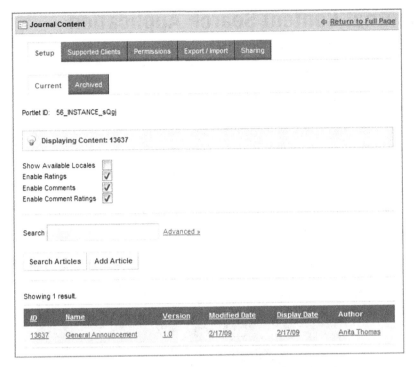

Figure 10-32. *The Setup screen of the Journal Content application*

A screen showing an article's comments, replies, and ratings is shown in Figure 10-33.

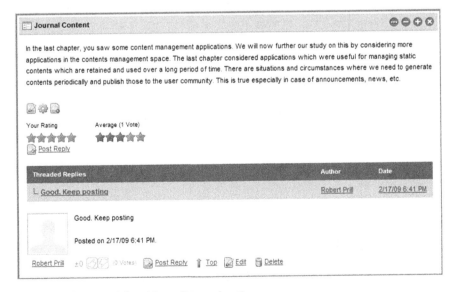

Figure 10-33. *An article with replies and ratings*

Using the Journal Content Search Application

Journal Content Search is an easy-to-use application that allows the user to locate an article from a huge database. To use this application on your portal, follow the steps listed here:

1. Log on using your *Administrator* account.

2. Navigate to the *Dynamic* public page you created earlier in this chapter, or move to any other page where you wish to add this application.

3. Select the *Add Application* menu option.

4. Select the *Journal Content Search* application under the *CMS* category.

5. Add the application to the portal page using the *Add* link. At this stage, your screen should like the one shown in Figure 10-34.

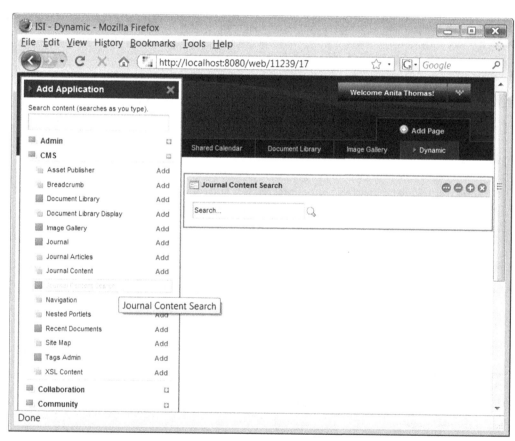

Figure 10-34. *Adding the Journal Content Search application*

6. To use the application, type your search criterion in the edit box and click the magnifying-glass icon. A list of articles matching the search criterion appears onscreen (see Figure 10-35).

Tip You can have more than one instance of the *Journal* application running on your portal. You can configure the *Journal Content Search* application to perform a search on a particular instance of the *Journal* application. You do this by setting the *Target Portal ID* field in the application configuration settings.

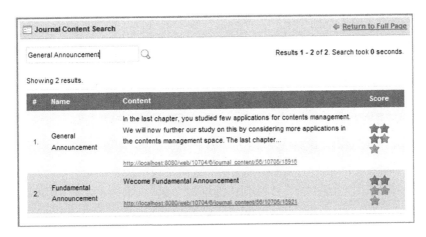

Figure 10-35. *List of searched articles*

7. Click an article name in the list to view it.

Summary

In this chapter, you studied four Liferay applications that allow community sharing of an article database: *Journal, Journal Articles, Journal Content,* and *Journal Content Search*. The *Journal* application facilitates the creation of journal articles. The users create articles and submit them to the portal for publishing. An administrator or a user with appropriate rights reviews the article, approves or rejects it, and publishes it on the portal if approved.

The *Journal* application allows you to create, modify, and save articles created by users. It also eases the article-creation process by allowing you to define structures and templates. A structure defines fields to be included in the article (such as text and images), whereas a template based on that structure specifies the article's formatting. With these structures and templates, users can easily fill in the required fields and submit their articles for consideration; they don't always have to create free-form articles from scratch.

Once you have your article database, you can use one of the other applications to view its contents. The *Journal Articles* portlet facilitates the display of an article list based on an article category. The *Journal Content* application's primary function is to display an individual article, but it also lets you create an individual article by giving you access to a limited version of the *Journal* application. The *Journal Content Search* portlet allows easy searching of a desired article within the portal's article database.

CHAPTER 11

■■■

Enhancing Your Portal

By now you've studied several applications provided in the Liferay package. Although Liferay has provided a wide variety of applications that you can use on your portal, they might not meet everyone's needs. So the Liferay community users started developing their own applications and making them available to others. Liferay officially encourages such application development and provides links to many good applications provided by the community. In this chapter, we will study some of the community applications that are relevant to the development of our ISI portal. In particular, you will learn to use these portlets and gadgets:

- The *Google Gadget* portlet
- The *Stock Ticker* gadget
- The *Stock Charts* gadget
- The *Google News* gadget
- The *Sun Notepad* portlet
- The *Google AdSense* portlet

The portlets provided by the Liferay community consist of a wide variety of applications including entertainment portlets, business and finance portlets, and even games. These can meet the requirements of most portal developers. For our ISI portal, we're particularly interested in the plugins related to finance, securities, and news. Many developers worldwide have written applications addressing these topics.

One way that third-party developers extend Liferay is through Google *gadgets*, which were introduced a couple years ago. Gadgets are "miniature objects" created by Google users that offer "cool and dynamic content"[1] and that can be placed on any web page. Google made the Gadgets API available to users worldwide and encouraged developers to build applications based on it. As a result, you have access to a myriad of applications of varying functionality, and new applications are continuously appearing on Google's ever-growing gadget list.

We will take advantage of these gadgets to enhance the functionality and thus usefulness of our portal. Note that a gadget is not a portlet, so you can't include it in the Liferay portal directly. It does need some conversion. Fortunately for us, Liferay has developed a portlet to bridge the gap between its portal and Google's gadgets. This is called the *Google Gadget* portlet. You will now use this portlet to incorporate gadget applications on your portal pages.

---

1 Google, "What are gadgets powered by Google?", http://www.google.com/webmasters/gadgets/.

The Google Gadget Portlet

The *Google Gadget* portlet gives us access to thousands of applications built on the Gadgets API, including several related to finance, securities, and news. First we'll download the portlet, then we'll look for the applications we want.

Downloading the Application

The *Google Gadget* portlet is listed in the *Downloads* section of Liferay's web site. Download the portlet by following these steps:

1. Open the official Liferay web site: `http://www.liferay.com`.

2. Click the *Downloads* tab.

3. Click the *Official Plugins* tab. This tab is highlighted in Figure 11-1.

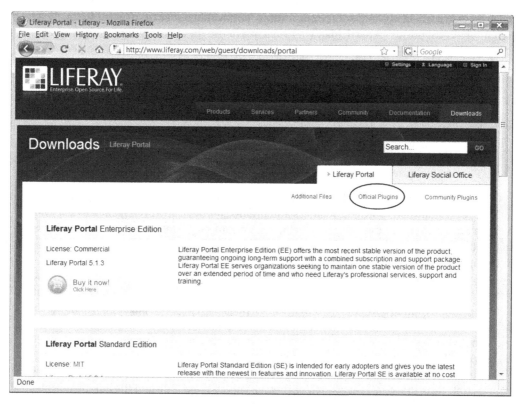

Figure 11-1. *The Official Plugins download area*

4. On the resulting page, enter **Google** in the Search edit box and click the *Search Products* button. You will get a list of products containing the "Google" keyword in their names (see Figure 11-2).

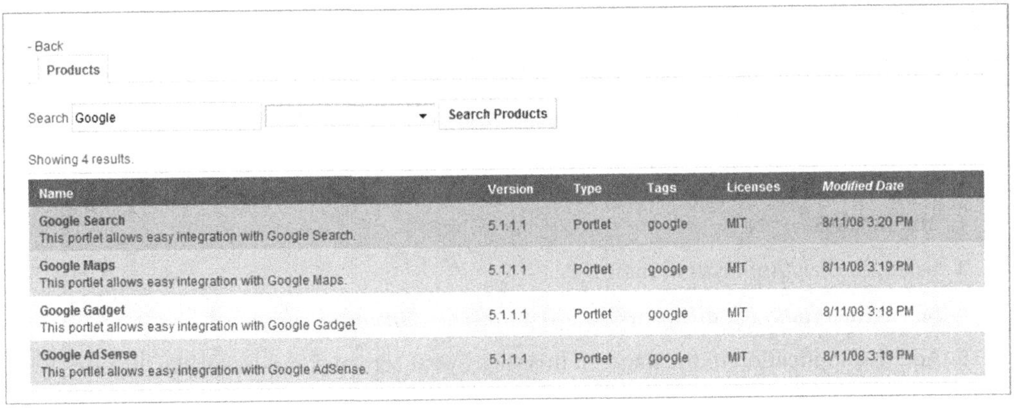

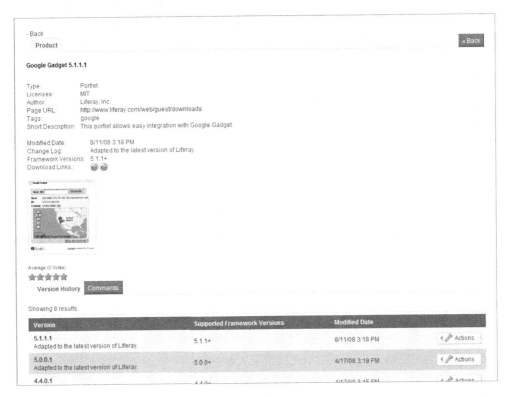

Figure 11-2. *Searching for portlets containing the keyword "Google"*

5. Click the *Google Gadget* product link to display the product information onscreen (see Figure 11-3). Note that the version number might differ from the one shown here.

Figure 11-3. *Product information for Google Gadget*

6. Under the *Version History* tab, click the *Actions* button associated with the product version you want. Select the *Download* option. Doing this downloads a .war file to your machine.

Installing the Application

After you have successfully downloaded the product's .war file, you are ready to install the product on your machine. Install the product by following these steps:

1. Log on to the portal using your *Administrator* account.

2. Create a new public page called *Products* for the purpose of testing our new gadgets and portlets.

3. Select the *Add Application* menu.

4. Select the *Plugin Installer* application under the *Admin* category.

5. Add the application to the page. At this stage, your screen should look like the one shown in Figure 11-4.

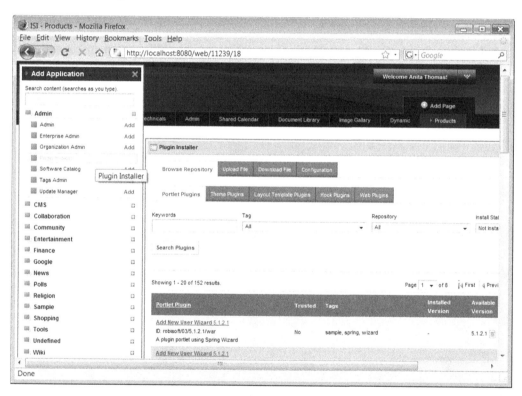

Figure 11-4. *Setting up the Plugin Installer application*

Note If you previously installed the *Plugin Installer* portlet on your site, you need not install it again.

6. Click the *Upload File* tab.

7. Browse and select the .war file you downloaded earlier (see Figure 11-5).

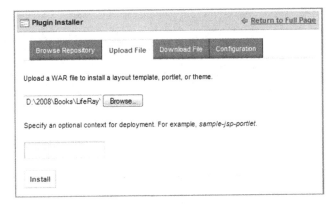

Figure 11-5. *Uploading the product's .war file*

8. Click the *Install* button to install the application on your portal. Note that it might take a while to install the .war file on your app server.

9. You can now remove the *Plugin Installer* application from the *Products* page.

Adding the Application

After you have successfully uploaded and installed the application on your portal, you need to add it to a page and use it. To add the application, follow the steps listed here:

1. Log on to the portal using your *Administrator* account.

2. Navigate to the *Products* page you created in the preceding "Installing the Application" section.

3. Select the *Add Application* menu.

4. Locate the new application category called *Google*.

5. Select the *Google Gadget* application under the newly added *Google* category.

6. Add the application to the page. At this stage, your screen should look like the one shown in Figure 11-6.

Figure 11-6. *Adding the Google Gadget application to a portal page*

Configuring the Application

By default, the *Google Gadget* portlet is configured to show you a gadget that lists YouTube videos (see Figure 11-7).

Figure 11-7. *Initial screen of the Google Gadget application*

You will need to configure the *Google Gadget* portlet to show a different gadget on the application screen. Follow these steps to do so:

1. Click the application-configuration icon or the *Configuration* menu option from the menu drop-down list, depending on the current page's theme. You will see a list of Google gadgets in the center of the screen and a category list on the left (see Figure 11-8).

2. Click the *Finance* category link. The resulting page shows many applications relevant to our ISI portal. We will work with a few applications from this category.

3. Locate the *Stock Ticker* application. You can use the *Search Gadgets* facility to find it.

4. Click the *Choose* button to add the gadget to your page.

5. Now return to full-page view by clicking the *Return to Full Page* link at the top-right corner of the page.

Figure 11-8. *Selecting a gadget*

You should now see a stock-price ticker displayed on the *Google Gadget* application's main screen (see Figure 11-9).

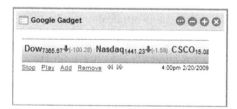

Figure 11-9. *Stock Ticker application screen*

For every gadget you want to include on your portal, you add an instance of the *Google Gadget* portlet and configure it by following the preceding steps. Now you'll learn to use a few of these gadgets, starting with *Stock Ticker*.

Caution Google provides a list of gadgets from developers worldwide and reserves the right to remove them from the list at any time. So you might find that a gadget of interest to you will have disappeared from the site the next time you look for it. However, some of the popular gadgets are available on the site for several months. Even if the gadget has been removed from the list on the Google site, you can always get it from the publisher's own site.

The Stock Ticker Gadget

The *Stock Ticker* application displays a ticker view of the selected securities based on data from the Yahoo! Finance web site. You will need to configure the securities that you wish to monitor on the ticker.

Selecting Securities

To select the securities to display, follow these steps:

1. Click the *Add* link on the *Stock Ticker* application's main screen. You'll get a dialog box asking you to enter the desired stock symbol (see Figure 11-10).

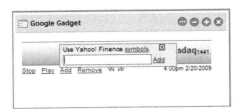

Figure 11-10. *Adding a stock symbol for the ticker display*

2. Enter a stock symbol such as **IBM** or **MSFT** in the edit box and click the *Add* link.

3. If you do not know the symbol for the desired stock, use the *symbols* link to find the code.

4. You can add multiple securities to the display by repeating step 2 for each one.

Caution The application permits multiple insertions of the same stock symbol.

5. Once you are done adding the stock symbols, close the *Add* dialog.

You now return to the main application screen, where the newly added stocks appear in the ticker.

Removing Securities

If you no longer want to monitor one of the securities that you added, follow these steps to remove it from the ticker:

1. Click the *Remove* link. You'll get a pop-up dialog showing a list of currently selected securities (see Figure 11-11).

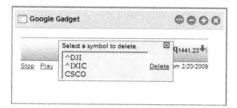

Figure 11-11. *Selecting a stock to delete*

2. Select the stock that you want to remove.

■**Note** The symbols that start with a ^ sign cannot be removed because they're stock-exchange symbols.

---

3. Click the *Delete* link.

4. You can delete multiple stocks by repeating steps 2 and 3 for each one.

5. After you are done, close the *Delete* dialog.

Your ticker now omits the securities that you removed from the display.

Other Features

The *Stock Ticker* application provides other features such as stopping the ticker, playing it again, and changing its scroll speed. Click the *Stop* link to prevent the ticker from scrolling, and click the *Play* link to enable scrolling again. To change the scrolling speed, click one of the two arrow buttons. The button with the right-facing arrows increases the scrolling speed, while the button with the left-facing arrows reduces the speed.

The Stock Charts Gadget

We will now look at another gadget that would interest our portal's technical analysts: the *Stock Charts* application provided by Stock Market Studio (http://www.stockmarketstudio.com).

Adding the Application

To add the *Stock Charts* application on your portal page, follow these steps:

1. Add another instance of the *Google Gadget* portlet to your portal page.

2. Click the portlet's application-configuration icon or the *Configuration* menu option from the menu drop-down list.

3. Click the *Finance* link in the category list.

4. Look for the *Stock Charts* gadget (highlighted in Figure 11-12). You can use the *Search Gadgets* facility to locate the application.

Figure 11-12. *Selecting the Stock Charts application from the list of finance-related gadgets*

5. Click the *Choose* button under the *Stock Charts* application.

6. Return to full-page view by clicking the *Return to Full Page* link. Your screen should now look like the one shown in Figure 11-13.

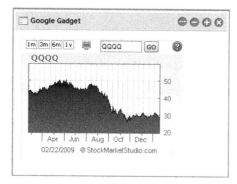

Figure 11-13. *The main screen of the Stock Charts application*

Using the Application

The *Stock Charts* application allows you to view stock charts from several companies. You simply need to provide the stock symbols for the companies whose data you want. To use this application, follow the steps listed here:

1. Suppose you wish to view the stock charts from IBM. Type **IBM** in the edit box on the application's main screen.

2. Click the *Go* button. Doing this displays IBM's chart onscreen. By default, a one-year chart is shown.

3. You can zoom into the chart by selecting smaller time periods. Click the provided buttons to view a one-month (*1m*) chart, a three-month (*3m*) chart, or a six-month (*6m*) chart. You can go back to the one-year chart by clicking the *1y* button.

4. If you click the *View Large Chart* icon in the center (it looks like a computer monitor), you'll pop up a new window that displays a full-fledged chart of the selected stock (see Figure 11-14).

Our technical analysts would find this charting application very useful in performing their analyses.

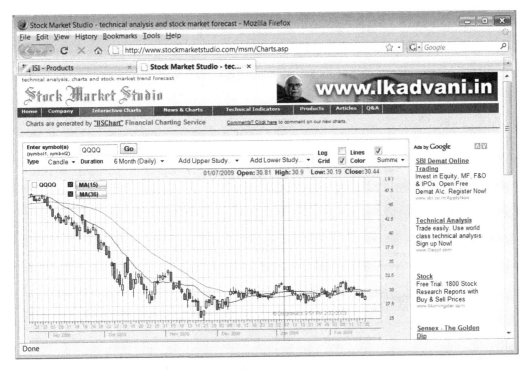

Figure 11-14. *A full-chart view in the Stock Charts application*

The Google News Gadget

A securities portal must have the latest news displayed on its web pages. To give our portal this feature, we will add yet another Google gadget called *Google News*.

Adding the Application

Follow these steps to add the *Google News* gadget to your portal:

1. Add another instance of the *Google Gadget* portlet to your portal page.

2. Click the portlet's application-configuration icon or the *Configuration* menu option from the menu drop-down list.

3. Click the *News* category.

4. Look for the *Google News* gadget (see Figure 11-15). You can use the search facility to locate the application.

5. Click the *Choose* button under the *Google News* application.

6. Return to full-page view by clicking the *Return to Full Page* link. Your screen should now look like the one shown in Figure 11-16.

Figure 11-15. *Selecting the Google News application from the gadget list*

Figure 11-16. *The Google News application main screen*

Using the Application

The *Google News* application displays news in various categories taken from authentic news sources. In the main application screen, you will see five different categories:

- *Top Stories*
- *World*

- *U.S.*

- *Business*

- *Sci/Tech*

The application is easy to use. Simply select the category of your choice to display the news from that category onscreen. Note that the application displays only the title and the news source. To view the details, click the desired title. Doing this pops up a new window that shows the contents from the source channel. Our ISI portal members will probably be most interested in the *Business* category, but they can access the other categories if desired.

So far, you've added several gadgets to the ISI portal: *Stock Ticker*, *Stock Charts*, and *Google News*. You'll probably find several Google gadgets that can enhance your portal's usefulness. Simply identify the applications from the list on the Google site, test them to determine their relevance, and add them to the portal pages using the *Google Gadget* portlet.

The Sun Notepad Portlet

As you've seen, the *Google Gadget* portlet provides a single gateway to thousands of useful applications. But you have access to even more third-party applications that aren't Google gadgets. These applications are simply portlets written in Java, PHP, Ruby, and so on. You can find a list of these applications on the Liferay web site.

You'll now learn how to install and use a typical third-party application: a notepad application from Sun Microsystems. Available through Liferay's list of community plugins, the application allows you to create personal notepad messages under categories that you can define yourself.

Downloading the Application

To use the *Sun Notepad* application, you first need to download it from Liferay's *Community Plugins* web page (or simply download it through the *Plugin Installer* portlet that you used in the section "The Google Gadget Portlet"). To download the application, follow these steps:

1. Go to Liferay's web site at `http://www.liferay.com`.

2. Click the *Downloads* tab.

3. Click the *Community Plugins* tab.

4. In the displayed list of products, locate the *Sun Notepad* portlet.

5. Click the *Notepad* link to pull up the product information (see Figure 11-17).

6. Under the *Version History* tab, click the *Actions* button associated with the product version you want. Select the *Download* option. Doing this downloads a .war file to your machine: `sun-notepad-portlet-5.1.1.1.war`.

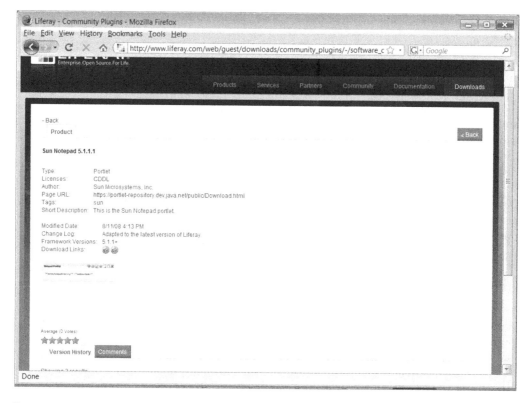

Figure 11-17. *Sun Notepad application information*

Installing the Application

After you have successfully downloaded the product's .war file, you are ready to install it on your machine. Follow these steps to install the product:

1. Log on to the portal using your *Administrator* account.

2. Navigate to the page containing the *Plugin Installer* application that you installed earlier. If you've removed the application since then, add it back to your page now.

3. Click the *Upload File* tab.

4. Browse and select the *Sun Notepad* application's downloaded .war file.

5. Click the *Install* button to install the application on your portal. Note that it might take a while to install the .war file on your app server.

Adding the Application

After you have successfully uploaded and installed the application on your portal, you need to add it to a page and use it. Perform these steps to add the application:

1. Log on to the portal using your *Administrator* account.

2. Navigate to the *Products* page that you created in the section "The Google Gadget Portlet."

3. Select the *Add Application* menu.

4. Locate the new application category called *Sun*.

5. Select the *Notepad Portlet* application under the *Sun* category.

6. Add the application to the page. At this stage, your screen should look like the one shown in Figure 11-18.

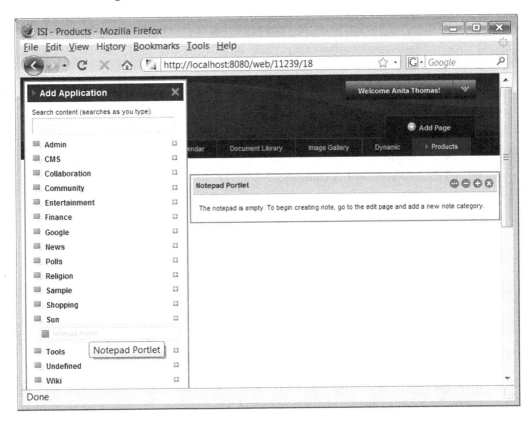

Figure 11-18. *Adding the Sun Notepad portlet to a portal page*

Using the Application

Initially, no notes are available for display in the application's main screen, so you need to create some. For this, you must first define a category. Follow these steps to create a category:

1. Click the *Preferences* (...) icon at the top-right corner of the application's main screen (see Figure 11-18). Note that depending on the currently used theme, *Preferences* might instead appear as a menu item in a drop-down list. Clicking *Preferences* brings up the screen in Figure 11-19.

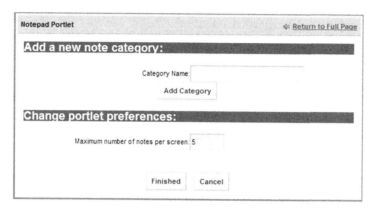

Figure 11-19. *Defining a new category in the Sun Notepad application*

2. Enter **Technical** in the *Category Name* edit box. We will categorize all our notes on technical analysis under this category.

3. Click the *Add Category* button to create the category with the specified name. You'll now see the newly added category onscreen.

4. Add one more category called **Fundamental** to store the notes pertaining to fundamentals analysis.

5. You can easily delete any of the created categories by marking the check box to the left of the unwanted category and clicking the *Delete Selected Category* button. Note that deleting a category will also delete the notes belonging to it, without asking for your confirmation.

6. Set the maximum number of notes to display on each screen by entering the desired number in the corresponding edit box.

7. Once you have completed all your edits, click the *Finished* button. You will now return to the application's main screen (see Figure 11-20).

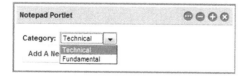

Figure 11-20. *List of categories in the Sun Notepad application*

Now you'll add a note under the *Fundamental* category. Follow these steps to do so:

1. Select the *Fundamental* category from the drop-down list on the main page of the *Sun Notepad* portlet.

2. Click the *Add A New Note* button. You will see the screen shown in Figure 11-21.

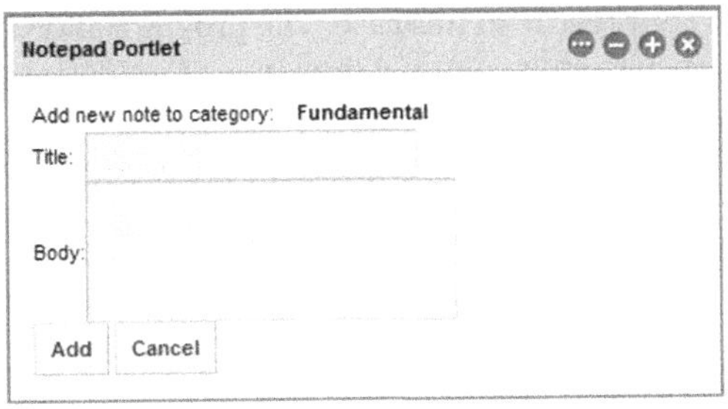

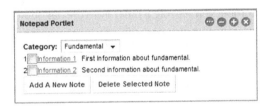

Figure 11-21. *Adding a new note*

3. Enter text for the *Title* and *Body* of the note.

4. Click the *Add* button to create the note.

5. Add one more note under the *Fundamental* category by repeating steps 1 through 4. Your application screen now displays the title and body of each note (see Figure 11-22).

Figure 11-22. *Displaying a list of notes under the Fundamental category*

6. To edit the note, simply click the corresponding link. You can change the note's title and/or body as desired.

7. To delete the note or multiple notes, mark the check box(es) to the left of the desired note(s) and click the *Delete Selected Note* button.

Note In addition to portlets, the Liferay web site also lists themes and layout templates developed by Liferay and its user communities. Enhancing the portal's look and feel with these community-developed themes and layouts was discussed in Chapter 2.

The Google AdSense Portlet

So far we have built a nice-looking, user-friendly portal for the benefit of those who aim to make money by investing in securities. But how do you yourself make money by hosting the portal? One way is to put advertisements on your site. This might not be easy, however; you face the hurdles of getting ads from customers and then doing the accounting.

The *Google AdSense* program comes to your rescue in this case. The program allows you to collect advertising revenue from your web portal with a minimal time investment on your part, and it does not demand any additional resources.

In this section, you will learn to use the *Google AdSense* portlet on your portal.

Downloading the Portlet

The *Google AdSense* portlet is listed on the Liferay web site in its *Downloads* section. To download this portlet application, follow the steps listed here:

1. Go to the Liferay web site at `http://www.liferay.com`.

2. Click the *Downloads* tab.

3. Click the *Official Plugins* tab.

4. On the resulting page, enter **Google** in the *Search* edit box and click the *Search Products* button. You will get a list of products containing the "Google" keyword in their names.

5. Click the *Google AdSense* product link to display the product information onscreen (see Figure 11-23). Note that the version number you see might differ from the one shown here.

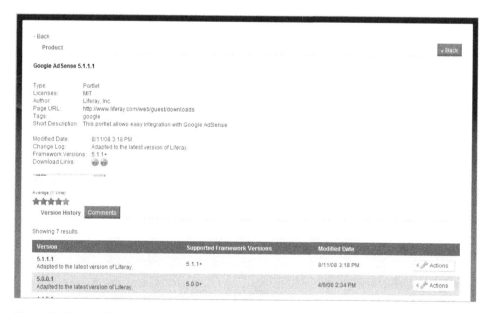

Figure 11-23. *Google AdSense application information*

6. Click on the *Actions* button associated with the product version you want, and select *Download* to download the .war file to your machine.

Installing the Portlet

After you have successfully downloaded the product's .war file, you are ready to install it on your machine. To install the product, follow the steps listed here:

1. Log on to the portal using your *Administrator* account.

2. Navigate to the *Products* page you created earlier. You'll use the *Plugin Installer* application that you previously added to this page.

3. Click the *Upload File* tab in the *Plugin Installer* application.

4. Browse and select the .war file that you just downloaded.

5. Click the *Install* button. The *Google AdSense* application will be installed on your portal.

Adding the Portlet

After you have successfully installed the application on your portal, you can add it to a page and use it. To add the application, follow the steps listed here:

1. Log on to the portal using your *Administrator* account.

2. Navigate to the *Products* page that you created in the section "The Google Gadget Portlet."

3. Select the *Add Application* menu.

4. Select the *Google AdSense* application under the new *Google* category.

5. Add the application to the page. At this stage, your screen should look like the one shown in Figure 11-24.

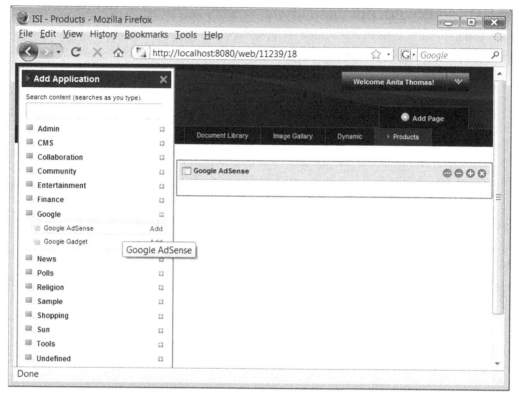

Figure 11-24. *Adding the Google AdSense application*

Configuring the Portlet

You must configure the *Google AdSense* application before it can display ads on your portal pages. Perform these steps to configure the application:

1. Click the application-configuration icon in the application's main screen, or select the *Configuration* menu option from the menu drop-down list (depending on the current page's theme). You will see the configuration settings as shown in Figure 11-25.

2. Enter the following information on this screen:

    a. *Ad Client*: Your Google AdSense client code

    b. *Ad Channel*: Name of a channel you created on the Google AdSense site

---

Tip You need to create a client code and an ad channel by signing on to the Google AdSense site (http://www.google.com/adsense). You can create any number of channels. Note that it is not necessary to sign up on Google AdSense to use this gadget. You can simply enter some dummy client code and channel information, and the gadget would display the ads—but you wouldn't make any revenue.

Figure 11-25. *The Google AdSense application-configuration screen*

c. *Ad Type*: This can be of any of the following three types:

  i. *Text*: This results in the display of text-only ads.

  ii. *Image*: This results in the display of image ads. Note that placing an image ad on your web pages will result in slower page loads.

  iii. *Text and Image*: This will display a mix of both text and image ads.

d. *Ad Format*: You get several choices here. Select the format depending on where you want to display the ad. Here are some selection guidelines:

  i. *(728 × 90) - Leaderboard*: This ad format nearly occupies the entire width of the web page, so it's ideal for placement at the top or bottom of the page.

  ii. *(468 × 60) - Banner*: This is a smaller banner compared to the leaderboard. It's ideally suited for a two-column display.

  iii. *(336 × 280) - Large Rectangle*: This format is useful for embedding the ad in your text; you let the text flow around the ad.

  iv. *(300 × 250) - Medium Rectangle*: This format is also useful for embedding the ad within the text.

  v. *(250 × 250) - Square*: This is a square ad ideally suited for the left or right column in a three-column display.

  vi. *(234 × 60) - Half Banner*: If you have a two-column web page, you can put this banner in one of the columns.

    vii. *(200 × 200) - Small Square*: An ad with this format ideally goes in one of the corners of your web page, or in the left column along with the portal-navigation portlet.

   viii. *(180 × 150) - Small Rectangle*: Use this format if you have limited real estate on your web page for ad display.

    ix. *(160 × 600) - Wide Skyscraper*: This is a vertical ad format that is highly visible when placed on the left or right side of your web page.

    x. *(125 × 125) - Button*: This format is handy if you want to place tiny ads.

    xi. *(120 × 600) - Skyscraper*: This is another full-height ad with high visibility, but with a lesser width than the wide skyscraper.

   xii. *(120 × 240) - Vertical Banner*: This is a vertical banner that uses about half of a page's height.

Tip You can preview the different ad formats by visiting the Google AdSense site.

Caution Google has the right to change its ad formats without alerting registered clients. Be sure to check the Google AdSense site for updates.

    e. *Color Border*: Generally, this is set to the background of your web page, so no border is visible. This way, the ad merges properly with the other content on your web page.

    f. *Color Background*: Again, this is generally set to the background color of your web page, so the ads blend well with other material on the page.

    g. *Color Link*: This sets the color for the hyperlinks in the ads. You can set this to match the color of the other hyperlinks on your web page.

    h. *Color Text*: Set this to the text color of your web page.

    i. *Color URL*: This sets the color for the URLs displayed in ads.

3. After you have completed the edits, click the *Save* button.

4. Return to the main application screen by clicking the *Return to Full Page* link. Your screen will now display ads as shown in Figure 11-26.

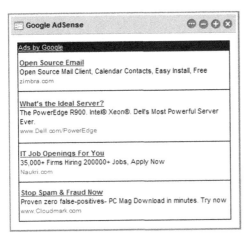

Figure 11-26. *The Google AdSense application screen*

Anybody who visits your portal page will see the ads displayed in the *Google AdSense* portlet. The ads are context-sensitive and thus relevant to the matter displayed on your web page. When the user clicks a displayed ad, you would earn some revenue from the click. Your revenue builds up as you get more users and more clicks. At the end of each month, if your account balance reaches a certain threshold that you specify (subject to a certain minimum), Google will send you a check for your earned revenue.

Summary

In this chapter, you learned to enhance your portal with the addition of third-party applications, starting with the *Google Gadget* portlet. This portlet serves as a gateway to gadget applications developed by Google community members, letting you incorporate those gadgets on your portal pages. It does this by providing an interface between Liferay's portlet specifications and Google's Gadgets API, on which the third-party applications are based. You studied how to download and install the *Google Gadget* portlet on your web pages.

Once you install the *Google Gadget* portlet, you can configure it with any of the available gadgets. You learned to configure this portlet with three different applications: *Stock Ticker*, *Stock Charts*, and *Google News*.

In addition to gadgets, you can enhance your site by adding community-developed portlets that adhere directly to Liferay's portlet specifications. You learned to use the *Sun Notepad* portlet as an example. Lastly, you learned to use the *Google AdSense* portlet to earn some revenue from your portal.

CHAPTER 12

Doing Portal Administration

Any portal requires proper administration. And as the number of users grows, administrative tasks become more demanding. Fortunately, Liferay has provided us with tools for managing a portal and controlling its activities to ensure user satisfaction. In this chapter, you will see how to perform several administrative tasks using Liferay's admin tools. In particular, you will learn to

- Install and use the *Admin* portlet
- Study resource utilization
- Set log levels
- Examine system properties and portal properties
- Shut down the server
- Integrate with OpenOffice
- Monitor server instances
- List plugins and manage plugin upgrades
- Use the *Password Generator* tool and the *Language* tool
- Monitor site traffic with Google Analytics

Using the Admin Portlet

Liferay provides a useful application called *Admin* that helps you perform several administrative tasks. Such tasks involve monitoring resource utilization to ensure optimal portal performance, logging messages from various classes in the system to get insight into what's happening under the hood, checking the various system and portal properties, monitoring server instances, shutting down the server, and so on.

You will now learn to use the *Admin* portlet. First, you need to install this portlet on your ISI portal. For this, you will create a private page in your own community. Users without administrator privileges will not be able to use the portlet, but it's still a good idea to put it on a private page rather than a public page. Perform these steps to create a private page:

1. Log on to the portal using your *Administrator* account.

2. Open the drop-down *Welcome* menu.

3. Navigate to the *Private Pages* menu item of the *Fundamental Analysts* community that you created in Chapter 3 (see Figure 12-1).

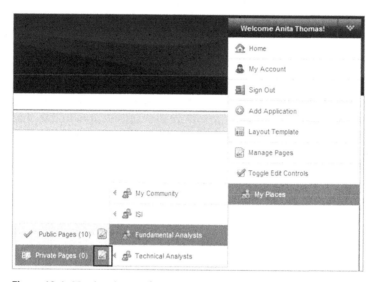

Figure 12-1. *Navigating to the Private Pages menu item*

4. Click the new-page icon on the right side of the menu item (highlighted in Figure 12-1). This opens the *Manage Pages* screen, which lets you create a new page (see Figure 12-2).

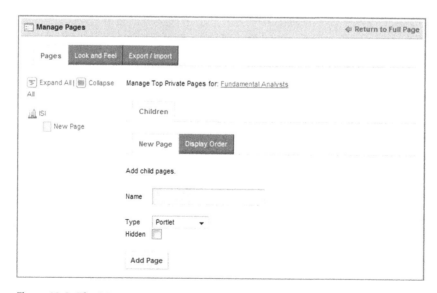

Figure 12-2. *The Manage Pages screen for creating a private page*

5. Enter **Administration** as the page name.

6. Click the *Add Page* button. This creates a new page and displays it in the navigation tree on the left side of the screen.

7. Click the *Return to Full Page* link to see the newly created private page onscreen. You can now add applications to the page.

Installing the Application

To install the *Admin* portlet on your portal, follow the steps listed here:

1. Log on to the portal using your *Administrator* account if you're not already logged in.

2. Open the *Administration* private page that you just created.

3. Select the *Add Application* menu.

4. Locate the *Admin* application under the *Admin* category.

5. Add the application to the *Administration* page by clicking the *Add* link. The screen at this stage should look like the one shown in Figure 12-3.

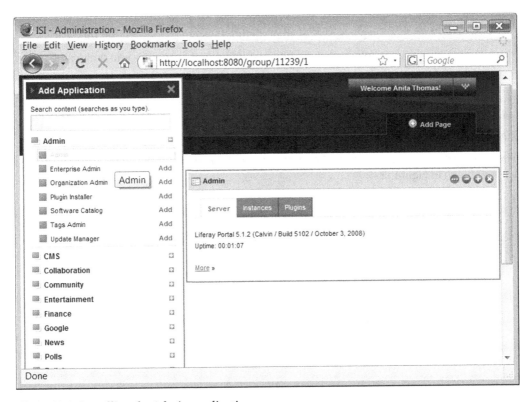

Figure 12-3. *Installing the Admin application*

You are now ready to use the *Admin* application.

Using the Application

Note that the *Admin* application screen shows the *Server* tab by default (see Figure 12-3). It displays the server's build version, date, and uptime (the time elapsed since the server was restarted).

These are the functions of the *Admin* application's three tabs:

- *Server*: Facilitates sever monitoring and management

- *Instances*: Displays a list of server instances

- *Plugins*: Displays a list of all installed plugins, including portlets, themes, and layouts

I will discuss each of these options in detail.

Examining Server Options

When you click the *More* link under the *Server* tab, you will see the following tabbed options:

- *Resources*: Displays memory usage and facilitates memory management

- *Log Levels*: Allows you to set the message-priority level for the server's various packages and classes

- *System Properties*: Displays a list of all predefined system properties and their values

- *Portal Properties*: Displays a list of all predefined portal properties and their values

- *Shutdown*: Facilitates shutting down the server

- *OpenOffice*: Facilitates integration with OpenOffice

Checking Resources

When you select the *Resources* tabbed option under the *Server* tab, your screen would look like the one shown in Figure 12-4.

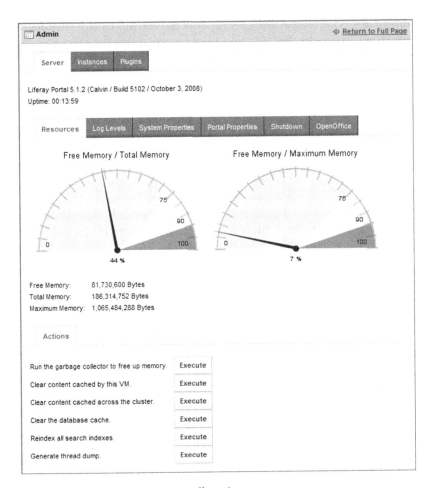

Figure 12-4. *Monitoring resource allocation*

This screen shows information related to memory usage, including a graphical representation of the percentage of free memory with respect to the total and maximum memory available for Liferay's use. The screen's secondary *Actions* tab offers you options to manage memory. You perform one of these actions by clicking the *Execute* button associated with it. Here are the various actions you can take:

- *Run the garbage collector*: Executing this action results in freeing the unreferenced (orphaned) resources from memory. It basically sends a request to the JVM (Java Virtual Machine) to begin the garbage-collection task.

- *Clear content cached by this VM*: The VM (Virtual Machine) periodically caches frequently used content to generate a faster response for the users. This action asks the JVM to clear the single VM cache. Doing this will free up some resources, but the VM cache will soon fill up again depending on the current load.

- *Clear content cached across the cluster*: The Liferay portal can run in a cluster environment. When it does, you can cache the frequently used content on several machines across the cluster. Performing this action clears this cache. This is useful when you want to synchronize the servers.

- *Clear the database cache*: Liferay can cache all your database resultsets. This action clears the database cache, which proves useful when you make direct modifications to the database.

- *Reindex all search indexes*: This action sends a request to regenerate all search indexes. Regenerating indexes will improve performance later, but it might affect the portal's immediate performance because the action takes a long time to process. You should schedule reindexing tasks at nonpeak hours when the server load is minimal. Also, because your indexes could become fragmented due to continuous additions, deletions, and updates, you should perform this task periodically to maintain optimal server performance.

- *Generate thread dump*: This action generates a system thread dump for later examination, which proves useful during testing and debugging.

Changing Log Levels

Logging application messages helps you debug your applications and also generally helps you get an inside view of what is happening in the system. During its lifetime, an object might generate several messages during the execution of its methods. You can prioritize such messages with different levels. Liferay provides several predefined priority levels: FATAL, ERROR, WARN, INFO, and DEBUG. Liferay classes use the log4j API (http://logging.apache.org/) to log these messages to an output device. Generally, this output device is redirected to a file, so you can view the messages later by opening a physical file.

You'll be happy to know that you can also log the messages generated by the plugins (classes) that you use to extend Liferay's functionality. I'll show you how to do that later in this section, but first let's look at how to select the message-priority levels for the various Liferay classes.

When you select the secondary *Log Levels* tab under the *Server* tab, you will see the screen shown in Figure 12-5.

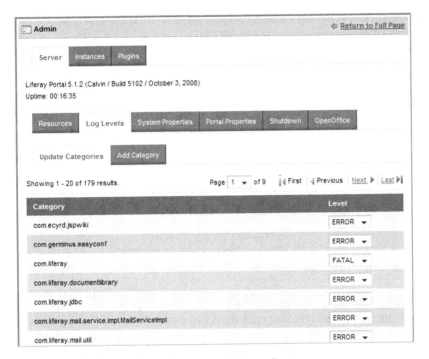

Figure 12-5. *Setting log levels for various Liferay classes*

In the *Category* column under the *Update Categories* tab, you will see a list of various Liferay classes and packages. The next column called *Level* displays the currently selected priority level for each item. By default, this level is set to ERROR for most of the classes and packages. You can select a different priority level or turn off the logging by making a choice from the drop-down combo box. After you have selected the desired priority levels for the various classes, click the *Save* button at the bottom of the screen. The changes take effect immediately, so all the new messages logged by the system will have updated priority levels.

The messages are generally saved to a physical file, the name and location of which depends on the application server where Liferay is running. If your portal is running on Tomcat, the file is stored in the `catalina.yyyy-mm-dd.log` file in the `<installation folder>\logs` folder, where the fields `yyyy`, `mm`, and `dd` designate the system date. So every day, a new log file is created.

Now let's go back to the topic of logging messages generated by user-created plugins. To do this, you first need to create a logging category.

Caution All user-created plugins must use the log4j API to log their messages. If they don't, the messages will not be logged.

Create a logging category by selecting the *Add Category* tab under the *Log Levels* tab. When you do so, you will see the screen shown in Figure 12-6.

Figure 12-6. *Adding a new category for logging*

Here, you will enter the fully qualified name of the plugin's class or package, select the message-priority level from the combo box, and click the *Save* button. When you return to the category list, you will find the newly added category at the end of the list on the last page. The logging is enabled immediately, so the system will log all the messages generated by the new category class matching the selected priority level.

As you can see from the category list (see Figure 12-5), Liferay allows you to select classes in its entire hierarchy starting from the com.liferay root. If you select a class higher up in the hierarchy, you will end up logging the messages for every class lower down in the hierarchy. This will make your log file too bulky to examine physically, so you might want to select only the classes you need.

■**Caution** Changes made to the log levels are stored in memory and thus are not permanent in nature. When you restart Liferay, all the changes are lost and the system reverts back to the default settings.

Checking System Properties

Selecting the *System Properties* tab under the *Server* tab displays all the predefined system properties and their values. A typical list of properties is shown in Figure 12-7.

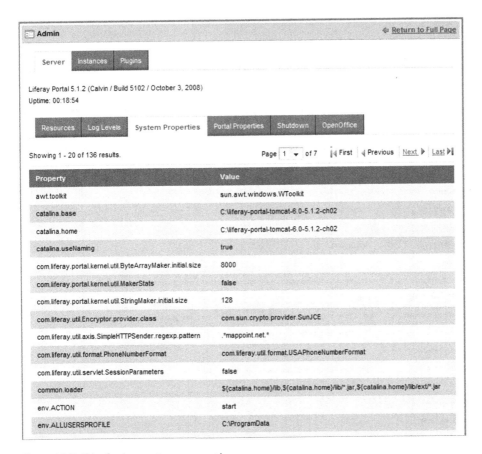

Figure 12-7. *Displaying system properties*

The list, which runs across several pages, helps you examine the value of any system variable. For example, suppose you want to know which copy of the Tomcat server on your machine is being used by Liferay. If you look up the catalina.home property, you will learn the location of the Tomcat server that Liferay is using. If you want to know which version of Java Runtime Environment (JRE) Liferay is using, you can check the value of the env.JAVA_HOME variable. And so on.

Checking Portal Properties

Selecting the *Portal Properties* tab under the *Server* tab displays the list of portal properties (see Figure 12-8).

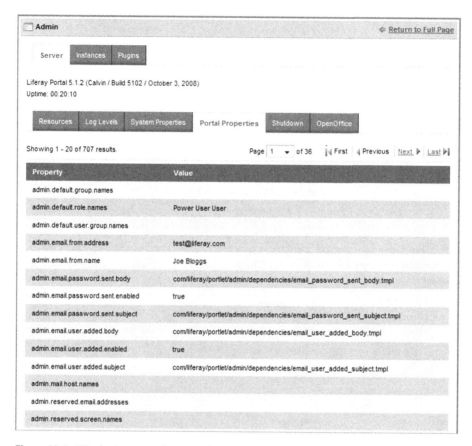

Figure 12-8. *Displaying portal properties*

This screen gives you the values of all the property variables used by the portal. For example, to learn the default *Email From* address used by the portal, you examine the value of the admin.email.from.address property. To know the default folder where your plugins are installed, you can examine the value of the auto.deploy.default.dest.dir property. These properties reside in the portal.properties file, which you can find in the Tomcat installation's WEB-INF\lib folder. This file is available in the portal-impl.jar archive.

Note Liferay's extension mechanism allows you to override the properties defined in the portal.properties file by defining the new values and properties in the portal-ext.properties file. This file is stored in the WEB-INF\classes folder.

Shutting Down the Portal

The *Shutdown* tabbed option allows you to initiate the portal shutdown. When you click this tab, you will see the screen shown in Figure 12-9.

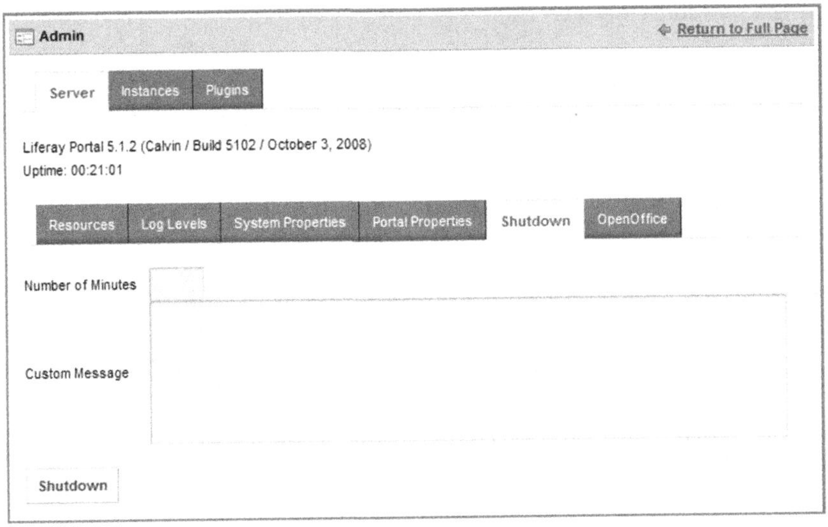

Figure 12-9. *Setting server-shutdown parameters*

Here, you need to enter the following information:

- *Number of Minutes*: Indicate the number of minutes after which the portal is to be shut down.

Note Unless you specify the time, the shutdown will not be initiated.

- *Custom Message*: Type the message to the user that indicates the reason for shutdown.

Entering the information and clicking the *Shutdown* button starts the shutdown process. Basically, the system notifies all logged-in users so that they can prepare for the shutdown. A typical shutdown message that appears on the user's terminal is shown in Figure 12-10.

Caution The maintenance-alert message is displayed on the user terminal only when the user performs some activity on the portal.

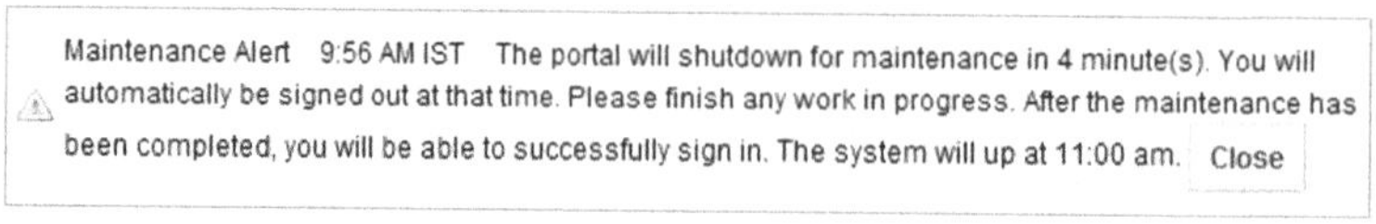

> Maintenance Alert   9:56 AM IST   The portal will shutdown for maintenance in 4 minute(s). You will
> ⚠ automatically be signed out at that time. Please finish any work in progress. After the maintenance has
> been completed, you will be able to successfully sign in. The system will up at 11:00 am.   Close

Figure 12-10. *Displaying a shutdown message*

You will notice that your custom message is appended to the system-generated message. After the specified shutdown time expires, a user will see this message if he tries any activity on the portal:

```
The system is shutdown. Please try again later.
```

After shutdown is initiated, you can cancel the process by clicking the *Cancel Shutdown* button.

Note Shutting down the portal does not result in shutting down the server. Even when the portal is shut down, other applications deployed on the server will continue running. To shut down the server, you need to carry out the shutdown procedures for the particular server that you are using.

Integrating with OpenOffice

OpenOffice is the leading open source office software suite consisting of word-processing, spreadsheet, presentation, and database applications. It's typically used in graphical mode to create documents, but you can also run it in server mode to convert documents from one format to another on the fly. Liferay's *Document Library* portlet incorporates this feature (see Chapter 9).

Examining Server Instances

Selecting the top-level *Instances* tab in the *Admin* portlet displays all the server instances (see Figure 12-11).

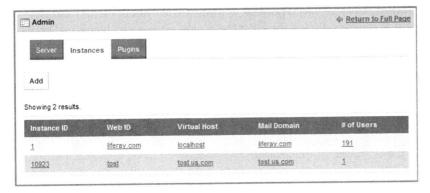

Figure 12-11. *Displaying server instances*

You can add more server instances by clicking the *Add* button. On the resulting screen, enter the following information:

- *Web ID*: Provide a user-specified ID, generally the domain name.

- *Virtual Host*: Specify the domain name that you have configured in your network. When the user opens the web site in her browser using this domain name, she will be redirected to the Liferay server. The server will send her the appropriate portal instance.

- *Mail Domain*: Specify the domain name for the mail host used by this portal instance. Liferay uses this mail domain to send notification messages.

After you have entered the information, click the *Save* button to save your changes. Now open the browser and navigate to the portal using the specified domain name. You will see the new instance of Liferay running in the browser. You can configure this new instance independently of the previous instance.

Listing Plugins

You've downloaded and installed plugins of various types using Liferay's *Plugin Installer* application. The top-level *Plugins* tab in the *Admin* application provides the same functionality, allowing you to list the plugins currently installed on your portal and to add new plugins to the portal. These are the types of plugins you can have:

- Portlet
- Theme
- Layout template
- Web
- Hook

By now you've worked extensively with portlets, and you learned about themes and layout templates in Chapter 2. I'll now discuss the other two plugin types: web plugins and hook plugins. A web plugin is essentially a Java EE module that helps integrate your Liferay portal with various Enterprise Service Bus (ESB) implementations, single sign-on (SSO) implementations, workflow engines, and so on.

Hook plugins, introduced in Liferay Portal version 5.1.0, are destined to replace EXT, Liferay's existing extension model. They're easier to use and they cause fewer maintenance and upgrade issues. Using hook plugins, you can *hook* into these entities:

- Liferay's eventing system

- Java model listeners

- JavaServer Pages (JSPs)

- Portal properties

- Language properties

To augment your portal with support for hook plugins, create a hook-configuration file with this structure:

```
<?xml version="1.0" encoding="UTF-8"?>
<!DOCTYPE hook PUBLIC "-//Liferay//DTD Hook 5.1.0//EN"
 "http://www.liferay.com/dtd/liferay-hook_5_1_0.dtd">

<hook>
</hook>
```

You'll be adding your plugin classes in the hook element. For example, you can place an event tag within the hook tag to extend event processing for any of the three types of events supported by Liferay: application-startup events, login events, and service events. If you wish to provide additional processing whenever a certain type of event occurs, add the following code in the event tag of your hook-configuration file:

```
<hook>
...
<event>
    <event-class>Event Processing Class</event-class>
    <event-type>Event Type Class</event-type>
</event>
</hook>
```

You provide the name of your event-processing class in the event-class tag and the event-type class name in the event-type tag. Now, whenever an event of the specified type occurs, the service code in your custom class would be executed.

Hooking into Java model listeners is similar to hooking into Liferay's eventing system. To extend the functionality provided in model listeners, you will write a custom class and specify it in the model-listener tag in the hook-configuration file:

```
<hook>
...
<model-listener>
    <model-listener-class> Listener Class</model-listener-class>
    <model-name> Model Class</model-name>
</model-listener>
</hook>
```

In addition to integrating model listeners, hook plugins allow you to easily integrate new JSPs in your portal. Rather than replace the existing JSPs with the new ones, you can use the plugin to invoke the new JSPs provided in an independent folder. You simply specify the new folder in the `custom-jsp-dir` tag of the hook-configuration file:

```
<hook>
...
<custom-jsp-dir>
    /WEB-INF/jsps
</custom-jsp-dir>
</hook>
```

This way, you can maintain several versions of JSPs and integrate them at any time by modifying only the configuration file.

Hook plugins also allow you to modify the portal properties easily. To modify the properties, write them in another file and specify the file name in the `portal-properties` tag of the hook-configuration file:

```
<hook>
...
<portal-properties>
    New Properties File
</portal-properties>
</hook>
```

Finally, you can use hook plugins to modify language properties. You could install new translations or override desired words in existing translations by using code like this:

```
<hook>
...
<language-properties>
    New Properties File
</language-properties>
</hook>
```

The major advantage offered by hook plugins is that you can easily revert to your original functionality; you simply remove the installed hook plugins from the portal. You can also disable each type of hook via the `portal.properties` file. Lastly, you can build, package, and deploy hook plugins, just as you can with other Liferay plugins.

Tip You need to install the Liferay Plugin SDK to create and add your own plugins. The purpose of this section was to provide an introduction to the new mechanism of extending Liferay's functionality; full details on creating plugins is beyond the scope of this book.

Managing Plugins

Over time, you'll likely accumulate many plugins on your Liferay portal. Some of these will undergo various updates, while some of them will become obsolete. You'll want to manage your plugins using Liferay's *Update Manager* application.

When *Update Manager* is installed, it will display a message at the top of your portal pages whenever new versions of your plugins are available (see Figure 12-12).

Updates are available for Liferay. Click here to open the Update Manager for details.
Close

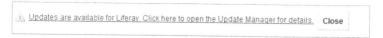

Figure 12-12. *Update Manager's notification message*

The *Update Manager* application is available in the *Admin* category. Install the application on your *Administration* private page and look at its main screen (see Figure 12-13).

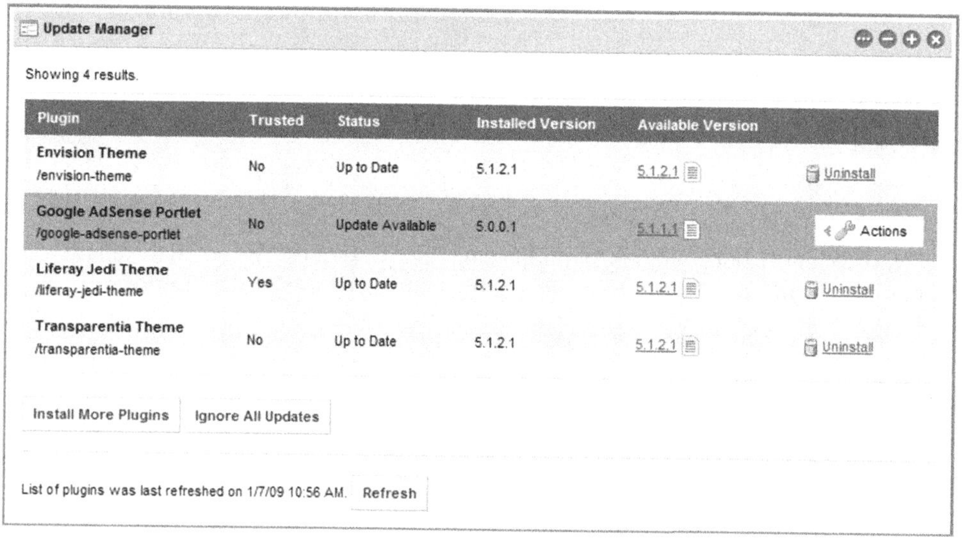

Update Manager
Showing 4 results.
Plugin
Trusted
Status
Installed Version
Available Version
Envision Theme
/envision-theme
No
Up to Date
5.1.2.1
5.1.2.1
Uninstall
Google AdSense Portlet
/google-adsense-portlet
No
Update Available
5.0.0.1
5.1.1.1
Actions
Liferay Jedi Theme
/liferay-jedi-theme
Yes
Up to Date
5.1.2.1
5.1.2.1
Uninstall
Transparentia Theme
/transparentia-theme
No
Up to Date
5.1.2.1
5.1.2.1
Uninstall
Install More Plugins
Ignore All Updates
List of plugins was last refreshed on 1/7/09 10:56 AM.
Refresh

Figure 12-13. *Displaying the upgrade status of installed applications*

The screen shows the currently installed plugins along with their status. If a newer version of an application is available, you'll see *Update Available* in the app's *Status* column (see the *Google AdSense Portlet* row in Figure 12-13). From here, you can upgrade the plugin to a newer version by clicking the *Actions* button to install the updates. If a plugin is outdated, on the other hand, you can uninstall it by clicking its *Uninstall* link.

To install more plugins, click the *Install More Plugins* button, which will take you to the *Plugin Installer* application.

Using Tools

As an administrator, you must perform several more functions other than monitoring the health of the portal. Such administrative tasks would include managing portal pages and their interfaces, user accounts, and so on. Liferay has provided a few tools to assist you in these tasks.

Generating User Passwords

When you create a new user, you will provide her with an initial password for her login. You also might have to regenerate a user's password because he has forgotten it. Liferay provides an application called *Password Generator* that creates random passwords for you. Find this application under the *Tools* category and add it to your *Administration* portal page. The application interface is shown in Figure 12-14.

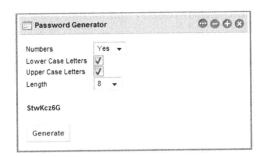

Figure 12-14. *The UI of the Password Generator application*

Before you generate a random password, you should set the password features, such as whether the password should contain a combination of uppercase letters, lowercase letters, and/or numbers. Additionally, you need to specify the desired password length. Once this is done, click the *Generate* button—you'll see a new password displayed on the screen. Every time you click the *Generate* button, the application generates a new random password. You can now send this password to your portal user after resetting his previous one.

Setting Language

As your portal becomes popular, you can expect users from all over the globe to visit it. When such a time comes, you probably want to add multilanguage support to your portal so that your portal pages can be viewed in different languages. Liferay provides an application called *Language* that facilities region selection. Find this application under the *Tools* category and add it to your *Administration* portal page. The application interface is shown in Figure 12-15, above the *Password Generator* application screen. *Password Generator* is the application that we'll translate using the Language tool.

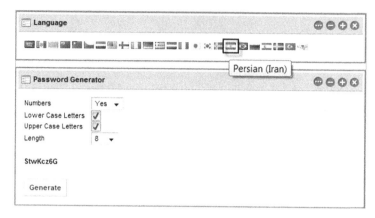

Figure 12-15. *The UI of the Language portlet*

The application shows the flags of different countries. The default language selection is American English. Now click the Persian (Iranian) flag (shown highlighted in Figure 12-15). Note that the *Password Generator* screen immediately changes to display translated text (see Figure 12-16).

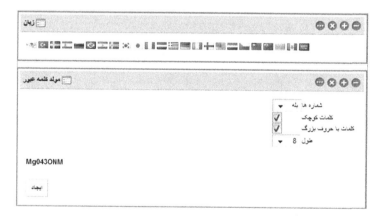

Figure 12-16. *Displaying Persian language output*

Clicking a different flag will display the text in the corresponding regional language.

Note Liferay provides language translations only for its own portlets. It will not automatically translate the text in your plugins or your portal pages; you must provide such translations yourself.

Monitoring Portal Traffic

It is always a good practice to monitor your site traffic on a regular basis. This allows you to make timely changes to the portal to keep your customers happy. Liferay provides integrated support for Google Analytics, a popular tool for analyzing site-traffic data. With this functionality, you can easily monitor and analyze the traffic generated on your community pages.

Before you enable this support, you must sign up with Google Analytics (http://www.google.com/analytics/) to receive an ID. You'll specify this ID on the community pages that you wish to monitor. Follow these steps to enable analytics support on your community pages:

1. Go to the *Communities* portlet application. If it's not currently installed on your portal page, install it from the *Community* category.

2. Get a list of available communities.

3. Select the name of the community that you wish to monitor.

4. Click the *Actions* button.

5. Select the *Manage Pages* menu option.

6. Click the *Settings* tab.

7. Click the *Monitoring* tab. You will see a screen similar to the one shown in Figure 12-17.

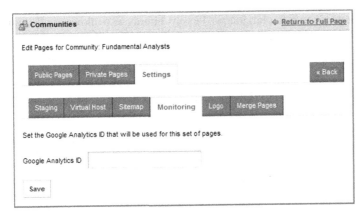

Figure 12-17. *Setting up Google Analytics*

8. Enter your Google Analytics ID.

9. Click the *Save* button.

The monitoring is now enabled. After a certain period of portal use by your community users, you can view the site-traffic data on the Google Analytics web site (http://www.google.com/analytics).

Summary

Proper administration is the key to a portal's success. In this chapter, you learned many techniques to monitor your portal's health.

First, you learned to use Liferay's *Admin* portlet to facilitate several administrative tasks such as monitoring system resources to ensure they're not running beyond critical limits; setting log levels for your system's instantiated classes so you can monitor its dynamic behavior; examining the various system and portal properties to ensure they're set properly; and integrating with the popular OpenOffice suite so you can convert documents from one format to another. You also used the *Admin* portlet to list and monitor the multiple instances of Liferay that can be started on a single server.

Then you delved into plugins. You used the *Admin* application to display a list of currently installed plugins and to install additional plugins. You can add various types of plugins, including portlets, themes, layout templates, web plugins, and hook plugins. With hook plugins, you can hook additional functionality into the portal by providing event-handling code or setting up new JSPs and portal properties. This feature lets you extend Liferay's functionality with minimal changes to the existing portal. You learned how to manage all your plugins using Liferay's *Update Manager* application, which allows you to upgrade plugins and remove ones that have become obsolete.

Finally, you learned to use a couple of Liferay's utility tools: *Password Generator* and *Language*. The former lets you generate new unique passwords for users, while the latter lets you translate Liferay's portlet pages to other languages. Finally, Liferay also allows easy integration with Google Analytics, which gives you site-traffic statistics for your portal.

Index

You Need the Companion eBook

Your purchase of this book entitles you to buy the companion PDF-version eBook for only $10. Take the weightless companion with you anywhere.

We believe this Apress title will prove so indispensable that you'll want to carry it with you everywhere, which is why we are offering the companion eBook (in PDF format) for $10 to customers who purchase this book now. Convenient and fully searchable, the PDF version of any content-rich, page-heavy Apress book makes a valuable addition to your programming library. You can easily find and copy code—or perform examples by quickly toggling between instructions and the application. Even simultaneously tackling a donut, diet soda, and complex code becomes simplified with hands-free eBooks!

Once you purchase your book, getting the $10 companion eBook is simple:

❶ Visit **www.apress.com/promo/tendollars/**.

❷ Complete a basic registration form to receive a randomly generated question about this title.

❸ Answer the question correctly in 60 seconds, and you will receive a promotional code to redeem for the $10.00 eBook.

2855 TELEGRAPH AVENUE | SUITE 600 | BERKELEY, CA 94705

Offer valid through 10/09.